# Alienation: Minority Groups

# Perception in Communication

GENERAL EDITOR: *Charles Sanders*

THE VOICES OF WAR, *James Shokoff*

MALE AND FEMALE: IDENTITY, *John Harrington*

ALIENATION: MINORITY GROUPS, *Don Rude*

WHO NEEDS NATURE? *Dixie Smith Jackson*

THE AMERICAN MOVIE GODDESS, *Marsha McCreadie*

# ALIENATION: MINORITY GROUPS

EDITED BY *Donald Rude*

*Texas Tech University*
*Lubbock, Texas*

JOHN WILEY AND SONS, INC.
NEW YORK · LONDON · SYDNEY · TORONTO

Library of Congress Cataloging in Publication Data

Rude, Donald, comp.
  Alienation: minority groups.

  (Perception in communication)
  CONTENTS: From The sane society, by E. Fromm.—The great American frustration, by A. MacLeish.—America, by A. Ginsberg. [etc.]
  1. Readers—Minorities—U. S. I. Title.
PE1127.M5R8      808.04'275      73-39168
ISBN 0-471-74456-5

Printed in the United States of A

10 9 8 7 6 5 4 3 2 1

# Series Preface

"Perception in Communication" is a series of brief topical readers presenting a collection of expository prose, verse, fiction, drama, and non-verbal media for the student of composition. No restrictive framework has been imposed upon any of the volumes. If a common framework exists, it stems from the editors' emphasis upon the principle of comparison and contrast and their mutual desire to make the questions and exercises participatory. The questions are focused on themes and matters of rhetorical technique that will provoke discussion between instructor and student in responses to the authors and editors.

Experience demonstrates that a student tends to write better when a timely, substantial subject engages his interest, or when the subject is elaborated and reviewed in a variety of modes of communication. Although the major emphasis of this series is on written communication, there are also a number of multimedia projects such as collages, comic routines, concrete poems, dramatic productions, films, pictorial essays, posters, songs, and tapes. The editors use this multimedia material in such a manner that they are very definitely assignments in composition.

By acknowledging several modes of communication and encouraging experimentation in more than one, the editors recognize the heterogeneity of today's college audience as well as its various commitments, concerns, goals, and needs. It is the editors' belief that presenting these various modes of communication will engage not only the reader's mind, but his sensory perception as well.

CHARLES SANDERS

*University of Illinois at Urbana*

# Contents

"*What a piece of work is man, how noble in reason, how infinite in faculties. . . .*"

William Shakespeare, Hamlet

*John Filo / Valley Daily News, Tarentum, Pa.*

*Being Different in America is . . .*

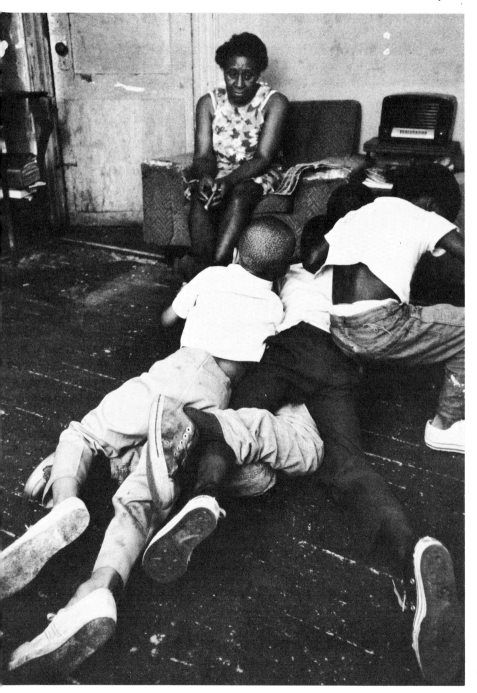

A Way of Life.

*Being Different in America is . . .*

*a Crime? ? ?*

*In America, Being Different is . . .*

*A Heritage!*

Should the Afro-American mother and the gay liberationist, the hard hat and the hippie meet, they might at first find little binding them together. Indeed, each might draw back from the other, seeing a threat, a rival, or an oppressor.

Although they are outwardly disparate, the struggle of the black man in the ghetto, the rebellion of the dissident college student, the protests of Chicago laborers, and the demands of women for equality do reflect a single impulse. They not only express discontentment with the material restraints placed upon them by a society that preaches equality while practicing exclusiveness, but they also question the validity of the moral and political goals of that society. Such discontentment has become so prevalent in the last decade that one can conclude with Jean François Revel that a new revolution is under way in America, a revolution in which "disagreement on values and goals is more pronounced than disagreement on the means of existence."

This book examines the values and goals of those individuals who have sought to reshape American society. It examines the paradox of a society that extols the expression of individuality but chastises those of its members set apart by their race, their sex, their politics, or their mores. The essays and works of fiction, poetry, and drama included in the book treat radically different social problems, ranging from racial oppression to homosexuality. Their juxtaposition here suggests the continuity of interests that binds America's diverse minority groups, and it clarifies the human concerns that lie hidden behind outbursts such as those that have flared in Watts and shattered Chicago's Gold Coast. Even though most of the writers presented here express particular concern for one segment of our society, all share a common interest in larger questions of self-definition and self-determination. How, they challenge us to ask, can "man" survive in a society not of his making and not under his control. And how, they force us to wonder, shall a man respond when he asks the question "Who am I?" only to be answered "Who you must not be"?

# *Alienation: Minority Groups*

# 1. from *The Sane Society*

## ERICH FROMM

Man first emerged from the animal world as a freak of nature. Having lost most of the instinctive equipment which regulates the animal's activities, he was more helpless, less well equipped for the fight for survival, than most animals. Yet he had developed a capacity for thought, imagination and self-awareness, which was the basis for transforming nature and himself. For many thousands of generations man lived by food gathering and hunting. He was still tied to nature, and afraid of being cast out from her. He identified himself with animals and worshiped these representatives of nature as his gods. After a long period of slow development, man began to cultivate the soil, to create a new social and religious order based on agriculture and animal husbandry. During this period he worshiped goddesses as the bearers of natural fertility, experienced himself as the child dependent on the fertility of the earth, on the life-giving breast of Mother. At a time some four thousand years ago, a decisive turn in man's history took place. He took a new step in the long-drawn-out process of his emergence from nature. He severed the ties with nature and with Mother, and set himself a new goal, that of being fully born, of being fully awake, of being fully human; of being free. Reason and conscience became the principles which were to guide him; his aim was a society bound by the bonds of brotherly love, justice and truth, a new and truly human home to take the place of the irretrievably lost home in nature.

And then again about five hundred years before Christ in the great religious systems of India, Greece, Palestine, Persia and China, the idea of the unity of mankind and of a unifying spiritual principle underlying all reality assumed new and more developed expressions. Lao-tse, Buddha, Isajah, Heraclitus and Socrates, and later, on Palestinian soil, Jesus and the Apostles, on American soil, Quetzalcoatl, and later again, on Arabian soil, Mohammed, taught the ideas of the unity of man, of reason, love and justice as the goals man must strive for.

Northern Europe seemed to sleep for a long time. Greek and Christian ideas were transmitted to its soil, and it took a thousand years before Europe was saturated with them. Around 1500 A.D. a new period began. Man discovered nature and the individual, he laid the foundations for the natural sciences, which began to transform the face of the earth. The closed world of the Middle Ages collapsed, the unifying heaven broke up, man found a new unifying principle in science, and was searching for a new unity in the social and political unification of the earth and in the domination of nature. Moral conscience, the heritage of the Judaeo-Christian tradition, and intellectual conscience, the heritage of the Greek tradition, fused and brought about a flowering of human creation as man had hardly ever known it before.

Europe, the youngest child of humanity, culturally speaking, developed such wealth and such weapons that it became the master of the rest of the world for several hundred years. But again, in the middle of the twentieth century, a drastic change is occurring, a change as great as ever occurred in the past. The new techniques replace the use of the physical energy of animals and men by that of steam, oil and electricity; they create means of communication which transform the earth into the size of one continent, and the human race into one society where the fate of one group is the fate of all; they create marvels of devices which permit the best of art, literature and music to be brought to every member of society; they create productive forces which will permit everybody to have a dignified material existence, and reduces work to such dimensions that it will fill only a fraction of man's day.

Yet today, when man seems to have reached the beginning of a new, richer, happier human era, his existence and that of the generations to follow is more threatened than ever. How is this possible?

Man had won his freedom from clerical and secular authorities, he stood alone with his reason and his conscience as his only judges, but he was afraid of the newly won freedom; he had achieved "freedom from"—without yet having achieved "freedom to"—to be himself, to be productive, to be fully awake. Thus he tried to escape from freedom. His very achievement, the mastery over nature, opened up the avenues for his escape.

In building the new industrial machine, man became so absorbed in the new task that it became the paramount goal of his life. His energies, which once were devoted to the search for God and salvation, were now directed toward the domination of nature and ever-increasing material comfort. He ceased to use production as a means for a better life, but hypostatized it instead to an end in itself, an end to which life was subordinated. In the process of an ever-increasing division of labor, ever-increasing mechanization of work, and an ever-increasing size of social agglomerations, man himself became a part of the machine, rather than its master. He experienced himself as a commodity, as an investment; his aim became to be a success, that is, to sell himself as profitably as possible on the market. His value as a person lies in his salability, not in his human qualities of love, reason, or in his artistic capacities. Happiness becomes identical with consumption of newer and better commodities, the drinking in of music, screen plays, fun, sex, liquor and cigarettes. Not having a sense of self except the one which conformity with the majority can give, he is insecure, anxious, depending on approval. He is alienated from himself, worships the product of his own hands, the leaders of his own making, as if they were above him, rather than made by him. He is in a sense back where he was before the great human evolution began in the second millennium B.C.

He is incapable to love and to use his reason, to make decisions, in fact incapable to appreciate life and thus ready and even willing to destroy everything. The world is again fragmentalized, has lost its unity; he is again worshiping diversified things, with the only exception that now they are man-made, rather than part of nature.

The new era started with the idea of individual initiative. Indeed, the discoverers of new worlds and sea lanes in the sixteenth and seventeenth centuries, the pioneers of science, and the founders of new philosophies, the statesmen and philosophers of the great English, French and American revolutions, and eventually, the industrial pioneers, and even the robber barons showed marvelous individual initiative. But with the bureaucratization and managerialization of Capitalism, it is exactly the individual initiative that is disappearing. Bureaucracy has little initiative, that is its nature; nor have automatons. The cry for individual initiative as an argument for Capitalism is at best a nostalgic yearning, and at worst a deceitful slogan used against those plans for reform which are based on the idea of truly human individual initiative. Modern society has started out with the vision of creating a culture which would fulfill man's needs; it has as its ideal the harmony between the individual and social needs, the end of the conflict between human nature and the social order. One believed one would arrive at this goal in two ways; by the increased productive technique which permitted feeding everybody satisfactorily, and by a rational, objective picture of man and of his real needs. Putting it differently, the aim of the efforts of modern man was to create a sane society. More specifically, this meant a society whose members have developed their reason to that point of objectivity which permits them to see themselves, others, nature, in their true reality, and not distorted by infantile omniscience or paranoid hate. It meant a society, whose members have developed to a point of independence when they know the difference between good and evil, where they make their own choices, where they have convictions rather than opinions, faith rather than superstitions or nebulous hopes. It meant a society whose members have developed the capacity to love their children, their neighbors, all men, themselves, all of nature; who can feel one with all, yet retain their sense of individuality and integrity; who transcend nature by creating, not by destroying.

So far, we have failed. We have not bridged the gap between a minority which realized these goals and tried to live according to them, and the majority whose mentality is far back, in the Stone Age, in totemism, in idol worship, in feudalism. Will the majority be converted to sanity—or will it use the greatest discoveries of human reason for its own purposes of unreason and insanity? Will we be able to create a vision of the good, sane life, which will stir the life forces of those afraid of marching forward? This time, mankind is at one crossroad where the wrong step could be the last step.

In the middle of the twentieth century, two great social collosi have developed which, being afraid of each other, seek security in ever-increasing military rearmament. The United States and her allies are wealthier; their standard of living is higher, their interest in comfort and pleasure is greater than that of their rivals, the Soviet Union and her satellites, and China. Both rivals claim that their system promises final salvation for man, guarantees the paradise of the future. Both claim that the opponent represents the exact opposite to himself, and that his system must be eradicated—in the short or long run—if mankind is to be saved. Both rivals speak in terms of nineteenth-century ideals. The West in the name of the ideas of the French Revolution, of liberty, reason, individualism. The East in the name of the socialist ideas of solidarity, equality. They both succeed in capturing the imagination and the fanatical allegiance of hundreds of millions of people.

There is today a decisive difference between the two systems. In the Western world there is freedom to express ideas critical of the existing system. In the Soviet world criticism and expression of different ideas is suppressed by brutal force. Hence, the Western world carries within itself the possibility for peaceful progressive transformation, while in the Soviet world such possibilities are almost non-existent; in the Western world the life of the individual is free from the terror of imprisonment, torture or death, which confront any member of the Soviet society who has not become a well-functioning automaton. Indeed, life in the Western world has been, and is even now sometimes as rich and joyous as it has ever been anywhere in human history; life in the Soviet system can never be joyous, as indeed it can never be where the executioner watches behind the door.

But without ignoring the tremendous differences between free Capitalism and authoritarian Communism today, it is shortsighted not to see the similarities, especially as they will develop in the future. Both systems are based on industrialization, their goal is ever-increasing economic efficiency and wealth. They are societies run by a managerial class, and by professional politicians. They both are thoroughly materialistic in their outlook, regardless of Christian ideology in the West and secular messianism in the East. They organize man in a centralized system, in large factories, political mass parties. Everybody is a cog in the machine, and has to function smoothly. In the West, this is achieved by a method of psychological conditioning, mass suggestion, monetary rewards. In the East by all this, plus the use of terror. It is to be assumed that the more the Soviet system develops economically, the less severely will it have to exploit the majority of the population, hence the more can terror be replaced by methods of psychological manipulation. The West develops rapidly in the direction of Huxley's *Brave New World,* the East *is* today Orwell's "1984." But both systems tend to converge.

What, then, are the prospects for the future? The first, and perhaps most likely possibility, is that of atomic war. The most likely outcome of such a war is the destruction of industrial civilization, and the regression of the world to a primitive agrarian level. Or, if the destruction should not prove to be as thorough as many specialists in the field believe, the result will be the necessity for the victor to organize and dominate the whole world. This could only happen in a centralized state based on force—and it would make little difference whether Moscow or Washington were the seat of government. But, unfortunately, even the avoidance of war alone does not promise a bright future. In the development of both Capitalism and of Communism as we can visualize them in the next fifty or a hundred years, the process of automatization and alienation will proceed. Both systems are developing into managerial societies, their inhabitants well fed, well clad, having their wishes satisfied, and not having wishes which cannot be satisfied; automatons, who follow without force, who are guided without leaders, who make machines which act like men and produce men who act like machines; men, whose reason deteriorates while their intelligence rises, thus creating the dangerous situation of equipping man with the greatest material power without the wisdom to use it.

This alienation and automatization leads to an ever-increasing insanity. Life has no meaning, there is no joy, no faith, no reality. Everybody is "happy"—except that he does not feel, does not reason, does not love.

In the nineteenth century the problem was that *God is dead;* in the twentieth century the problem is that *man is dead.* In the nineteenth century inhumanity meant cruelty; in the twentieth century it means schizoid self-alienation. The danger of the past was that men became slaves. The danger of the future is that men may become robots. True enough, robots do not rebel. But given man's nature, robots cannot live and remain sane, they become "Golems," they will destroy their world and themselves because they cannot stand any longer the boredom of a meaningless life.

Our dangers are war and robotism. What is the alternative? To get out of the rut in which we are moving, and to take the next step in the birth and self-realization of humanity. The first condition is the abolishment of the war threat hanging over all of us now and paralyzing faith and initiative. We must take the responsibility for the life of all men, and develop on an international scale what all great countries have developed internally, a relative sharing of wealth and a new and more just division of economic resources. This must lead eventually to forms of international economic co-operation and planning, to forms of world government and to complete disarmament. We must retain the industrial method. But we must decentralize work and state so as to give it *human proportions,* and permit centralization only to an optimal point which is necessary because of the requirements of industry. In the economic sphere we need co-management of all who work in an enterprise, to permit their active and responsible participation. The new forms for such participation can be found. In the political sphere, return to the town meetings, by creating thousands of small face-to-face groups, which are well informed, which discuss, and whose decisions are integrated in a new "lower house." A cultural renaissance must combine work education for the young, adult education and a new system of popular art and secular ritual throughout the whole nation.

Our only alternative to the danger of robotism is humanistic communitarianism. The problem is not primarily the legal problem of property ownership, nor that of sharing *profits;* it is that of sharing *work,* sharing *experience.* Changes in ownership must be made to the extent to which they are necessary to create a community of work, and to prevent the profit motive from directing production into socially harmful directions. Income must be equalized to the extent of giving everybody the material basis for a dignified life, and thus preventing the economic differences from creating a fundamentally different experience of life for various social classes. Man must be restituted to his supreme place in society, never being a means, never a thing to be used by others or by himself. Man's use by man must end, and economy must become the servant for the development of man. Capital must serve labor, things must serve life. Instead of the exploitative and hoarding orientation, dominant in the nineteenth century, and the receptive and marketing orientation dominant today, the *productive orientation* must be the end which all social arrangements serve.

No change must be brought about by force, it must be a simultaneous one in the economic, political and cultural spheres. Changes restricted to *one* sphere are destructive of every change. Just as primitive man was helpless before natural forces, modern man is helpless before the social and economic forces created by himself. He worships the works of his own hands, bowing to the new idols, yet swearing by the name of the God who commanded him to destroy all idols. Man can protect himself from the consequences of his own madness only by creating a sane society which conforms with the needs of man, needs which are rooted in the very conditions of his existence. A society in which man relates to man lovingly, in which he is rooted in bonds of brotherliness and solidarity, rather than in the ties of blood and soil; a society which gives him the possibility of transcending nature by creating rather than by destroying, in which everyone gains a sense of self by experiencing himself as the subject of his powers rather than by conformity, in which a system of orientation and devotion exists without man's needing to distort reality and to worship idols.

Building such a society means taking the next step; it means the end of "humanoid" history, the phase in which man had not become fully human. It does not mean the "end of days," the "completion," the state of perfect harmony in which no conflicts or problems confront men. On the contrary, it is man's fate that his existence is beset by contradictions, which he has to solve without ever solving them. When he has overcome the primitive state of human sacrifice, be it in the ritualistic form of the Aztecs or in the secular form of war, when he has been able to regulate his relationship with nature reasonably instead of blindly, when things have truly become his servants rather than his idols, he will be confronted with the truly human conflicts and problems; he will have to be adventuresome, courageous, imaginative, capable of suffering and of joy, but his powers will be in the service of life, and not in the service of death. The new phase of human history, if it comes to pass, will be a new beginning, not an end.

Man today is confronted with the most fundamental choice; not that between Capitalism or Communism, but that between *robotism* (of both the capitalist and the communist variety), or Humanistic Communitarian Socialism. Most facts seem to indicate that he is choosing robotism, and that means, in the long run, insanity and destruction. But all these facts are not strong enough to destroy faith in man's reason, good will and sanity. As long as we can think of other alternatives, we are not lost; as long as we can consult together and plan together, we can hope. But, indeed, the shadows are lengthening; the voices of insanity are becoming louder.

We are in reach of achieving a state of humanity which corresponds to the vision of our great teachers; yet we are in danger of the destruction of all civilization, or of robotization. A small tribe was told thousands of years ago: "I put before you life and death, blessing and curse—and you chose life." This is our choice too.

## Study Guide

1. Erich Fromm begins this essay with a description of man's social evolution from primitive times until the present. What were the major steps in this evolutionary process? Write a brief paraphrase of Fromm's view of man's emergence from nature.

2. Fromm states that when man had severed his ties with nature, he attempted to create a "truly human home to take the place of the irretrievably lost home in nature." What does Fromm mean when he suggests that man had severed his ties with nature? How does he characterize the "human home" men have tried to create for themselves?

3. What dramatic change in human life does the author suggest has taken place in the twentieth century?

4. How has this change affected men? How has it interfered with creation of a "truly human" society?

5. Fromm writes that modern man has won "freedom from clerical and secular authorities . . ." but that he has "achieved 'freedom from'—without yet having achieved 'freedom to'—to be himself, to be productive, to be fully awake. Thus he tried to escape from freedom." Fromm suggests that man's technological advances provided him the means with escaping from his newfound freedom. What does Fromm mean to distinguish by the phrases "freedom from" and "freedom to"? From what does he suggest modern man is seeking to escape? In what ways does he suggest that man's technological triumphs over nature facilitate escapism?

6. Fromm thinks man's spiritual goals have been superseded by technological ones. Man, he writes, has become "a part of the machine rather than its master. He experiences himself as a commodity, as an investment; his aim became to be a success, that is, to sell himself as profitably as possible on the market. His value as a person lies in his salability, not in his human qualities of love, reason, or in his artistic capacities. Happiness becomes identical with consumption of new and better commodities . . . ." To what extent do you feel that these statements accurately express modern man's view of himself? What evidence can you find in our society that supports or contradicts Fromm's statements?

7. Fromm states that modern man is "alienated from himself, worships the product of his own hands, the leaders of his own

making, as if they were above him, rather than made by him." What does the word "alienated" mean in this context? Is the dictionary's definition an adequate one? Write a definition of the word that you feel adequately explains its usage by Fromm.

8. Modern man, Fromm states, lives, like his primitive ancestors, in a fragmentalized world. What similarities does he find that link modern and primitive life?

9. Fromm thinks modern man originally set out to create a "sane society." How does he characterize that society? What has prevented man from realizing this goal?

10. Fromm criticizes both capitalism and socialism. What flaws does he find in the two systems? What similarities does he see linking them?

11. Fromm writes that "the death of man" is the central problem of the twentieth century. Modern men, he suggests, have become robots. In your opinion, is Fromm justified in making such an assertion?

12. In what way does Fromm propose to solve the problem of a dehumanized society?

13. Fromm states that modern men worship the products of their technology, that they have become indifferent to spiritual and human values. Does this statement characterize the attitudes of all Americans? What groups do you feel do not share these attitudes?

14. Are the racial, economic, and sexual minorities now striving for greater acceptance in American society motivated in their demands and protests by what Fromm would feel are primarily human or spiritual goals?

15. Do you think that the dehumanization of modern man accounts for the indifference, antagonism, and hostility with which affluent Americans greet protests and demands of minority groups today? If so, how are the two attitudes connected?

16. Select a prominent minority group with which you are familiar. Then analyze its goals. When you have done so, write an essay in which you try to determine whether or not the group is motivated by concerns that Fromm would see as valid spiritual or human ones.

17. In this essay, Fromm discusses the "death of man" in the twentieth century. In what areas of life do you see the sort of robotism he discusses? Plan a scenario in which you dramatize Fromm's thesis. (If you have access to the necessary equipment, you might carry the project one step further and film your scenario.)

18. Fromm discusses the unifying spiritual principle that emphasized the "idea of the unity of man, of reason, love and justice as the goals man must strive for." What is your conception of reason, love, or justice? Write an essay in which you determine the extent to which that concept is fully realized in our society. For instance, you might consider whether or not current demands for "law and order" are in harmony with our traditional belief in justice.

19. Fromm describes the Renaissance view of man, a view that stressed moral and intellectual conscience, secular and clerical freedom, and individual achievement. Such a view, he suggests, is now anachronistic. What view of man now prevails in our culture? Take a group of photographs that express that view. Then gather illustrations that express the Renaissance view of man. Use these photos and illustrations as the basis for a collage in which you contrast the two attitudes toward human life. When you have completed the collage, explain your comparison in a brief essay.

20. To survive, Fromm suggests, modern man must choose life. What does Fromm mean? How does his understanding of life differ from yours? From that commonly held by society?

21. Fromm states that modern man sees himself as a "commodity," and values himself according to his "salability." Do you feel that this statement is true? If so, how has it affected the quality of your life? When you have answered these questions, write an essay in which you discuss some of the ways in which modern men and women try to enhance their salability.

# 2. The Great American Frustration[1]

## ARCHIBALD MacLEISH

That Americans have changed their nature since Andrew Jackson's day or Theodore Roosevelt's or even Harry Truman's is now taken as self-evident—at least among the Americans. No visiting European from Crèvecoeur to Somerset Maugham would have reported us to the world in the terms in which we now report ourselves, nor would Charles Dickens, who liked us least and used almost every other derogatory term to describe us, have used the word we repeat most frequently today. Arrogant, perhaps. Self-confident and bumptious, certainly. But frustrated? If there was one people on earth incapable of frustration it was the people who inhabited the United States . . . a hundred years ago.

But not now. Not to us. Not in the newspapers or the television programs or the lecture circuits or anywhere else our national mania for prodding and poking at our national psyche indulges itself. For a time last winter the word frustration was almost as frequently seen and heard in those quarters as the word America itself, and when Robert Kennedy was shot in Los Angeles, though the talk was all of the "sickness of American society," it was still

[1] This article is based on the first Milton Eisenhower Lecture, delivered by Mr. Mac-Leish at the Johns Hopkins University.

the American sense of frustration and helplessness which spoke. We have not only accepted our frustration, we have embraced it. To the young it seems somehow to explain what is otherwise inexplicable in the numb uneasiness with which they approach their lives. To the old it provides an alternative to the exhausting labor of struggling to comprehend an increasingly incomprehensible epoch.

But what the great frustration actually means is not so obvious. Most of us, questioned about it, would reply Vietnam, meaning one of two quite different things: either that the stupidity of our involvement in the war in Vietnam has shaken our confidence in our ability to manage our own affairs, or that our astonishing failure to win the war once we had involved ourselves has undermined our belief in our greatness as a world power. But is either reply correct? Would we believe in our greatness as a world power today if we had used our incontestable superiority in weapons to blast what Governor Reagan refers to as "a water buffalo economy" off the earth? Or would we now regain our political self-confidence if we were to repudiate the President, whoever he was, who involved us in Vietnam in the first place? I doubt it. I think any such washing of the hands would end where, indeed, it has already ended; in the realization that no one, whether Eisenhower or Kennedy or Johnson, can usefully be blamed for the events which led to our involvement in Vietnam because no one of them was really in control of those events. And that realization, far from curing our sense of frustration, would only deepen it.

Or, more precisely, it would show us what this frustration which we confess so readily really is. It is not, as we like to think, Vietnam. Not the sense of individual helplessness which plagues the citizens of a large country when they become aware of the blindness and ineptitude of their rulers, the stupidity of those in power. Not the impotent rage which follows the failure of events to conform to expectations, the failure of history to keep to the plot as written—the refusal of the water buffalo economy to collapse before the electronic power. Not the first mistake which committed us to the Asian war, or the last mistake which has left us in it, or anything else which has to do with Vietnam alone—which began in Vietnam and will end there. It is none of these things but something larger and more troubling: a numb, unformed, persistent sense, like the hinting pinch of a pain which is not yet brutal hurt but will be, that we, as Americans, we perhaps as members of our generation on this earth, have somehow lost control of the management of our human affairs, of the direction of our lives, of what our ancestors would have called our destiny.

It is a sense we have had in one form or another for a long time now, but not as an explicit, a formulated fear until we found ourselves deep in the present century with its faceless slaughters, its mindless violence, its fabulous triumphs over space and time and matter ending in terrors space and time and matter never held. Before that there were only hints and intimations, but they were felt, they were recorded where all the hints and intimations are recorded —in poems, fictions, works of art. From the beginning of what we used to call the industrial revolution—what we see today more clearly as a sort of technological coup d'état—men and women, particularly men and women of imaginative sensibility, have seen that something was happening to the human role in the shaping of civilization.

A curious automatism, human in origin but not human in action, seemed to be taking over. Cities were being built and rebuilt not with human purposes in mind but with technological means at hand. It was no longer the neighborhood which fixed the shape and limits of the town but the communications system, the power grid. Technology, our grandfathers said, "advanced" and it was literally true: it was technology which was beating the tambours, leading the march. Buildings crowded into the air not because their occupants had any particular desire to lift them there, but because the invention of electric elevators and new methods of steel and glass construction made these ziggurats possible and the possibility presented itself as economic compulsion.

Wildness and silence disappeared from the countryside, sweetness fell from the air, not because anyone wished them to vanish or fall but because throughways had to floor the meadows with cement to carry the automobiles which advancing technology produced first by the thousands and then by the thousand thousands. Tropical beaches turned into high-priced slums where thousand-room hotels elbowed each other for glimpses of once-famous surf not because those who loved the beaches wanted them there but because enormous jets could bring a million tourists every year—and therefore did.

The result, seen in a glimpse here, a perception there, was a gradual change in our attitude toward ourselves as men, toward the part we play as men in the direction of our lives. It was a confused change. We were proud—in England, and even more in America, raucously proud—of our technological achievements, but we were aware also, even from the beginning, that these achievements were not altogether ours or, more precisely, not altogether ours to direct, to control—that the *process* had somehow taken over leaving the purpose to shift for itself so that we, the ostensible managers of the process, were merely its beneficiaries.

Not, of course, that we complained of that, at least in the beginning. A hundred years ago, with the rare exception of a Dickens or a Zola, we were amenable enough—amenable as children at a Christmas party. Inventions showered on our heads: steam engines and electric lights and telegraph messages and all the rest. We were up to our knees, to our necks, in Progress. And technology had made it all possible. Science was the giver of every good and perfect gift. If there were aspects of the new world which were not perfect— child labor for example—progress would take care of them. If the ugliness and filth and smoke of industrial cities offended us, we put up with them for the sake of the gas lights and the central heating. We were rich and growing richer.

But nevertheless the uneasiness remained and became more and more evident in our books, our paintings, our music—even the new directions of our medical sciences. Who were *we* in this strange new world? What part did *we* play in it? Someone had written a new equation somewhere, pushed the doors of ignorance back a little, entered the darkened room of knowledge by one more step. Someone else had found a way to make use of that new knowledge, put it to work. Our lives had changed but without *our* changing them, without our intending them to change. Improvements had appeared and we had accepted them. We had bought Mr. Ford's machines by the hundreds of thousands. We had ordered radios by the millions and then installed TVs. And now we took to the air, flew from city to city, from continent to continent, from climate to climate, following summer up and down the earth like birds. We were new men in a new life in a new world . . . but a world *we* had not made—had not, at least, intended to make.

And a new world, moreover, that we were increasingly unsure, as time went by, we would have wanted to make. We wanted its conveniences, yes. Its comforts, certainly. But the world as a world to live in? As a human world? It was already obvious by the beginning of this century that many of our artists and writers—those not so silent observers of the human world who sit in its windows and lurk in its doorways watching—were not precisely in love with the modern world, were, indeed, so little in love with it that they had turned against life itself, accepting absurdity and terror in its place and making of human hopelessness the only human hope. And there were other nearer, stranger witnesses. Before the century was two-thirds over numbers of our children—extraordinary numbers if you stop to think about it—were to reject, singly and secretly, or publicly in curious refugee encampments, the whole community of our modern lives, and most particularly those aspects of our lives which were most modern: their conveniences, their comforts . . . their affluence.

It was inevitable under these circumstances that some sort of confrontation should occur between the old idea of man as the liver of his own life, the shaper of his own existence, and the new idea of world, the newly autonomous world—world autonomous in its economic laws, as the Marxists hoped, or autonomous in its scientific surge, its technological compulsions, as some in the West began to fear. And, of course, the confrontation did occur: first in rather fatuous academic ructions in which science and the humanities were made to quarrel with each other in the universities, and then, in 1945, at Hiroshima. What happened at Hiroshima was not only that a scientific breakthrough—"breakthrough" in the almost literal sense —had occurred and that a great part of the population of a city had been burned to death, but that the problem of the relation of the triumphs of modern science to the human purposes of man had been explicitly defined and the whole question of the role of humanity in the modern scientific age had been exposed in terms not even the most unthinking could evade.

Prior to Hiroshima it had still been possible—increasingly diffi-cult but still possible—to believe that science was by nature a human tool obedient to human wishes and that the world science and its technology could create would therefore be a human world reflect-ing our human needs, our human purposes. After Hiroshima it was obvious that the loyalty of science was not to humanity but to truth —its own truth—and that the law of science was not the law of the good—what humanity thinks of as good, meaning moral, decent, humane—but the law of the possible. What it is *possible* for science to know science must know. What it is possible for technology to do technology will have done. If it is possible to split the atom, then the atom must be split. Regardless. Regardless of . . . anything.

There was a time, just after Hiroshima, when we tried—we in the United States, at least—to escape from that haunting problem by blaming the scientists as individuals: the scientists, in particular, who had made the bomb—the mysterious workers in the cellars at Stagg Field and the laboratories of the Manhattan Project. And the scientists themselves, curious as it now may seem, cooperated; many of them, many of the best, assuming, or attempting to assume, burdens of personal guilt or struggling, somehow, anyhow, to undo what had been done.

I remember—more vividly perhaps than anything else which happened to me in those years—a late winter evening after Hiroshima in a study at the Institute at Princeton—Einstein's study, I think—when Niels Bohr, who was as great a man as he was a physicist, walked up and down for hours beside the rattling radiators urging me to go to President Truman, whom I did not know, to remind him that there had been an understanding between Mr. Roosevelt and the scientists about the future neutralization of the bomb. I guessed that Bohr, even as he talked that evening, realized there was nothing Mr. Truman or anyone on earth could do to unknow what was known. And yet he walked up and down the freezing study talking. Things, of course, *were* "done"—attempted anyway. In the brief time when we alone possessed what was called "the secret," the American Government offered to share it with the world (the Baruch Plan) for peaceful exploitation. What we proposed, though we did not put it in these words, was that humanity as a whole should assert its control of science, or at least of this particular branch of science, nuclear physics, limiting its pursuit of possibility to possibilities which served mankind. But the Russians, with their faith in the dialectics of matter, demurred. They preferred to put their trust in *things,* and within a few short months their trust was justified: they had the bomb themselves.

The immediate effect in the United States was, of course, the soaring fear of Russia which fed the Cold War abroad and made the black plague of McCarthyism possible at home. But there was also a deeper and more enduring consequence. Our original American belief in our human capability, our human capacity to manage our affairs ourselves, "govern ourselves," faltered with our failure to control the greatest and most immediate of human dangers. We began to see science as a kind of absolute beyond our reach, beyond our understanding even, known, if it was known at all, through proxies who, like priests in other centuries, could not tell us what they knew.

In short, our belief in ourselves declined at the very moment when the Russian belief in the mechanics of the universe confirmed itself. No one talked any longer of a Baruch Plan, or even remembered that there had been one. The freedom of science to follow the laws of absolute possibility to whatever conclusions they might lead had been established, or so we thought, as the unchallengeable fixed assumption of our age, and the freedom of technology to invent whatever world it happened to invent was taken as the underlying law of modern life. It was enough for a manufacturer of automobiles to announce on TV that he had a better idea—any better idea: pop-open gas-tank covers or headlights that hide by day. No one thought any longer of asking whether his new idea matched a human purpose.

What was happening in those years, as the bitterly satirical fictions of the period never tired of pointing out, was that we were ceasing to think of ourselves as men, as self-governing men, as proudly self-governing makers of a new nation, and were becoming instead a society of consumers: recipients—grateful recipients—of the blessings of a technological civilization. We no longer talked in the old way of The American Proposition, either at home or abroad —particularly abroad. We talked instead of The American Way of Life. It never crossed our minds apparently—or if it did we turned our minds away—that a population of consumers, though it may constitute an affluent society, can never compose a nation in the great, the human, sense.

But the satirical novels, revealing as they were, missed the essential fact that we were becoming a population of consumers, an affluent society, not because we preferred to think of ourselves in this somewhat less than noble role but because we were no longer able to think of ourselves in that other role—the role our grandfathers had conceived for us two hundred years ago. We were not, and knew we were not, Whitman's Pioneers O Pioneers.

It is here, rather than in the floundering failures and futile disappointments of Vietnam, that this famous frustration of ours is rooted. Vietnam alone, disastrous as that whole experience has been, could never have produced, in a confident and self-reliant people such as the Americans once were, a mood like the American mood of these past months. Not even the riots of last summer and this spring could have afflicted us as we are now afflicted if we had still believed that our principal business was the making of a nation, the government of ourselves. Indeed the riots are, if anything, the consequence, not the cause, of our self-doubt—or, more precisely, the consequence of the *actual* causes of that doubt. It is not without significance that the targets of the mobs in the burning streets are supermarkets and television outlets rather than the courthouses and city halls which would have drawn the mobs of earlier times. Courthouses and city halls stand—or stood once—for The American Proposition. Supermarkets and television outlets are the symbols of The American Way of Life. Mobs strike for the Bastille in any rising and the Bastille in the United States today is whatever stands for The American Way of Life: the goods and services, the material wealth, which the majority claim as the mark of their Americanism and which the minority are denied.

It is because we are unwilling to recognize this fact and unable to face the crisis as a crisis in the long struggle for the creation of a true Republic—because, indeed, we are no longer primarily concerned with the creation of a true Republic—that the majority respond to these riots with nothing but a demand for more police and more repression, while the Congress sits impotent and paralyzed in Washington.

Which means, of course, however we put it, that we no longer believe in man. And it is that fact which raises, in its turn, the most disturbing of all the swarming questions which surround us: how did we come to this defeated helplessness? How were we persuaded of our impotence as men? What convinced us that the fundamental law of a scientific age must be the scientific law of possibility and that our human part must be a passive part, a subservient part, the part of the recipient, the beneficiary . . . the victim? Have the scientists taught us this? A few months ago one of the greatest of living scientists told an international gathering composed of other scientists: "We must not ask where science and technology are taking us, but rather how we can manage science and technology so that they can help us get where we want to go." It is not reported that Dr. René Dubos was shouted down by his audience, and yet what he was asserting was precisely what we as a people seem to have dismissed as unthinkable: that "we," which apparently means mankind, must abandon our modern practice of asking where science and technology are "taking *us*," and must ask instead how *we* can "manage" science and technology so that they will help us to achieve *our* purposes—our purposes, that is to say, as men.

Dr. Dubos, it appears, scientist though he is and great scientist, believes rather more in man than we do. Why, then, do we believe so little? Perhaps we can answer that question best by asking another: how was our original, American belief in man achieved?

Where did it come from? Thomas Jefferson, who had as much to do with the definition of our American belief as anyone, reflected on that subject toward his life's end. It was that famous trio at William and Mary, he decided, who "fixed" his "destinies." It was his education in his college, the teaching of Small and Wythe and the rest, which shaped his mind, gave it its direction. John Adams would have said the same and doubtless did: it was in Harvard College that he found those Greeks and Romans who taught him what a man could be and therefore *should*.

Is it *our* education, then, which has shaped the very different estimate of man we live by? In part, I think; in considerable part. Education, particularly higher education, has altered its relation to the idea of man in fundamental ways since Adams's day and Jefferson's. From the time when Harvard President Charles Eliot introduced the elective system there—from the time, that is to say, of the renunciation by the university of an intention to produce a certain *kind* of man, a man shaped by certain models, certain texts—the university's concern with "man" as such has grown less and less and its concern with what it calls "subjects" has become greater and greater. The important thing has become the academic "offering" (revealing word): the range of subjects from which the student, with his eye on his career, may choose. And the ultimate consequence, only too evident in the time we live in, has been the vocationalization of the higher schools. The college no longer exists to produce men *qua* men, men prepared for life in a society of men, but men as specialized experts, men prepared for employment in an industry or a profession.

"Getting ahead in the world," says Professor Allen Tate of the University of Minnesota, "is now the purpose of education and the University must therefore provide education for our time, not for all time: it must discover and then give to society what society thinks it wants. . . ." Some of us, looking at the present state of American society—the decay of its cities, the bewilderment of its citizens—may wonder whether the university has really provided "education for our time," but no one, I think, will deny that Professor Tate's emphatic irony has its bite. The vocationalism which a technological society demands of the graduate schools has produced a secondary vocationalism which the graduate schools impose on the colleges, and the result is that undergraduate education—far more important to the preparation for citizenship than graduate education—is increasingly affected by the vocational taint.

What is happening, and in the greatest universities as well as in the less great, is that the entire educational process is becoming fixed—hung-up as the phrase goes now—on its vocational end result. The job out there in the profession or the industry dictates the "training" (their word, not mine) in the graduate schools, and the graduate schools dictate the preparation in the colleges, and the whole system congeals from the top down like a pond freezing. The danger is that, the society may congeal with it, for nothing is more certain in the history of our kind than the fact that frozen societies perish.

As specialized, professional training, higher education in the United States today is often magnificent. Young doctors are better and better as their specialties become more specialized: so much better that it is now a recommendation in almost any field to say of a young doctor that he is young. Student physicists in the great graduate schools are so notoriously productive at twenty-two that a professional physicist of thirty regards himself, or is regarded by his juniors, as middle-aged. But the educated *man,* the man capable not of providing specialized answers, but of asking the great and liberating questions by which humanity makes its way through time, is not more frequently encountered than he was two hundred years ago. On the contrary, he is rarely discovered in public life at all.

I am not arguing—though I deeply believe—that the future of the Republic and the hope for a recovery of its old vitality and confidence depend on the university. I am confining myself to Dr. Dubos's admonition that we must give up the childishness of our present attitude toward science and technology, our constant question where *they* are taking *us,* and begin instead to ask how *we* can manage *them* "so that they can help us get where we want to go." "Where we want to go" depends, of course, on ourselves and, more particularly, on our conception of ourselves. If our conception of ourselves as the university teaches it or fails to teach it is the conception of the applicant preparing for his job, the professional preparing for his profession, then the question will not be answered because it will not be asked. But if our conception of ourselves as the university teaches it is that of men preparing to be men, to achieve themselves as men, then the question will be asked *and* answered because it cannot be avoided. Where do we want to go? Where men can be most themselves. How should science and technology be managed? To help us to become what we can be.

There is no quarrel between the humanities and the sciences.

There is only a need, common to them both, to put the idea of man back where it once stood, at the focus of our lives; to make the end of education the preparation of men to be men, and so to restore to mankind—and above all to this nation of mankind—a conception of humanity with which humanity can live.

The frustration—and it is a real and debasing frustration—in which we are mired today will not leave us until we believe in ourselves again, assume again the mastery of our lives, the management of our means.

## Study Guide

1. In describing our world as "a world we had not made—had not, at least, intended to make," MacLeish borrows a phrase from the poem, "The Laws of God, The Laws of Man," by A. E. Housman. Find a copy of this poem in the library and read it carefully. Do you think that the statement Housman makes concerning the human condition clarifies MacLeish's view of the plight of the modern American in any way? Does the modern American's response to his technological and depersonalized society resemble the response of the narrator in Housman's poem?

2. MacLeish suggests that man has lost control of his own destiny, that the directions of his life and his society are no longer determined by human values. What do you think he means by human values? What values does the author suggest have replaced human concerns? Does his view resemble that of Fromm?

3. In your opinion, how do most Americans feel about technology and its products? Does MacLeish share their views?

4. As you examine your society, can you find any evidence that suggests Americans may be changing their attitudes toward technology? Is the belief that science is "the giver of every good and perfect gift" as prevalent in the 1970's as it was in the 1950's? If it is not, how do you account for the change?

5. MacLeish thinks that as technology developed men ceased to be "the ostensible managers of the processes" of life and became merely "its beneficiaries." Explain this idea in your own words. Then, look around you and attempt to find evidence confirming or denying MacLeish's point in your own experience. You might consider whether or not the housewife is trapped by her appliances, or whether workers in business and industry are negatively affected by the technologies at their control.

6. In the statement quoted in question 5, MacLeish seems to be suggesting that men have lost control of their machines. Using a nonwritten media, create a visual or sound collage in which you demonstrate this idea. For example, you might record the sounds produced by the machines men use on a typical working day, beginning with the sound of an electric clock ringing and concluding with the TV test signal that follows sign-off. What could you suggest about modern life by assembling these sounds along with

those of the electric percolator, traffic on the freeway, computers and electronic office equipment, the sound of coins in food vending machines, and so on?

7.   The idea that men no longer control their own destinies is one which was current in the popular arts during the last decade. Examine some of the lyrics of songs by the Beatles (e.g., "Eleanor Rigby"), Simon and Garfunkel ("He was a most Peculiar Man" and "Mrs. Robinson"), and other popular groups. Then write a report on alienation as a theme in popular music.

8.   MacLeish quotes the criticism of Professor Allen Tate who states that modern universities educate students "for our time" rather than "for all time." How would you distinguish the two types of education? Examine your own education in an essay and try to determine whether it is for our time or for all time.

9.   In an essay, consider the way that technology has changed one of the following:

(a)   Warfare
(b)   Morality
(c)   Education
(d)   Art
(e)   Government

To fulfill this assignment, you must narrow your topic carefully. For instance, you might wish to consider the effects of technology on education. Has the widespread use of televised lectures, for instance, had a beneficial or detrimental effect on the student?

# 3. America

ALLEN GINSBERG

America I've given you all and now I'm nothing.
America two dollars and twentyseven cents January 17, 1956.
I can't stand my own mind.
America when will we end the human war?
Go fuck yourself with your atom bomb.
I don't feel good don't bother me.
I won't write my poem till I'm in my right mind.
America when will you be angelic?
When will you take off your clothes?
When will you look at yourself through the grave?
When will you be worthy of your million Trotskyites?
America why are your libraries full of tears?
America when will you send your eggs to India?
I'm sick of your insane demands.
When can I go into the supermarket and buy what I need with my
    good looks?
America after all it is you and I who are perfect not the next world.
Your machinery is too much for me.
You made me want to be a saint.
There must be some other way to settle this argument.

Burroughs is in Tangiers I don't think he'll come back it's sinister.
Are you being sinister or is this some form of practical joke?
I'm trying to come to the point.
I refuse to give up my obsession.
America stop pushing I know what I'm doing.
America the plum blossoms are falling.
I haven't read the newspapers for months, everyday somebody goes
    on trial for murder.
America I feel sentimental about the Wobblies.
America I used to be a communist when I was a kid I'm not sorry.
I smoke marijuana every chance I get.
I sit in my house for days on end and stare at the roses in the closet.
When I go to Chinatown I get drunk and never get laid.
My mind is made up there's going to be trouble.
You should have seen me reading Marx.
My psychoanalyst thinks I'm perfectly right.
I won't say the Lord's Prayer.
I have mystical visions and cosmic vibrations.
America I still haven't told you what you did to Uncle Max after
    he came over from Russia.

I'm addressing you.
Are you going to let your emotional life be run by Time Magazine?
I'm obsessed by Time Magazine.
I read it every week.
Its cover stares at me every time I slink past the corner candystore.
I read it in the basement of the Berkeley Public Library.
It's always telling me about responsibility. Businessmen are serious.
    Movie producers are serious. Everybody's serious but me.
It occurs to me that I am America.
I am talking to myself again.

Asia is rising against me.
I haven't got a chinaman's chance.
I'd better consider my national resources.
My national resources consist of two joints of marijuana millions of
    genitals an unpublishable private literature that goes 1400
    miles an hour and twentyfive-thousand mental institutions.
I say nothing about my prisons nor the millions of underprivileged
    who live in my flowerpots under the light of five hundred
    suns.

I have abolished the whorehouses of France, Tangiers is the next
to go.
My ambition is to be President despite the fact that I'm a Catholic.

America how can I write a holy litany in your silly mood?
I will continue like Henry Ford my strophes are as individual as
his automobiles more so they're all different sexes.
America I will sell you strophes $2500 apiece $500 down on your
old strophe
America free Tom Mooney
America save the Spanish Loyalists
America Sacco & Vanzetti must not die
America I am the Scottsboro boys.
America when I was seven momma took me to Communist Cell
meetings they sold us garbanzos a handful per ticket
a ticket costs a nickel and the speeches were free
everybody was angelic and sentimental about the workers
it was all so sincere you have no idea what a good thing
the party was in 1835 Scott Nearing was a grand old man
a real mensch Mother Bloor made me cry I once saw
Israel Amter plain. Everybody must have been a spy.
America you don't really want to go to war.
America it's them bad Russians.
Them Russians them Russians and them Chinamen. And them
Russians.
The Russia wants to eat us alive. The Russia's power mad. She
wants to take our cars from out our garages.
Her wants to grab Chicago. Her needs a Red Readers' Digest.
Her wants our auto plants in Siberia. Him big bureaucracy
running our fillingstations.
That no good. Ugh. Him make Indians learn read. Him need
big black niggers. Hah. Her make us all work sixteen hours
a day. Help.
America this is quite serious.
America this is the impression I get from looking in the television
set.
America is this correct?
I'd better get right down to the job.
It's true I don't want to join the Army or turn lathes in precision
parts factories, I'm nearsighted and psychopathic anyway.
America I'm putting my queer shoulder to the wheel.

## Study Guide

1.  Ginsberg's "America" deals with the paradoxical nature of the United States and the conflict between the American ideal and American reality. What social and political attitudes lie beneath the surface of the poem? What implicit criticisms of America and Americans does the poet make?

2.  Is America the true subject of the poem? Is its subject Americans? If it is the latter, with what characteristics of Americans is the narrator concerned?

3.  Who is the speaker in the poem? What attitude does he have toward his subject? Toward his audience? How are these attitudes conveyed through his use of language?

4.  The narrator writes "You made me want to be a saint." To what extent is the poem an ironic reversal of a beatific vision? What stands in the way of the author's achieving sainthood? What qualities does the narrator share with an Old Testament prophet?

5.  In many ways, "America" is a poem about the American consciousness (perhaps even the American conscience). How might you characterize the American consciousness as it is expressed in this poem?

6.  Near the conclusion of the poem, the narrator says "I don't want to join the army or turn lathes in precision parts factories . . ." How does this statement provide a symbolic focus for the criticisms set out earlier? What relationship links the military and industry?

7.  Assume you are an illustrator and that you have been asked to illustrate this poem. Take a group of photographs (or collect magazine illustrations) that visualize the central ideas in the poem or illustrate key lines. Using the photos, create a montage in which you make a visual statement expressing the central ideal of the poem without quoting its text.

8.  Write a critical assessment of the poem. What are its strengths and weaknesses as a poem? What are its strengths and weaknesses as a sociological criticism of American life?

9.  When you have completed your critical analysis of the poem, assume that you are one of the following individuals:

      (a)  A member of the D.A.R.

(b)  A Vietnam veteran who was wounded in action
(c)  A Black militant
(d)  Thomas Jefferson

Write a second critical assessment of the poem from the point of view of the individual whose identity you have assumed.

# 4. The Gangster as Tragic Hero

## ROBERT WARSHOW

America, as a social and political organization, is committed to a cheerful view of life. It could not be otherwise. The sense of tragedy is a luxury of aristocratic societies, where the fate of the individual is not conceived of as having a direct and legitimate political importance, being determined by a fixed and supra-political—that is, non-controversial—moral order or fate. Modern equalitarian societies, however, whether democratic or authoritarian in their political forms, always base themselves on the claim that they are making life happier; the avowed function of the modern state, at least in its ultimate terms, is not only to regulate social relations, but also to determine the quality and the possibilities of human life in general. Happiness thus becomes the chief political issue—in a sense, the only political issue—and for that reason it can never be treated as an issue at all. If an American or a Russian is unhappy, it implies a certain reprobation of his society, and therefore, by a logic of which we can all recognize the necessity, it becomes an obligation of citizenship to be cheerful; if the authorities find it necessary, the citizen may even be compelled to make a public display of his cheerfulness on important occasions, just as he may be conscripted into the army in time of war.

Robert Warshow, "The Gangster as Tragic Hero," from *The Immediate Experience*, pp. 127–133, © Doubleday Publishing Company. Permission granted by author's son.

Naturally, this civic responsibility rests most strongly upon the organs of mass culture. The individual citizen may still be permitted his private unhappiness so long as it does not take on political significance, the extent of this tolerance being determined by how large an area of private life the society can accommodate. But every production of mass culture is a public act and must conform with accepted notions of the public good. Nobody seriously questions the principle that it is the function of mass culture to maintain public morale, and certainly nobody in the mass audience objects to having his morale maintained.[1] At a time when the normal condition of the citizen is a state of anxiety, euphoria spreads over our culture like the broad smile of an idiot. In terms of attitudes towards life, there is very little difference between a "happy" movie like *Good News,* which ignores death and suffering, and a "sad" movie like *A Tree Grows in Brooklyn,* which uses death and suffering as incidents in the service of a higher optimism.

But, whatever its effectiveness as a source of consolation and a means of pressure for maintaining "positive" social attitudes, this optimism is fundamentally satisfying to no one, not even to those who would be most disoriented without its support. Even within the area of mass culture, there always exists a current of opposition, seeking to express by whatever means are available to it that sense of desperation and inevitable failure which optimism itself helps to create. Most often, this opposition is confined to rudimentary or semi-literate forms: in mob politics and journalism, for example, or in certain kinds of religious enthusiasm. When it does enter the field of art, it is likely to be disguised or attenuated: in an unspecific form of expression like jazz, in the basically harmless nihilism of the Marx Brothers, in the continually reasserted strain of hopelessness that often seems to be the real meaning of the soap opera. The gangster film is remarkable in that it fills the need for disguise (though not sufficiently to avoid arousing uneasiness) without requiring any serious distortion. From its beginnings, it has been a consistent and astonishingly complete presentation of the modern sense of tragedy.[2]

---

[1] In her testimony before the House Committee on Un-American Activities, Mrs. Leila Rogers said that the movie *None But the Lonely Heart* was un-American because it was gloomy. Like so much else that was said during the unhappy investigation of Hollywood, this statement was at once stupid and illuminating. One knew immediately what Mrs. Rogers was talking about; she had simply been insensitive enough to carry her philistinism to its conclusion.

[2] Efforts have been made from time to time to bring the gangster film into line with

In its initial character, the gangster film is simply one example of the movies' constant tendency to create fixed dramatic patterns that can be repeated indefinitely with a reasonable expectation of profit. One gangster film follows another as one musical or one Western follows another. But this rigidity is not necessarily opposed to the requirements of art. There have been very successful types of art in the past which developed such specific and detailed conventions as almost to make individual examples of the type interchangeable. This is true, for example, of Elizabethan revenge tragedy and Restoration comedy.

For such a type to be successful means that its conventions have imposed themselves upon the general consciousness and become the accepted vehicles of a particular set of attitudes and a particular aesthetic effect. One goes to any individual example of the type with very definite expectations, and originality is to be welcomed only in the degree that it intensifies the expected experience without fundamentally altering it. Moreover, the relationship between the conventions which go to make up such a type and the real experience of its audience or the real facts of whatever situation it pretends to describe is of only secondary importance and does not determine its aesthetic force. It is only in an ultimate sense that the type appeals to its audience's experience of reality; much more immediately, it appeals to previous experience of the type itself: it creates its own field of reference.

Thus the importance of the gangster film, and the nature and intensity of its emotional and aesthetic impact, cannot be measured in terms of the place of the gangster himself or the importance of the problem of crime in American life. Those European movie-goers who think there is a gangster on every corner in New York are certainly deceived, but defenders of the "positive" side of American culture are equally deceived if they think it relevant to point out that most Americans have never seen a gangster. What matters is that the experience of the gangster *as an experience of art* is universal to Americans. There is almost nothing we understand better or react to more readily or with quicker intelligence. The Western film, though it seems never to diminish in popularity, is for most of us no more than the folklore of the past, familiar and understandable

---

the prevailing optimism and social constructiveness of our culture; *Kiss of Death* is a recent example. These efforts are usually unsuccessful; the reasons for their lack of success are interesting in themselves, but I shall not be able to discuss them here.

only because it has been repeated so often. The gangster film comes much closer. In ways that we do not easily or willingly define, the gangster speaks for us, expressing that part of the American psyche which rejects the qualities and the demands of modern life, which rejects "Americanism" itself.

The gangster is the man of the city, with the city's language and knowledge, with its queer and dishonest skills and its terrible daring, carrying his life in his hands like a placard, like a club. For everyone else, there is at least the theoretical possibility of another world—in that happier American culture which the gangster denies, the city does not really exist; it is only a more crowded and more brightly lit country—but for the gangster there is only the city; he must inhabit it in order to personify it: not the real city, but that dangerous and sad city of the imagination which is so much more important, which is the modern world. And the gangster—though there are real gangsters—is also, and primarily, a creature of the imagination. The real city, one might say, produces only criminals; the imaginary city produces the gangster: he is what we want to be and what we are afraid we may become.

Thrown into the crowd without background or advantages, with only those ambiguous skills which the rest of us—the real people of the real city—can only pretend to have, the gangster is required to make his way, to make his life and impose it on others. Usually, when we come upon him, he has already made his choice or the choice has already been made for him, it doesn't matter which: we are not permitted to ask whether at some point he could have chosen to be something else than what he is.

The gangster's activity is actually a form of rational enterprise, involving fairly definite goals and various techniques for achieving them. But this rationality is usually no more than a vague background; we know, perhaps, that the gangster sells liquor or that he operates a numbers racket; often we are not given even that much information. So his activity becomes a kind of pure criminality: he hurts people. Certainly our response to the gangster film is most consistently and most universally a response to sadism; we gain the double satisfaction of participating vicariously in the gangster's sadism and then seeing it turned against the gangster himself.

But on another level the quality of irrational brutality and the quality of rational enterprise become one. Since we do not see the rational and routine aspects of the gangster's behavior, the practice of brutality—the quality of unmixed criminality—becomes the totality of his career. At the same time, we are always conscious that the whole meaning of this career is a drive for success: the typical gangster film presents a steady upward progress followed by a very precipitate fall. Thus brutality itself becomes at once the means to success and the content of success—a success that is defined in its most general terms, not as accomplishment or specific gain, but simply as the unlimited possibility of aggression. (In the same way, film presentations of businessmen tend to make it appear that they achieve their success by talking on the telephone and holding conferences and that success *is* talking on the telephone and holding conferences.)

From this point of view, the initial contact between the film and its audience is an agreed conception of human life: that man is a being with the possibilities of success or failure. This principle, too, belongs to the city; one must emerge from the crowd or else one is nothing. On that basis the necessity of the action is established, and it progresses by inalterable paths to the point where the gangster lies dead and the principle has been modified: there is really only one possibility—failure. The final meaning of the city is anonymity and death.

In the opening scene of *Scarface,* we are shown a successful man; we know he is successful because he has just given a party of opulent proportions and because he is called Big Louie. Through some monstrous lack of caution, he permits himself to be alone for a few moments. We understand from this immediately that he is about to be killed. No convention of the gangster film is more strongly established than this: it is dangerous to be alone. And yet the very conditions of success make it impossible not to be alone, for success is always the establishment of an *individual* pre-eminence that must be imposed on others, in whom it automatically arouses hatred; the successful man is an outlaw. The gangster's whole life is an effort to assert himself as an individual, to draw himself out of the crowd, and he always dies *because* he is an individual; the final bullet thrusts him back, makes him, after all, a failure. "Mother of God," says the dying Little Caesar, "is this the end of Rico?"—speaking of himself thus in the third person because what has been brought low is not the undifferentiated *man,* but the individual with a name, the gangster, the success; even to himself he is a creature of the imagination. (T. S. Eliot has pointed out that a number of Shakespeare's tragic heroes have this trick of looking at themselves dramatically; their true identity, the thing that is destroyed when they die, is something outside themselves—not a man, but a style of life, a kind of meaning.)

At bottom, the gangster is doomed because he is under the obligation to succeed, not because the means he employs are unlawful. In the deeper layers of the modern consciousness, *all* means are unlawful, every attempt to succeed is an act of aggression, leaving one alone and guilty and defenseless among enemies: one is *punished* for success. This is our intolerable dilemma: that failure is a kind of death and success is evil and dangerous, is—ultimately—impossible. The effect of the gangster film is to embody this dilemma in the person of the gangster and resolve it by his death. The dilemma is resolved because it is *his* death, not ours. We are safe; for the moment, we can acquiesce in our failure, we can choose to fail.

## Study Guide

1.  Warshow states that "America, as a social and political organization, is committed to a cheerful view of life." Is this statement as valid today as it was when Warshow wrote it in 1948? What segments of our society are, in your opinion, committed to such a view of life? Which ones are not?

2.  Examining the films of the late 1940's, Warshow concludes that the organs of mass culture reflected the view that "happiness is the chief political issue in America." Is this assessment of the entertainment media valid today?

Develop an essay on the point of view of the entertainment media. You might approach your subject in one of many ways. For example, compare the view of American life implicit in the film *Good News,* the college musical Warshow discusses, with that in more recent films about American youth such as *Getting Straight* or *The Strawberry Statement.*

You might compare the attitudes toward our society expressed in standard television fare with that expressed in such recent films as *Easy Rider, Five Easy Pieces,* or *M\*A\*S\*H.* Do the entertainment media express a single cultural standard?

3.  A noted news commentator recently stated that Americans are upset by TV news coverage because they expect it to entertain them as they are entertained by other television programs. Does this view confirm or deny Warshow's statement that we are committed to the view that happiness is a political issue in America?

4.  In analyzing the classic gangster film, what characteristics does Warshow feel the gangster possesses that elevate him to the status of tragic hero? Are these characteristics possessed by any culture heroes today?

5.  Warshow states that the gangster expresses a "part of the American psyche . . . which rejects Americanism." Explain this idea in a paragraph of your own composition. What does the gangster reject? What attitude does he have toward himself that sets him apart from others? In what ways is he an inversion of some American ideal? What is lost when he dies?

6.  Consider the political assumptions Warshow uses in developing his theory. Can one account for the virtual disappearance of gangster

films as a genre in the past decade by looking at the political climate in America? Can one account for its continued popularity with the young?

7.   Do any of the heroes of American youth or American minority groups share characteristics with the classic screen gangster? In an essay, compare and contrast the classic gangster hero with some current culture hero.

8.   Warshow suggests that the screen gangster captured the American imagination partly because his story expressed the "drive for success." This drive also entailed the possibility of unlimited aggression. Do these statements tell us anything about our culture?

9.   If possible, view some of the classic gangster films (*Scarface, Little Caesar, Public Enemy,* or *Kiss of Death*). Then prepare a scenario for a modern gangster film. What changes might you have to make to adapt the classic genre to contemporary tastes? When you have prepared your scenario, write an analysis of the changes you have made.

10.   Warshow suggests that the popularity of the gangster film rested in part on social and political conditions in America in the 1930's. Select some popular art form of the 1970's. Does its popularity reflect today's social or political conditions? Present your findings in an essay.

# 5. My Dungeon Shook

JAMES BALDWIN

Dear James:

I have begun this letter five times and torn it up five times. I keep seeing your face, which is also the face of your father and my brother. Like him, you are tough, dark, vulnerable, moody—with a very definite tendency to sound truculent because you want no one to think you are soft. You may be like your grandfather in this, I don't know, but certainly both you and your father resemble him very much physically. Well, he is dead, he never saw you, and he had a terrible life; he was defeated long before he died because, at the bottom of his heart, he really believed what white people said about him. This is one of the reasons that he became so holy. I am sure that your father has told you something about all that. Neither you nor your father exhibit any tendency towards holiness: you really *are* of another era, part of what happened when the Negro left the land and came into what the late E. Franklin Frazier called "the cities of destruction." You can only be destroyed by believing that you really are what the white world calls a *nigger*. I tell you this because I love you, and please don't you ever forget it.

I have known both of you all your lives, have carried your Daddy in my arms and on my shoulders, kissed and spanked him

From *The Fire Next Time,* by James Baldwin. Copyright © 1962, 1963 by James Baldwin. Reprinted by permission of the publisher, The Dial Press.

and watched him learn to walk. I don't know if you've known anybody from that far back; if you've loved anybody that long, first as an infant, then as a child, then as a man, you gain a strange perspective on time and human pain and effort. Other people cannot see what I see whenever I look into your father's face, for behind your father's face as it is today are all those other faces which were his. Let him laugh and I see a cellar your father does not remember and a house he does not remember and I hear in his present laughter his laughter as a child. Let him curse and I remember him falling down the cellar steps, and howling, and I remember, with pain, his tears, which my hand or your grandmother's so easily wiped away. But no one's hand can wipe away those tears he sheds invisibly today, which one hears in his laughter and in his speech and in his songs. I know what the world has done to my brother and how narrowly he has survived it. And I know, which is much worse, and this is the crime of which I accuse my country and my countrymen, and for which neither I nor time nor history will ever forgive them, that they have destroyed and are destroying hundreds of thousands of lives and do not know it and do not want to know it. One can be, indeed one must strive to become, tough and philosophical concerning destruction and death, for this is what most of mankind has been best at since we have heard of man. (But remember: *most* of mankind is not *all* of mankind.) But it is not permissible that the authors of devastation should also be innocent. It is the innocence which constitutes the crime.

Now, my dear namesake, these innocent and well-meaning people, your countrymen, have caused you to be born under conditions not very far removed from those described for us by Charles Dickens in the London of more than a hundred years ago. (I hear the chorus of the innocents screaming, "No! This is not true! How *bitter* you are!"—but I am writing this letter to *you,* to try to tell you something about how to handle *them,* for most of them do not yet really know that you exist. I *know* the conditions under which you were born, for I was there. Your countrymen were *not* there, and haven't made it yet. Your grandmother was also there, and no one has ever accused her of being bitter. I suggest that the innocents check with her. She isn't hard to find. Your countrymen don't know that *she* exists, either, though she has been working for them all their lives.)

Well, you were born, here you came, something like fourteen years ago; and though your father and mother and grandmother, looking about the streets through which they were carrying you, staring at the walls into which they brought you, had every reason to be heavyhearted, yet they were not. For here you were, Big James, named for me—you were a big baby, I was not—here you were: to be loved. To be loved, baby, hard, at once, and forever, to strengthen you against the loveless world. Remember that: I know how black it looks today, for you. It looked bad that day, too, yes, we were trembling. We have not stopped trembling yet, but if we had not loved each other none of us would have survived. And now you must survive because we love you, and for the sake of your children and your children's children.

This innocent country set you down in a ghetto in which, in fact, it intended that you should perish. Let me spell out precisely what I mean by that, for the heart of the matter is here, and the root of my dispute with my country. You were born where you were born and faced the future that you faced because you were black and *for no other reason*. The limits of your ambition were, thus, expected to be set forever. You were born into a society which spelled out with brutal clarity, and in as many ways as possible, that you were a worthless human being. You were not expected to aspire to excellence: you were expected to make peace with mediocrity. Wherever you have turned, James, in your short time on this earth, you have been told where you could go and what you could do (and *how* you could do it) and where you could live and whom you could marry. I know your countrymen do not agree with me about this, and I hear them saying, "You exaggerate." They do not know Harlem, and I do. So do you. Take no one's word for anything, including mine—but trust your experience. Know whence you came. If you know whence you came, there is really no limit to where you can go. The details and symbols of your life have been deliberately constructed to make you believe what white people say about you. Please try to remember that what they believe, as well as what they do and cause you to endure, does not testify to your inferiority but to their inhumanity and fear. Please try to be clear, dear James, through the storm which rages about your youthful head today, about the reality which lies behind the words *acceptance* and *integration*. There is no reason for you to try to become like white people and there is no basis whatever for their impertinent assumption that *they* must accept *you*. The really terrible thing, old buddy, is that *you* must accept *them*. And I mean that very seriously. You must accept them and accept them with love. For these innocent people have no other hope. They are, in effect, still trapped in a history which they do not understand; and until they understand it, they cannot be released from it. They have had to believe for many years, and for innumerable reasons, that black men are inferior to white men. Many of them, indeed, know better, but, as you will discover, people find it very difficult to act on what they know. To act is to be committed, and to be committed is to be in danger. In this case, the danger, in the minds of most white Americans, is the loss of their identity. Try to imagine how you would feel if you woke up one morning to find the sun shining and all the stars aflame. You would be frightened because it is out of the order of nature. Any upheaval in the universe is terrifying because it so profoundly attacks one's sense of one's own reality. Well, the black man has functioned in the white man's world as a fixed star, as an immovable pillar: and as he moves out of his place, heaven and earth are shaken to their foundations. You, don't be afraid. I said that it was intended that you should perish in the ghetto, perish by never being allowed to go behind the white man's definitions, by never being allowed to spell your proper name. You have, and many of us have, defeated this intention; and, by a terrible law, a terrible paradox, those innocents who believed that your imprisonment made them safe are losing their grasp of reality. But these men are your brothers—your lost, younger brothers. And if the word *integration* means anything, this is what it means: that we, with love, shall force our brothers to see themselves as they are, to cease fleeing from reality and begin to change it. For this is your home, my friend, do not be driven from it; great men have done great things here, and will again, and we can make America what America must become. It will be hard, James, but you come from sturdy, peasant stock, men who picked cotton and dammed rivers and built railroads, and, in the teeth of the most terrifying odds, achieved an unassailable and monumental dignity. You come from a long line of great poets, some of the greatest poets since Homer. One of them said, *The very time I thought I was lost, My dungeon shook and my chains fell off.*

You know, and I know, that the country is celebrating one hundred years of freedom one hundred years too soon. We cannot be free until they are free. God bless you, James, and Godspeed.

Your uncle,
James

## Study Guide

1.   Baldwin's essay was addressed to his nephew. Is the boy the only audience for whom the letter is intended? Is there another audience? Who is it? How is the nature of the second audience revealed by Baldwin's use of language?

2.   Examine Baldwin's idea that self-deception has been an element in the suppression of black men in America. How have the suppressors and the suppressed been self-deceived?

3.   In the second paragraph, Baldwin contrasts the innocent world of his brother as a child with the world of his adult experience. To what extent are these distinctions universal ones? To what extent are they peculiar to black people in America?

4.   Baldwin says that most white Americans feel innocent of having suppressed blacks and that this feeling of innocence constitutes a crime. Examine and explain this idea fully.

5.   Baldwin states that the vast majority of Americans are unaware of the true conditions in the ghettos. How does this assertion relate to the theme of innocence and experience in his essay?

6.   Baldwin tells his nephew to "accept white people with love" because this acceptance is "their only hope." What common assumptions about American racial problems does his statement contradict? Why does he place the burden on black people? How do you feel contemporary black militants might react to this admonition?

7.   The loss of identity is a prominent idea in Baldwin's essay. How does Baldwin feel black men look at themselves? What has been the traditional source of their identity? Are the identities of white Americans shaped in a similar manner?

8.   Compare Baldwin's comments on the black man's loss of identity with the view of Fromm and MacLeish. Does the white man's treatment of blacks reflect his own loss of identity?

9.   Investigate the response of recent black authors to Baldwin. (You might begin with Eldridge Cleaver's "Notes on a Native Son" in *Soul on Ice*.) Write a report on the critical reaction of other blacks to his works.

10.  Select one of James Baldwin's novels for outside reading.

After you have read it, try to determine whether or not it reflects the ideas contained in "My Dungeon Shook." Present your findings in a report.

11. Baldwin uses the dungeon as a central metaphor in this essay. Take this metaphor and use it as the basis for a nonverbal project such as a collage or sculpture. Try to express Baldwin's concept of the dungeon visually.

12. "My Dungeon Shook" was written long before the current black power movement had attained prominence. If Baldwin were writing to his nephew today, how might his letter differ? Assume the persona of a black militant and write a comparable letter.

# 6. Nice Day for a Lynching

## KENNETH PATCHEN

The bloodhounds look like sad
  old judges
In a strange court. They point
  their noses
At the Negro jerking in the
  tight noose
His feet spread crow-like above
  these
Honorable men who laugh as
  he chokes.

I don't know this black man.
I don't know these white men.

But I know that one of my hands
Is black, and one white. I know
  that
One part of me is being strangled,
While another part horribly
  laughs.

Until it changes,
I shall be forever killing; and
  be killed.

*Max Tharpe / Black Star*

# Government Injunction Restraining Harlem Cosmetic Co.

JOSEPHINE MILES

They say La Jac Brite Pink Skin Bleach avails not,
They say its Orange Beauty Glow does not glow,
Nor the face grow five shades lighter nor the heart
Five shades lighter. They say no.

They deny good luck, love, power, romance, and inspiration
From La Jac Brite ointment and incense of all kinds,
And condemn in writing skin brightening and whitening
And whitening of minds.

There is upon the federal trade commission a burden of glory
So to defend the fact, so to impel
The plucking of hope from the hand, honor from the complexion,
Sprite from the spell.

From *Poems: 1930–1960,* by Josephine Miles. Copyright © 1960 by Indiana University Press. Reprinted by permission of the publisher.

## Study Guide

1. Who is the speaker in Patchen's poem? From what point of view does he write?

2. From what vantage point does he view the lynching? What is his attitude toward it?

3. Can you relate the conclusion of Patchen's poem to Baldwin's statements about the crime of innocence in "My Dungeon Shook"?

4. In Miss Miles's poem, the question of identity is touched upon. Does her poem relate to Baldwin's contention that black people have not been allowed to establish their own identities?

5. Are the ideas in Miss Miles's poem anachronistic?

6. Is the form of the poem "Government Injunction . . ." traditional or antitraditional? Is there anything ironic about the author's choice of forms?

# 7. Wigs for Freedom

## LANGSTON HUGHES

"You ought to of heard my Cousin Minnie last night telling about her part in the riots," said Simple, leaning on one of the unbroken bars on Lenox Avenue that summer, beer in hand. "After hearing three rebroadcasts of Mayor Wagner's speech after he flew back home from Europe, Minnie was so mad she wanted to start rioting again. She said old Wagner did not say one constructive thing. Anyhow, Minnie come in the bar with a big patch on the top of her head, otherwise she was O.K., talking about all the big excitement and how she was in the very middle of it.

"Cousin Minnie told me, 'Just as I was about to hit a cop, a bottle from on high hit me.' Then she described what happened to her.

" 'They taken me to Harlem Hospital and stitched up my head, which is O.K. now and thinking better than before,' Minnie said. 'But, you know, them first-aid doctors and nurses or somebody in Harlem Hospital took my forty-dollar wig and I have not seen it since. I went back to Harlem Hospital after the riots and asked for my wig, an orange-brown chestnut blonde for which I paid cash money. But they said it were not in the Lost and Found. They said my wig had blood on it, anyhow, so it got throwed away.

" 'I told them peoples in the Emergency Room, "Not just my

From *Simple's Uncle Sam*, by Langston Hughes. Copyright © 1965 by Langston Hughes. Reprinted by permission of Hill and Wang, Inc.

wig, but my head had blood on it, too. I am glad you did not throw my head away." Whereupon one of them young doctors had the nerve to say, "Don't sass me!" But since he was colored, I did not cuss him out.

" 'I knowed that young doctor had been under a strain—so many busted heads to fix up—so I just let his remarks pass. All I said was, "I wish I had back my wig. That were a real-hair wig dyed to match my complexion and styled to compliment my cheekbones." Only thing I regret about them riots is, had it not been for me wanting to get even with white folks, I would still have my wig. My advice to all womens taking part in riots is to leave their wigs at home.'

"I said, 'Miss Minnie, you look good with your natural hair, African style. I did not like you with that blonde wig on, nohow. Fact is, I did not hardly know you the first time I run into you on 125th Street under that wig. Now you look natural again.'

" 'The reason I bought that wig is, I do not want to look natural,' said Miss Minnie. 'What woman wants to look her natural self? That is why powder and rouge and wigs is made, to make a woman look like Elizabeth Taylor or Lena Horne—and them stars do not look like natural-born womens at all. I paid forty dollars for my wig just to look *unnatural*. It were *fine* hair, too! All wigs should always be saved in hospitals, bloody or not, and given back to the patients after their heads is sewed up. Since I were unconscious from being hit with a bottle, also grief-stricken from little Jimmy Powell's pistol funeral, when they ambulancetized me and laid me out in the hospital, I did not even know they had taken my wig off.'

" 'Do you reckon you will be left with a scar in the top of your head?' I asked.

" 'If I do,' said Miss Minnie, 'I am proud of it. What is one little scar in the fight for freedom when some people lose their life? Medgar Evers lost his life in Mississippi. All I lost was my wig in Harlem Hospital. And I know that cop did not hit me. He was busy hitting somebody else when I started to hit him; he didn't see me. Some Negro on a roof aimed a bottle at that cop's head—but hit me by accident instead. Bullets, billy clubs, and bottles was flying every whichaway that Sunday night after that Powell boy's funeral. Lenox Avenue were a *sweet* battleground. But I would not have been in action myself had not I seen a cop hit an old man old enough to be his father. He were a young white cop and the man was an old black man who did not do nothing except not move fast enough when that cop spoke. That young cop whaled him. WHAM! WHAM!

WHAM! I did not have no weapon with me but my purse, but I was going to wham that cop dead in the face with that—when a bottle whammed me on the head. God saved that cop from being slapped with a pocketbook full of knockout punches from poker chips to a bottle of Evening in Paradise, also a big bunch of keys which might of broke his nose.'

" 'Don't you believe in nonviolence?' I asked.

" 'Yes,' said Miss Minnie, 'when the other parties are nonviolent, too. But when I have just come out of a funeral parlor from looking at a little small black boy shot three times by a full-grown cop, I think it is about time I raised my pocketbook and strike at least one blow for freedom. I come up North ten years ago to find freedom, Jesse B. Semple. I did not come to Harlem to look a white army of white cops in the face and let them tell me I can't be free in my own black neighborhood on my own black street in the very year when the Civil Rights Bill says *you shall be free.* No, I didn't! It is a good thing that bottle struck me down, or I would of tore that cop's head every way but loose.'

" 'Then you might not of been here today,' I said.

" 'That is right,' agreed Miss Minnie, 'but my soul would go marching on. Was I to have gone to the morgue instead of Harlem Hospital, I would go crying, *"Freedom now,"* and I would come back to haunt them that struck me low. The ghost of Miss Minnie would walk among white folks till their dying day and keep them scared to death. I would incite to riot every week-end in Harlem. I would lead black mobs—which is what the papers said we is—from Friday night to Monday morning. It would cost New York a million dollars a week to just try to keep us Negroes and *me* quiet. They would wonder downtown what got into Harlem. It would just be my spirit egging us on. I would gladly die for freedom and come back to haunt white folks. Yes, I would! Imagine me floating down Lenox Avenue, a white ghost with a blonde wig on!'

" 'I would hate to see you,' I said.

" 'I would hate to see myself,' said Miss Minnie. *'Freedom now!'* She raised her beer glass and I raised mine. Then Miss Minnie said, 'I might not of gave my head to the cause, but I gave my wig.'

"Peoples like to hear Cousin Minnie talk and sometimes when she gets an audience, she goes to town. It being kind of quiet in the bar last night, folks started listening at Minnie instead of playing the juke box, and Minnie proceeded to expostulate on the subject of riots and white and colored leaders advising Harlem to go slow and be cool. Says Minnie, 'When I was down South picking cotton, didn't a soul tell me to go slow and cool it. "Pick more! Pick more! Can't you pick a bale a day? What's wrong with you?" That's what they said. Did not a soul say, "Wait, don't over-pick yourself." Nobody said slow down in cotton-picking days. So what is this here now? When Negroes are trying to get something for themselves, I must wait, *don't demonstrate?* I'll tell them big shots, "How you sound?"

" 'Be cool?' asked Miss Minnie. 'Didn't a soul say, "Be cool," when I was out in that hot sun down South. I heard not nary a word about "be cool." So who is telling me to be cool now? I have not no air cooler in Harlem where I live, neither air conditioner. And you talking about be cool! How you sound?

" 'Get off the streets!' Huh! Never did nobody say, 'Get out of the fields,' when I was down home picking cotton in them old cotton fields which I have *not* forgotten. In slavery times, I better not get out of no fields if I wanted to save my hide, or save my belly from meeting my backbone from hunger when freedom came. No! I better stay in them fields and work. But now that I got a street to stand on, how do you sound telling me to get off the street? Just because some little old disturbance come up and a few rocks is throwed in a riot, I am supposed to get off of my street in Harlem and leave it to the polices to rule? I am supposed to go home and be cool? Cool what, where, baby? How do you sound?

" ' "My name is Minnie and I lost my forty-dollar wig in the riots, so I am reduced to my natural hair," I'll tell them leaders. But what is one wig more or less to give for freedom? One wig not to go slow. One wig not to be cool. One wig not to get off the streets. When it is a long hot summer, where else but in the streets, fool, can I be cool? Uncontrollable? Who says I was uncontrollable? Huh! I knowed what I was doing. I did not lose my head because when I throwed a bottle, I knowed what I was throwing at. I were throwing at Jim Crow, Mr. K. K. Krow—at which I aimed my throw. How do you sound, telling me not to aim at Jim Crow?

" 'Did not a soul in slavery time tell old bull-whip marster not to aim his whip at me, at me—a woman. Did not a soul tell that mean old overseer not to hit Harriet Tubman (who is famous every Negro History Week), not to hit her in the head with a rock whilst she was a young girl. She were black, and a slave, and her head was made to be hit with a rock by her white overseer. Did not a soul tell that man who shot Medgar Evers in the back with a bullet to be cool. Did not a soul say to them hoodlums what slayed them three white and colored boys in Mississippi to cool it. Now they calling me hoodlums up here in Harlem for wanting to be free. Hoodlums? Me, a hoodlum? Not a soul said "hoodlums" about them night riders who ride through the South burning black churches and lighting white crosses. Not a soul said "hoodlums" when the bombs went off in Birmingham and blasted four little Sunday School girls to death, little black Sunday School girls. Not a soul said "hoodlums" when they tied an auto rim to Emmett Till's feet and throwed him in that Mississippi river, a kid just fourteen years old. But me, I am a hoodlum when I don't cool it, won't cool it, or lose my wig on a riot gig. They burnt down fourteen colored churches in Mississippi in one summer, yet, I'm supposed to be cool? Even our colored leaders telling Harlem to be cool! Well, I am my own leader, and I am not cool.

" 'Everywhere they herd my people in jail like cattle, and I am supposed to be cool. I read in one of our colored papers the other day where it has cost Mississippi four million dollars just to keep Negroes in jail. And Savannah, Georgia, spent eighteen thousand in one year feeding black boycotters in jail. One town in North Carolina spent twelve hundred dollars a day on beans for colored students they locked up for marching to be free. One paper said it cost the State of Maryland one hundred thousand dollars a month to send the militia to Cambridge to keep Negroes from getting a cup of coffee in them crumby little old white restaurants which has no decent coffee, nohow, but which everybody ought to have the right to go into on general principles. But me, I can't go in. Yet them that's supposed to be my leaders tell me, 'Give up! Don't demonstrate! Wait!' To tell the truth, I believe my own colored leaders is ashamed of me. So how are they going to lead anybody they are ashamed of? Telling me to be cool. Huh! I'm too hot to be cool—so I guess I will just have to lead my own self—which I dead sure will do. I will lead myself.' "

## Study Guide

1. "Wigs for Freedom" was written in the early 1960's. How does the author's attitude toward the Afro-American's struggle in America differ from James Baldwin's attitude? From that of other black writers such as Eldridge Cleaver, George Jackson, or Malcolm X?

2. Hughes' story has a serious point to make, but there are many elements of humor contained in it. Discuss the author's use of humor.

3. Cousin Minnie loses her wig in a riot. What does she gain?

4. Does Cousin Minnie's insistence on wearing a blond wig have any relationship to the ideas in Miss Miles's poem "Government Injunction . . ."? What is paradoxical about the wig?

5. In "My Dungeon Shook," Baldwin urged his nephew to respond with love to white society. How do you suppose Cousin Minnie might respond to this notion? Why? Assuming the persona of Cousin Minnie, write a letter to James Baldwin, expressing her response to his statements.

6. Freedom is seldom easily gained. Write a narrative describing some event in your own life through which you gained or lost freedom. Does the word have the same meaning for you that it did for the characters in Hughes' story?

7. Hughes's story might serve as the basis for a teleplay or screen play. Write a scenario for such a presentation. Then produce your play for your class.

# 8. *Prison Letter*

## GEORGE JACKSON

April 1970

Dear Fay,[1]

On the occasion of your and Senator Dymally's tour and investigation into the affairs here at Soledad, I detected in the questions posed by your team a desire to isolate some rationale that would explain why racism exists at the prison with "particular prominence." Of course the subject was really too large to be dealt with in one tour and in the short time they allowed you, but it was a brave scene. My small but mighty mouthpiece, and the black establishment senator and his team, invading the state's maximum security row in the worst of its concentration camps. I think you are the first woman to be allowed to inspect these facilities. Thanks from all. The question was too large, however. It's tied into the question of why all these California prisons vary in character and flavor in general. It's tied into the larger question of why racism exists in this whole society with "particular prominence," tied into history. Out of it comes another question: Why do California

---

[1] Mrs. Fay Stender, the author's lawyer.

joints produce more Bunchy Carters and Eldridge Cleavers than those over the rest of the country?

I understand your attempt to isolate the set of localized circumstances that give to this particular prison's problems of race is based on a desire to aid us right now, in the present crisis. There are some changes that could be made right now that would alleviate some of the pressures inside this and other prisons. But to get at the causes, you know, one would be forced to deal with questions at the very center of Amerikan political and economic life, at the core of the Amerikan historical experience. This prison didn't come to exist where it does just by happenstance. Those who inhabit it and feed off its existence are historical products. The great majority of Soledad pigs are southern migrants who do not want to work in the fields and farms of the area, who couldn't sell cars or insurance, and who couldn't tolerate the discipline of the army. And of course prisons attract sadists. After one concedes that racism is stamped unalterably into the present nature of Amerikan sociopolitical and economic life in general (the definition of fascism is: a police state wherein the political ascendancy is tied into and protects the interests of the upper class—characterized by militarism, *racism,* and imperialism), and concedes further that criminals and crime arise from material, economic, sociopolitical causes, we can then burn *all* of the criminology and penology libraries and direct our attention where it will do some good.

The logical place to begin any investigation into the problems of California prisons is with our "pigs are beautiful" Governor Reagan, radical reformer turned reactionary. For a real understanding of the failure of prison policies, it is senseless to continue to study the criminal. All of those who can afford to be honest know that the real victim, that poor, uneducated, disorganized man who finds himself a convicted criminal, is simply the end result of a long chain of corruption and mismanagement that starts with people like Reagan and his political appointees in Sacramento. After one investigates Reagan's character (what makes a turncoat) the next logical step in the inquiry would be a look into the biggest political prize of the state—the directorship of the Department of Correction.

All other lines of inquiry would be like walking backward. You'll never see where you're going. You must begin with directors, assistant directors, adult authority boards, roving boards, supervisors, wardens, captains, and guards. You have to examine these people from director down to guard before you can logically examine their product. Add to this some concrete and steel, barbed wire, rifles, pistols, clubs, the tear gas that killed Brother Billingslea in San Quentin in February 1970 while he was locked in his cell, and the pick handles of Folsom, San Quentin, and Soledad.

To determine how men will behave once they enter the prison it is of first importance to know that prison. Men are brutalized by their environment—not the reverse.

I gave you a good example of this when I saw you last. Where I am presently being held, they never allow us to leave our cell without first handcuffing us and belting or chaining the cuffs to our waists. This is preceded always by a very thorough skin search. A force of a dozen or more pigs can be expected to invade the row at any time searching and destroying personal effects. The attitude of the staff toward the convicts is both defensive and hostile. Until the convict gives in completely it will continue to be so. By giving in, I mean prostrating oneself at their feet. Only then does their attitude alter itself to one of paternalistic condescension. Most convicts don't dig this kind of relationship (though there are some who do love it) with a group of individuals demonstrably inferior to the rest of the society in regard to education, culture, and sensitivity. Our cells are so far from the regular dining area that our food is always cold before we get it. Some days there is only one meal that can be called cooked. We *never* get anything but cold-cut sandwiches for lunch. There is no variety to the menu. The same things week after week. One is confined to his cell 23½ hours a day. Overt racism exists unchecked. It is not a case of the pigs trying to stop the many racist attacks; they actively encourage them.

They are fighting upstairs right now. It's 11:10 A.M., June 11. No black is supposed to be on the tier upstairs with anyone but other blacks but—mistakes take place—and one or two blacks end up on the tier with nine or ten white convicts frustrated by the living conditions or openly working with the pigs. The whole ceiling is trembling. In hand-to-hand combat we always win; we lose sometimes if the pigs give them knives or zip guns. Lunch will be delayed today, the tear gas or whatever it is drifts down to sting my nose and eyes. Someone is hurt bad. I hear the meat wagon from the hospital being brought up. Pigs probably gave them some weapons. But I must be fair. Sometimes (not more often than necessary) they'll set up one of the Mexican or white convicts. He'll be one who has not been sufficiently racist in his attitudes. After the brothers (enraged by previous attacks) kick on this white convict whom the officials have set up, he'll fall right into line with the rest.

I was saying that the great majority of the people who live in this area of the state and seek their employment from this institution have overt racism as a *traditional* aspect of their characters. The only stops that regulate how far they will carry this thing come from the fear of losing employment here as a result of the outside pressures to control the violence. That is O Wing, Max (Maximum Security) Row, Soledad—in part anyway.

Take an individual who has been in the general prison population for a time. Picture him as an average convict with the average twelve-year-old mentality, the nation's norm. He wants out, he wants a woman and a beer. Let's say this average convict is white and has just been caught attempting to escape. They may put him on Max Row. This is the worst thing that will ever happen to him. In the general population facility there are no chains and cuffs. TVs, radios, record players, civilian sweaters, keys to his own cell for daytime use, serve to keep his mind off his real problems. There is also a recreation yard with all sorts of balls and instruments to strike or thrust at. There is a gym. There are movies and a library well stocked with light fiction. And of course there is work, where for two or three cents an hour convicts here at Soledad make paper products, furniture, and clothing. Some people actually like this work since it does provide some money for the small things and helps them to get through their day—*without thinking* about their real problems.

Take an innocent con out of this general population setting (because a pig "thought" he may have seen him attempting a lock). Bring him to any part of O Wing (the worst part of the adjustment center of which Max Row is a part). He will be cuffed, chained, belted, pressured by the police who think that every convict should be an informer. He will be pressured by the white cons to join their racist brand of politics (they *all* go under the nickname "Hitler's Helpers"). If he is predisposed to help black he will be pushed away—by black. Three weeks is enough. The strongest hold out no more than a couple of weeks. There has been *one* white man only to go through this O Wing experience without losing his balance, without allowing himself to succumb to the madness of ribald, protrusive racism.

It destroys the logical processes of the mind, a man's thoughts become completely disorganized. The noise, madness streaming from every throat, frustrated sounds from the bars, metallic sounds from the walls, the steel trays, the iron beds bolted to the wall, the hollow sounds from a cast-iron sink or toilet.

The smells, the human waste thrown at us, unwashed bodies, the rotten food. When a white con leaves here he's ruined for life. No black leaves Max Row walking. Either he leaves on the meat wagon or he leaves crawling licking at the pig's feet.

Ironic, because one cannot get a parole to the outside prison directly from O Wing, Max Row. It's positively not done. The parole board won't even consider the Max Row case. So a man licks at the feet of the pig not for a release to the outside world but for the privilege of going upstairs to O Wing adjustment center. There the licking process must continue if a parole is the object. You can count on one hand the number of people who have been paroled to the streets from O Wing proper in all the years that the prison has existed. No one goes from O Wing, Max Row straight to the general prison population. To go from here to the outside world is unthinkable. A man *must* go from Max Row to the regular adjustment center facility upstairs. Then from there to the general prison population. Only then can he entertain thoughts of eventual release to the outside world.

One can understand the depression felt by an inmate on Max Row. He's fallen as far as he can into the social trap, relief is so distant that it is very easy for him to lose his holds. In two weeks that little average man who may have ended up on Max Row for *suspicion* of *attempted* escape is so brutalized, so completely without holds, that he will never heal again. It's worse than Vietnam.

He's dodging lead. He may be forced to fight a duel to the death with knives. If he doesn't sound and act more zealous than everyone else he will be challenged for not being loyal to his race and its politics, fascism. Some of these cons support the pigs' racism without shame, the others support it inadvertently by their own racism. The former are white, the latter black. But in here as on the street black racism is a forced *reaction*. A survival adaptation.

The picture that I have painted of Soledad's general population facility may have made it sound not too bad at all. That mistaken impression would result from the absence in my description of one more very important feature of the main line—terrorism. A frightening, petrifying diffusion of violence and intimidation is emitted from the offices of the warden and captain. How else could a small group of armed men be expected to hold and rule another much larger group except through *fear?*

We have a gym (inducement to throw away our energies with a ball instead of revolution). But if you walk into this gym with a cigarette burning, you're probably in trouble. There is a pig waiting to trap you. There's a sign "No Smoking." If you miss the sign, trouble. If you drop the cigarette to comply, trouble. The floor is regarded as something of a fire hazard (I'm not certain what the pretext is). There are no receptacles. The pig will pounce. You'll be told in no uncertain terms to scrape the cigarette from the floor with your hands. It builds from there. You have a gym but only certain things may be done and in specified ways. Since the rules change with the pigs' mood, it is really safer for a man to stay in his cell.

You have to work with emoluments that range from nothing to three cents an hour! But once you accept the pay job in the prison's industrial sector you cannot get out without going through the bad conduct process. When workers are needed, it isn't a case of accepting a job in this area. You take the job or you're automatically refusing to work, even if you clearly stated that you would cooperate in other employment. The same atmosphere prevails on the recreation yard where any type of minor mistake could result not in merely a bad conduct report and placement in adjustment center, but death. A fistfight, a temporary, trivial loss of temper will bring a fusillade of bullets down on the darker of the two men fighting.

You can't begin to measure the bad feeling caused by the existence of one TV set shared by 140 men. Think! One TV, 140 men. If there is more than one channel, what's going to occur? In Soledad's TV rooms there has been murder, mayhem, and destruction of many TV sets.

The blacks occupy one side of the room and the whites and Mexicans the other. (Isn't it significant in some way that our numbers in prison are sufficient to justify the claiming of half of all these facilities?)

We have a side, they have a side. What does your imagination envisage out of a hypothetical situation where Nina Simone sings, Angela Davis speaks, and Jim Brown "splits" on one channel, while Merle Haggard yodels and begs for an ass kicking on another. The fight will follow immediately after some brother, who is less democratic than he is starved for beauty (we did vote, but they're sixty to our forty), turns the station to see Angela Davis. What lines do you think the fighting will be along? Won't it be Angela and me against Merle Haggard?

But this situation is tolerable at least up to a point. It was worse. When I entered the joint on this offense, they had half and we had half, but our half was in the back.

In a case like the one just mentioned, the white convicts will start passing the word among themselves that all whites should be in the TV room to vote in the "Cadillac cowboy." The two groups polarize out of a situation created by whom? It's just like the outside. Nothing at all complicated about it. When people walk on each other, when disharmony is the norm, when organisms start falling apart it is the fault of those whose responsibility it is to govern. They're doing something wrong. They shouldn't have been trusted with the responsibility. And long-range political activity isn't going to help that man who will die tomorrow or tonight. The apologists recognize that these places are controlled by absolute terror, but they justify the pig's excesses with the argument that we exist outside the practice of any civilized codes of conduct. Since we are convicts rather than men, a bullet through the heart, summary execution for fistfighting or stepping across a line is not extreme or unsound at all. An official is allowed full range in violent means because a convict can be handled no other way.

Fay, have you ever considered what type of man is capable of handling absolute power. I mean how many would not abuse it? Is there any way of isolating or classifying generally who can be trusted with a gun and *absolute* discretion as to who he will kill? I've already mentioned that most of them are KKK types. The rest, all the rest, in general, are so stupid that they shouldn't be allowed to run their own bath. A *responsible* state government would have found a means of weeding out most of the savage types that are drawn to gunslinger jobs long ago. How did all these pigs get through?! Men who can barely read, write, or reason. How did they get through!!? You may as well give a baboon a gun and set him loose on us!! It's the same in here as on the streets out there. *Who* has loosed this thing on an already suffering people? The Reagans, Nixons, the men who have, who own. Investigate them!! There are no qualifications asked, no experience necessary. Any fool who falls in here and can sign his name might shoot me tomorrow from a position thirty feet above my head with an automatic military rifle!! He could be dead drunk. It could really be an accident (a million to one it won't be, however), but he'll be protected still. He won't even miss a day's wages.

The textbooks on criminology like to advance the idea that prisoners are mentally defective. There is only the merest suggestion that the system itself is at fault. Penologists regard prisons as asylums. Most policy is formulated in a bureau that operates under the heading Department of Corrections. But what can we say about these asylums since *none* of the inmates are ever cured. Since in every instance they are sent out of the prison more damaged physically and mentally than when they entered. Because that is the reality. Do you continue to investigate the inmate? Where does administrative responsibility begin? Perhaps the administration of the prison cannot be held accountable for every individual act of their charges, but when things fly apart along racial lines, when the breakdown can be traced so clearly to circumstances even beyond the control of the guards and administration, investigation of anything outside the tenets of the fascist system itself is futile.

Nothing has improved, nothing has changed in the weeks since your team was here. We're on the same course, the blacks are fast losing the last of their restraints. Growing numbers of blacks are openly passed over when paroles are considered. They have become aware that their only hope lies in resistance. They have learned that resistance is actually possible. The holds are beginning to slip away. Very few men imprisoned for economic crimes or even crimes of passion against the oppressor feel that they are really guilty. Most of today's black convicts have come to understand that they are the most abused victims of an unrighteous order. Up until now, the prospect of parole has kept us from confronting our captors with any real determination. But now with the living conditions deteriorating, and with the sure knowledge that we are slated for destruction, we have been transformed into an implacable army of liberation. The shift to the revolutionary antiestablishment position that Huey Newton, Eldridge Cleaver, and Bobby Seale projected as a solution to the problems of Amerika's black colonies has taken firm hold of these brothers' minds. They are now showing great interest in the thoughts of Mao Tse-tung, Nkrumah, Lenin, Marx, and the achievements of men like Che Guevara, Giap, and Uncle Ho.

Some people are going to get killed out of this situation that is growing. That is not a warning (or wishful thinking). I see it as an "unavoidable consequence" of placing and leaving control of our lives in the hands of men like Reagan.

These prisons have always borne a certain resemblance to Dachau and Buchenwald, places for the bad niggers, Mexicans, and poor whites. But the last ten years have brought an increase in the percentage of blacks for crimes that can *clearly* be traced to political-economic causes. There are still some blacks here who consider themselves criminals—but not many. Believe me, my friend, with the time and incentive that these brothers have to read, study, and think, you will find no class or category more aware, more embittered, desperate, or dedicated to the ultimate remedy—revolution. The most dedicated, the best of our kind—you'll find them in the Folsoms, San Quentins, and Soledads. They live like there was no tomorrow. And for most of them there isn't. Somewhere along the line they sensed this. Life on the installment plan, three years of prison, three months on parole; then back to start all over again, sometimes in the same cell. Parole officers have sent brothers back to the joint for selling newspapers (the Black Panther paper). Their official reason is "Failure to Maintain Gainful Employment," etc.

We're something like 40 to 42 percent of the prison population. Perhaps more, since I'm relying on material published by the media. The leadership of the black prison population now definitely identifies with Huey, Bobby, Angela, Eldridge, and antifascism. The savage repression of blacks, which can be estimated by reading the obituary columns of the nation's dailies, Fred Hampton, etc., has not failed to register on the black inmates. The holds are fast being broken. Men who read Lenin, Fanon, and Che don't riot, "they mass," "they rage," they dig graves.

When John Clutchette was first accused of this murder he was proud, conscious, aware of his own worth but uncommitted to any specific remedial action. Review the process that they are sending this beautiful brother through now. It comes at the end of a long train of similar incidents in his prison life. Add to this all of the things he has witnessed happening to others of our group here. Comrade Fleeta spent eleven months here in O Wing for possessing photography taken from a newsweekly. It is such things that explain why California prisons produce more than their share of Bunchy Carters and Eldridge Cleavers.

Fay, there are only two types of blacks ever released from these places, the Carters and the broken men.

The broken men are so damaged that they will never again be suitable members of any sort of social unit. Everything that was still good when they entered the joint, anything inside of them that may have escaped the ruinous effects of black colonial existence, anything that may have been redeemable when they first entered the joint—is gone when they leave.

This camp brings out the very best in brothers or destroys them entirely. But none are unaffected. None who leave here are normal. If I leave here alive, I'll leave nothing behind. They'll never count me among the broken men, but I can't say that I am normal either. I've been hungry too long. I've gotten angry too often. I've been lied to and insulted too many times. They've pushed me over the line from which there can be no retreat. I *know* that they will not be satisfied until they've pushed me out of this existence altogether. I've been the victim of so many racist attacks that I could never relax again. My reflexes will never be normal again. I'm like a dog that has gone through the K—9 process.

This is not the first attempt the institution (camp) has made to murder me. It is the most determined attempt, but not the first.

I look into myself at the close of every one of these pretrial days for any changes that may have taken place. I can still smile now, after ten years of blocking knife thrusts and pick handles of faceless sadistic pigs, of anticipating and reacting for ten years, seven of them in solitary. I can still smile sometimes, but by the time this thing is over I may not be a nice person. And I just lit my seventy-seventh cigarette of this twenty-one-hour day. I'm going to lay down for two or three hours, perhaps I'll sleep . . . .

Seize the Time.

## Study Guide

1. Is Jackson's point of view that of a prisoner? Of a black militant? In what ways does the author trace black militantism to the prison system? How valid is his logic?

2. What attitude does Jackson have toward the government that imprisoned him? How does he reveal this attitude through his use of language?

3. In arguing his case, is Jackson ever guilty of using fallacious logic? Can you, for instance, find examples of arguments directed against men rather than issues or of reasoning that might conceal rationalizations?

4. How does Jackson feel the prison system openly encourages racism? Paraphrase his ideas in two or three paragraphs.

5. Write a brief definition of racism. How does your definition differ from that implicit in Jackson's essay?

6. In what ways are the prisoners Jackson writes about dehumanized? Are members of minority groups treated in a comparable fashion outside of prisons?

7. Jackson suggests that violence and rebellion are the only alternatives to dehumanization. Does this suggest anything to you concerning the success or failure of our nation's penal institutions?

8. How do you think Jackson might have responded to James Baldwin's admonition to meet the world that oppresses the individual with love?

9. Jackson's letter describes the prison experiences of one man. Do some outside research on the effect of penal institutions on the prisoners whom they are expected to reform. Try to determine whether or not our prisons succeed in rehabilitating convicts, and present your conclusions in a documented essay.

10. Since this letter was first published, the author was killed in a prison disturbance. Numerous other rebellions and riots in our prisons have drawn attention to the civil rights of prisoners. Investigate the conditions in our prisons and the grievances of prisoners. To what extent are conditions such as those Jackson describes prevalent? When you have concluded your research, write an essay on the civil rights and liberties that you feel prisoners should have.

# 9. *The Man Who Worked for Thirty Years Without Pay*

## STAN STEINER

On the old Montoya Ranch in the hills to the north of Albuquerque, the boy came looking for a job. It was in the summer of 1933. He was then thirteen and he was hired as a ranch hand, for 75 cents a day. Abernicio Gonzales remembers the day with wincing, distant eyes. He remembers his mother had borrowed $50 to pay for the wedding of an older brother. He worked off the debt in about three months. Yet he went on working at the ranch for thirty-three years, and he says he was never paid a penny.

In those Depression days he was happy to have any job. He had been convinced, he says, to go on working for 50 cents a day and board. He was a hard worker; the rancher liked him and promised, since he was so young, to put his wages away for him. That way he would have money to live on when he was too old to work. He reluctantly agreed to this. Whenever the boy asked to see his bank account, he was cowed into silence. He was beaten when he tried to leave the remote ranch. The boy grew to be a man, but he was afraid to run away lest he lose the years of promised savings. He was a serf in the middle of the twentieth century in the United States.

One day in 1966 Gonzales fled from the Montoya Ranch. He was forty-six, penniless, a novice in the world, bewildered by his discovery of hatred. He sued for his thirty-three years of back pay, at 50 cents a day, with 6 per cent interest, but obviously no court could repay him for his lost youth and stolen manhood.

A boy may be intimidated. But why would the grown man go on as the boy began? Year after year he lived as if he were a slave. He had enslaved himself. The habits and fears of a man who feels he has no rights bind him to servitude as tightly as if he were chained.

"There are hundreds of people kept in slavery on remote ranches throughout the Southwest of the United States," declares *El Malcriado,* the newspaper of the farm workers. "It is well known. . . ."

No man has fewer rights. The campesino earns less in wages and respect than anyone else. If he is a migrant worker "his earnings are the lowest of our Nation's work force," the Senate Subcommittee on Migratory Labor reports in *The Migratory Farm Labor Problem in the United States* (1967). In recent years these migrants averaged little over $1,100 annually from field work. And they were lucky to add $600 from odd jobs, off season. The hired hands who were regularly employed did somewhat better, but not much.

There are more farm workers in the country than steel workers, auto workers, or aircraft workers. In spite of Rube Goldberg farm machines the census counters say there are 1,400,000 farm workers. Of these over 200,000 are migrants. Since the census counters do not reach the remote ranches, the unseen alleys of the barrios, and the elusive "commuters" from across the Rio Grande, there are undoubtedly many more who are uncounted. Farm workers are a hungry army.

In the fields wages are not only "the lowest," but are getting lower. The output per man on the farm zoomed 270 per cent from 1947 to 1964, while wages increased only 64 per cent, but in the factories, during the same years, output per man went up 160 per cent, while wages increased only 107 per cent. Unlike farm workers the factory workers have unions. "The gap between agricultural and nonagricultural earnings has continually widened," reports the Senate Subcommittee. Not only that, but "between 1940 and 1964 gross farm income increased from $11.1 to $42.2 billion. Yet the average farm worker today still earns a daily wage under $9. No other segment of our population is so poorly paid yet contributes so much to our Nation's health and welfare."

So I tell my friends
Not to sell themselves;
He who sells himself
Always will be the loser.

It is a song of the campesinos by the young grape picker, poet, and singer of El Teatro Campesino, Agustín Lira. He sings:

Look, look, look, look,
Look, look, how they work;
If they stop to rest
They lose their jobs.

The campesino often feels he is trapped by his labor in the fields of a stranger. Says a campesino in Delano, "You just don't get out of the fields. I think it's very heavy. It's something you are stuck with for the rest of your life. You just can't start anywhere else because you don't have the education, you don't have the experience."

"I am nothing," says another campesino. "My children, they will get an education and they will be someone."

"We have nothing but our hands. Empty hands," a woman says.

It is a feeling of nothingness voiced in the lament of *El Malcriado*: "We have seen how they have taken the work of our hands and our bodies and made themselves rich while we are left with empty hands between the earth and the sky. We who are farm workers have been insulted. We have seen ourselves treated like cattle. We have seen our children treated like inferiors in the schools. We have seen in the face of the cop our inequality before the law. We have known what it is like to be less respected, to be unwanted, to live in a world which did not belong to us."

In a small house on the edge of town the campesino lives quietly. He bothers no one. Usually he stays as far away from the downtown streets as he can. He feels uncomfortable there.

A man says, "They want our business. But they do not like us. We do not go where we are not wanted."

He is an urban man, nonetheless. Most campesinos nowadays live in the cities. Even in the supermetropolis of Los Angeles, a state of California study of employment shows that 7 per cent of the men in the barrios of East Los Angeles are farm workers. The myth of the "foot-loose" and "shiftless" migrant eternally wandering in an old jalopy, like a poor, dirty, gypsy, no longer exists in the urban Southwest—except in old movies.

Still he does not take part in urban life. He is ignored by the city elites, of whatever group. He pays little in taxes, for his income is too low, and so he has no voice. He is unrepresented in the city where he lives.

"You see, the farm worker is an outsider, even though he may be a resident worker," says Cesar Chavez. "He is an outsider economically, and he is an outsider racially. Most farm workers are of ethnic backgrounds other than white.

"And so, with very few exceptions, they have not been part of the communities where they live. Most of them don't know how or why or by whom laws are made. Who governs them. None of these things. They don't really care," Chavez says.

It is his isolation from the sources of power over his own life that has made the campesino abject. The gap between the two sections of town, much less two societies, has seemed unbridgeable. "Our color, or our language, or our job, have kept us apart," says *El Malcriado.* "And the people who are profiting from our separateness are determined to keep it that way."

A campesino looks around and sees that he is treated as though he were nonexistent. The laws that protect other workers do not apply to him. In the fields the health codes are often ignored. In the farm towns the normal sanitation and civic services often do not reach his little house. Even his ordinary needs on the job—like water to drink and the use of toilets—are ignored. Housing regulations are not enforced in his barrios and *colonias.* "The same labor camps which were used thirty years ago, at the time of the La Follette Committee hearings, are still housing our workers," Chavez tells the Senate Subcommittee on Migratory Labor. "Nothing has changed."

Campesinos are not the invisible men of the ghetto. They are vigorous, sensuous, full of life, strenuous sinews, bright as the sun itself, and at times darkly emotional. In the bars they are boisterous, yelling *"Viva!"* to the TV; and in the churches they are reverent, passionately and publicly. They suffer few identity crises. Yet, these same men will say, "I am nothing!"

The nothingness of the campesino is the recognition of what exists, the way life is. It is not simply self-denial, nor is it the humility of the poor. His is a world of nothings. It descends on the labor camps and barrio homes from the world outside with an almost physical force. Like an impenetrable white fog, it is sometimes so dense it hides the identity of a man from himself.

"I will tell you the truth," says a young campesino in Del Rio, Texas. "When I am among you people, I am not the man I am. I am the man you think I am. A fool!"

"Who emasculated us? I say we emasculate our own manhood," says Rodolfo Gonzales. "For what? The crumbs on the table we have been promised—someday. So we stoop to lick up the crumbs on the floor, saying, 'Yes sir! Yes, sir! Thank you, sir!' "

He scowls. "It's mental stoop labor."

It is "a world of fantasy," Cesar Chavez feels, a "mental attitude" that is the remnant of the old *patrón* syndrome that enslaves the campesinos through their own sense of helplessness and servility, as much as by the power of the ranchers. "It has lot to do with paternalism. Before, when the employer came by, if the worker was dying of thirst, he would say, 'I'm not thirsty, *patrón*.' And whatever ailed him, or hurt him, he never complained. Now they come back, although they would want a union, more money, [they] keep believing these things. It's really a world of fantasy."

Not all of their fears are fantasies. There is the real fear of the invisible man who feels that he, or a relative, may be deported if he becomes too visible.

In retelling her tale of twenty years in the fields—of illnesses, deaths, hungers, and inhuman treatment—Mrs. Guadalupe Olivarez was questioned by the Senate Subcommittee on Migratory Labor:

SENATOR ROBERT KENNEDY:   Have you reported it to anybody?

MRS. OLIVAREZ:   No, sir.

SENATOR ROBERT KENNEDY:   Why?

MRS. OLIVAREZ:   Well, the one thing I will tell you why, we farm workers, we are afraid.

SENATOR ROBERT KENNEDY:   Why are you afraid?

MRS. OLIVAREZ:   Because I have seen it, sir. Well, I wouldn't mention names. We were not contented about what they did to us in the company we were working for, so we rebelled, and this was sort of a strike. And so there was one woman, you know, who spoke for all of us, and so that woman was fired because she was called an agitator. So, you see, sir, that's why we are afraid to speak.

There is the fear of hunger. . . .

In the kitchens the hunger is visible on the bare tables, in the motley dishes of beans and cereals. The odd and battered pots on the rickety kerosene stoves have a nauseous odor that mingles with the delicious aroma of hot chili cooking. And there is the rancid smell of powdered eggs and surplus food rations. These are the aromas of hunger.

The eyes of the children grow cold in the winter, although the kerosene stoves in the campesinos' homes exude an odorous heat. The work in the fields is seasonal, and during the winter there is not much to do. Men sit and wait. In the farm towns there is little to do but sit and wait—jobs are few, the jobless are many.

It is nonsense to talk of high wages and low wages in work so seasonal. The campesino has to earn enough in the growing and harvesting seasons, his entire family working, to last all winter. His family starves if they cannot save. The income of the campesinos is disputed. Statistics are hard to get. And those that are given are inadequate and inaccurate and contradictory. It is enough to say that they all seem to show that the annual income of the average campesino is about one-third of the national family income of a factory worker.

And this too makes a man fearful. He gets no wage he dare depend on. When the season comes, he never knows what it will bring. The drought and the rain that worry the farmer are worse for the campesino. His family may starve in the winter. So he works harder, travels faster, goes farther, complains less. Once the crops are harvested, there will be little for him to do but sit and wait for the spring.

Waiting demeans a man. He becomes sullen. He is nothing who does nothing.

"People who are hungry have no spirit, have no strength to fight. People who are hungry don't care who makes decisions for them, so long as their families don't starve," Cesar Chavez says. He says it emphatically, unusually so for him, with knowing harshness. "People who are hungry have to eat first of all.

" 'Eating comes before religion and art,' " he says. "That's an old Mexican proverb."

I ask him, "Even before love?"

"No," Chavez says with a half smile, "but certainly before politics. Bread and eggs on the table are the important thing."

In Starr County, Texas, a mother of six children talks of hunger. Her name is Mrs. E. F. Gutierrez. She has been the director of a

Community Action Program for farm workers, going from barrio to barrio to soothe the hungry with her words.

"There is out-and-out starvation," she says. "I have been in a home where I have seen a small, two-year-old child eating oatmeal from the original paper container, with her fingers. Dry and raw.

"And I said, 'Why don't you put it in a pot and cook it? It will taste better.'

"And the mother said, 'I don't have a stove.'

"So I said, 'Why don't you mix it with a little water and sugar to make it taste better?'

"And she said, 'I don't have a cup. I don't have sugar. I don't have a spoon.' "

In the vineyards of Delano, a farm worker talks of hunger. His lips are burnt by the sun. When he talks his words expose the scar tissue.

"When a man is hungry, he either gives up, or he becomes ruthless," he says.

"A man will kill for food. He will not kill another man. He will kill himself. If a man becomes ruthless, he destroys love. Without love there is no family. There is no life. There is nothing.

"Hunger does not kill a man," he says. "I know. The hungry man kills himself, his senses, his morals, his manhood. I know."

## Study Guide

1. Stan Steiner begins his examination of the plight of Mexican-American farm laborers with the story of Abernicio Gonzales. What generalizations about the lot of the migrant farm laborer does the story illustrate?

2. At the conclusion of the illustration, Steiner states that Gonzales was "a serf in the middle of the twentieth century in the United States." Is he justified in using this analogy? What characteristics of serfdom does he associate with the life of the farm laborer?

3. To what extent does Steiner suggest that the conditions of the migrant's life are self-imposed? How does he explain the laborer's willingness to accept the low pay, inadequate living conditions, and the menial status that attaches to his job?

4. In examining working conditions of the Mexican-American farm laborer, Steiner reveals the exploitation of a sizable segment of the American labor force. What other groups have been similarly exploited? How does exploitation extend beyond economic conditions? How are minority group members affected other than as workers? Consider the creation of reservations for Indians, ghettos for black and Mexican-Americans, segregation in education, and so on.

5. Steiner relates the exploitation of the Mexican laborer to the *"patrón* syndrome." To what is he referring? Is paternalism always a factor when there are minority groups? How might it apply in specific ways to women, Indians, homosexuals, or members of other minorities discussed in this text?

6. The phrase *"patrón* syndrome" has negative connotations in the context of Steiner's discussion. Is paternalism always negative? Consider the example of a struggling white business man who exploits minority group workers by paying them barely subsistence wages, but who is willing to bankrupt himself to support the widows of several of his employees who are killed while working for him. In this case, does his paternalism justify the exploitation of the workers, or is this self-sacrifice yet another way for the businessman to maintain his superiority?

7. Steiner writes that the "campesinos are not the invisible men of the ghetto." What distinctions set the migrant Mexican laborer

apart from the black residents of inner-city slums? How are the problems of the two groups different?

8.   Throughout the essay, Steiner emphasizes the importance of fear in the lives of migratory workers. What are the sources of their fears?

9.   Which fears have the most important role in shaping the lives of the laborers whom Steiner discusses?

10.   Steiner frequently cites Cesar Chavez. Do outside research on the career of this California labor leader. What specific problems has Chavez been concerned with? What solutions did he propose for them? What means did he use to accomplish his goals. Present your findings in an expository essay.

11.   Investigate the working and living conditions of some ethnic minority in your community. Are the lives of its members like those of the migrant workers described by Steiner? If so, what are the means society has used to enforce the social and economic im-mobility of the group? In an essay, compare and contrast the living or working conditions of the local minority you have investigated with those of the Mexican-Americans discussed by Steiner.

12.   One of the workers Steiner interviewed stated: "Hunger does not kill a man . . . I know. The hungry man kills himself, his senses, his morals, his manhood. I know." This statement suggests that poverty dehumanizes men. Earlier, we have seen that Erich Fromm believes that affluence can also dehumanize men. In an essay, explore the relationship between the two forms of dehumanization. Do the conditions that Steiner describes grow out of an affluent, technologically advanced society?

13.   Have you ever been exploited? What were the circumstances? What effect did the experience have on you? Explore such an experience in a narrative essay.

# 10. *Cecilia Rosas*

AMADO MURO

When I was in the ninth grade at Bowie High School in El Paso, I got a job hanging up women's coats at La Feria Department Store on Saturdays. It wasn't the kind of a job that had much appeal for a Mexican boy or for boys of any other nationality either. But the work wasn't hard, only boring. Wearing a smock, I stood around the Ladies' Wear Department all day long waiting for women customers to finish trying on coats so I could hang them up.

Having to wear a smock was worse than the work itself. It was an agonizing ordeal. To me it was a loathsome stigma of unmanly toil that made an already degrading job even more so. The work itself I looked on as onerous and effeminate for a boy from a family of miners, shepherds, and ditchdiggers. But working in Ladies' Wear had two compensations: earning three dollars every Saturday was one; being close to the Señorita Cecilia Rosas was the other.

This alluring young woman, the most beautiful I had ever seen, more than made up for my mollycoddle labor and the smock that symbolized it. My chances of looking at her were almost limitless. And like a good Mexican, I made the most of them. But I was only

"Cecilia Rosas," by Amado Muro, Winter 1964–65 Issue of the *New Mexico Quarterly,* Volume XXXIV:4, copyright © 1965 by the University of New Mexico Press. Reprinted by permission of the author.

too painfully aware that I wasn't the only one who thought this saleslady gorgeous.

La Feria had water fountains on every one of its eight floors. But men liked best the one on the floor where Miss Rosas worked. So they made special trips to Ladies' Wear all day long to drink water and look at her.

Since I was only fourteen and in love for the first time, I looked at her more chastely than most. The way her romantic lashes fringed her obsidian eyes was especially enthralling to me. Then, too, I never tired of admiring her shining raven hair, her Cupid's-bow lips, the warmth of her gleaming white smile. Her rich olive skin was almost as dark as mine. Sometimes she wore a San Juan rose in her hair. When she did, she looked so very lovely I forgot all about what La Feria was paying me to do and stood gaping at her instead. My admiration was decorous but complete. I admired her hourglass figure as well as her wonderfully radiant face.

Other men admired her too. They inspected her from the water fountain. Some stared at her boldly, watching her trimly rhythmic hips sway. Others, less frank and open, gazed furtively at her swelling bosom or her shapely calves. This effrontery made me indignant. I, too, looked at these details of Miss Rosas. But I prided myself on doing so more romantically, far more poetically than they did, with much more love than desire.

Then, too, Miss Rosas was the friendliest as well as the most beautiful saleslady in Ladies' Wear. But the other salesladies, Mexican girls all, didn't like her. She was so nice to them all they were hard put to justify their dislike. They couldn't very well admit they disliked her because she was pretty. So they all said she was haughty and imperious. Their claim was partly true. Her beauty was Miss Rosas' only obvious vanity. But she had still another. She prided herself on being more American than Mexican because she was born in El Paso. And she did her best to act, dress, and talk the way Americans do. She hated to speak Spanish, disliked her Mexican name. She called herself Cecile Roses instead of Cecilia Rosas. This made the other salesladies smile derisively. They called her La Americana or the Gringa from Xochimilco every time they mentioned her name.

Looking at this beautiful girl was more important than money to me. It was my greatest compensation for doing work that I hated. She was so lovely that a glance at her sweetly expressive face was enough to make me forget my shame at wearing a smock and my dislike for my job with its eternal waiting around.

Miss Rosas was an exemplary saleslady. She could be frivolous, serious or demure, primly efficient too, molding herself to each customer's personality. Her voice matched her exotically mysterious eyes. It was the richest, the softest I had ever heard. Her husky whisper, gentle as a rain breeze, was like a tender caress. Hearing it made me want to dream and I did. Romantic thoughts burgeoned up in my mind like rosy billows of hope scented with Miss Rosas' perfume. These thoughts made me so languid at my work that the floor manager, Joe Apple, warned me to show some enthusiasm for it or else suffer the consequences.

But my dreams sapped my will to struggle, making me oblivious to admonitions. I had neither the desire nor the energy to respond to Joe Apple's warnings. Looking at Miss Rosas used up so much of my energy that I had little left for my work. Miss Rosas was twenty, much too old for me, everyone said. But what everyone said didn't matter. So I soldiered on the job and watched her, entranced by her beauty, her grace. While I watched I dreamed of being a hero. It hurt me to have her see me doing such menial work. But there was no escape from it. I needed the job to stay in school. So more and more I took refuge in dreams.

When I had watched her as much, if not more, than I could safely do without attracting the attention of other alert Mexican saleslades, I slipped out of Ladies' Wear and walked up the stairs to the top floor. There I sat on a window ledge smoking Faro cigarettes, looking down at the city's canyons, and best of all, thinking about Miss Rosas and myself.

They say Chihuahua Mexicans are good at dreaming because the mountains are so gigantic and the horizons so vast in Mexico's biggest state that men don't think pygmy thoughts there. I was no exception. Lolling on the ledge, I became what I wanted to be. And what I wanted to be was a handsome American Miss Rosas could love and marry. The dreams I dreamed were imaginative masterpieces, or so I thought. They transcended the insipid realities of a casual relationship, making it vibrantly thrilling and infinitely more romantic. They transformed me from a colorless Mexican boy who put women's coats away into the debonair American, handsome, dashing and worldly, that I longed to be for her sake. For the first time in my life I revelled in the magic of fantasy. It brought happiness. Reality didn't.

But my window-ledge reveries left me bewildered and shaken. They had a narcotic quality. The more thrillingly romantic fantasies I created, the more I needed to create. It got so I couldn't get enough dreaming time in Ladies' Wear. My kind of dreaming demanded disciplined concentration. And there was just too much hubbub, too much gossiping, too many coats to be put away there.

So I spent less time in Ladies' Wear. My flights to the window ledge became more recklessly frequent. Sometimes I got tired sitting there. When I did, I took the freight elevator down to the street floor and brazenly walked out of the store without so much as punching a time clock. Walking the streets quickened my imagination, gave form and color to my thoughts. It made my brain glow with impossible hopes that seemed incredibly easy to realize. So absorbed was I in thoughts of Miss Rosas and myself that I bumped into Americans, apologizing mechanically in Spanish instead of English, and wandered down South El Paso Street like a somnambulist, without really seeing its street vendors, cafes and arcades, tattoo shops, and shooting galleries at all.

But if there was confusion in these walks there was some serenity too. Something good did come from the dreams that prompted them. I found I could tramp the streets with a newly won tranquillity, no longer troubled by, or even aware of, girls in tight skirts, overflowing blouses, and drop-stitch stockings. My love for Miss Rosas was my shield against the furtive thoughts and indiscriminate desires that had made me so uneasy for a year or more before I met her.

Then, too, because of her, I no longer looked at the pictures of voluptuous women in the *Vea* and *Vodevil* magazines at Zamora's newsstand. The piquant thoughts Mexicans call *malos deseos* were gone from my mind. I no longer thought about women as I did before I fell in love with Miss Rosas. Instead, I thought about a woman, only one. This clear-cut objective and the serenity that went with it made me understand something of one of the nicest things about love.

I treasured the walks, the window-ledge sittings, and the dreams that I had then. I clung to them just as long as I could. Drab realities closed in on me chokingly just as soon as I gave them up. My future was a time clock with an American Mister telling me what to do and this I knew only too well. A career as an ice-dock laborer stretched ahead of me. Better said, it dangled over me like a Veracruz machete. My uncle, Rodolfo Avitia, a straw boss on the ice docks, was already training me for it. Every night he took me to the mile-long docks overhanging the Southern Pacific freight yards. There he handed me tongs and made me practice tripping three-hundred-pound ice blocks so I could learn how to unload an entire boxcar of ice blocks myself.

Thinking of this bleak future drove me back into my fantasies, made me want to prolong them forever. My imagination was taxed to the breaking point by the heavy strain I put on it.

I thought about every word Miss Rosas had ever said to me, making myself believe she looked at me with unmistakable tenderness when she said them. When she said: "Amado, please hang up this fur coat," I found special meaning in her tone. It was as though she had said: "Amadito, I love you."

When she gave these orders, I pushed into action like a man blazing with a desire to perform epically heroic feats. At such times I felt capable of putting away not one but a thousand fur coats, and would have done so joyously.

Sometimes on the street I caught myself murmuring: "Cecilia, *linda amorcita,* I love you." When these surges swept over me, I walked down empty streets so I could whisper: "Cecilia, *te quiero con toda mi alma"* as much as I wanted to and mumble everything else that I felt. And so I emptied my heart on the streets and window ledge while women's coats piled up in Ladies' Wear.

But my absences didn't go unnoticed. Once an executive-looking man, portly, gray, and efficiently brusque, confronted me while I sat on the window ledge with a Faro cigarette pasted to my lips, a cloud of tobacco smoke hanging over my head, and many perfumed dreams inside it. He had a no-nonsense approach that jibed with his austere mien. He asked me what my name was, jotted down my work number, and went off to make a report on what he called "sordid malingering."

Other reports followed this. Gruff warnings, stern admonitions, and blustery tirades developed from them. They came from both major and minor executives. These I was already inured to. They didn't matter anyway. My condition was far too advanced, already much too complex to be cleared up by mere lectures, fatherly or otherwise. All the threats and rebukes in the world couldn't have made me give up my window-ledge reveries or kept me from roaming city streets with Cecilia Rosas' name on my lips like a prayer.

The reports merely made me more cunning, more doggedly determined to city-slick La Feria out of work hours I owed it. The net result was that I timed my absences more precisely and contrived better lies to explain them. Sometimes I went to the men's room and looked at myself in the mirror for as long as ten minutes at a time. Such self-studies filled me with gloom. The mirror reflected an ordinary Mexican face, more homely than comely. Only my hair gave me hope. It was thick and wavy, deserving a better face to go with it. So I did the best I could with what I had, and combed it over my temples in ringlets just like the poets back in my hometown of Parral, Chihuahua, used to do.

My inefficiency, my dreams, my general lassitude could have gone on indefinitely, it seemed. My life at the store wavered between bright hope and leaden despair, unrelieved by Miss Rosas' acceptance or rejection of me. Then one day something happened that almost made my overstrained heart stop beating.

It happened on the day Miss Rosas stood behind me while I put a fur coat away. Her heady perfume, the fragrance of her warm healthy body, made me feel faint. She was so close to me I thought about putting my hands around her lissome waist and hugging her as hard as I could. But thoughts of subsequent disgrace deterred me, so instead of hugging her I smiled wanly and asked her in Spanish how she was feeling.

"Amado, speak English," she told me. "And pronounce the words slowly and carefully so you won't sound like a country Mexican."

Then she looked at me in a way that made me the happiest employee who ever punched La Feria's time clock.

"Amadito," she whispered the way I had always dreamed she would.

"Yes, Señorita Cecilia," I said expectantly.

Her smile was warmly intimate. "Amadito, when are you going to take me to the movies?" she asked.

Other salesladies watched us, all smiling. They made me so nervous I couldn't answer.

"Amadito, you haven't answered me," Miss Rosas said teasingly. "Either you're bashful as a village sweetheart or else you don't like me at all."

In voluble Spanish, I quickly assured her the latter wasn't the case. I was just getting ready to say "Señorita Cecilia, I more than like you, I love you" when she frowned and told me to speak English. So I slowed down and tried to smooth out my ruffled thoughts.

"Señorita Cecilia," I said. "I'd love to take you to the movies any time."

Miss Rosas smiled and patted my cheek. "Will you buy me candy and popcorn?" she said.

I nodded, putting my hand against the imprint her warm palm had left on my face.

"And hold my hand?"

I said "yes" so enthusiastically it made her laugh. Other salesladies laughed too. Dazed and numb with happiness, I watched Miss Rosas walk away. How proud and confident she was, how wholesomely clean and feminine. Other salesladies were looking at me and laughing.

Miss Sandoval came over to me. *"Ay papacito,"* she said. "With women you're the divine tortilla."

Miss de la Rosa came over too. "When you take the Americana to the movies, remember not to speak Christian," she said. "And be sure you wear the pants that don't have any patches on them."

What they said made me blush and wonder how they knew what we had been talking about. Miss Arroyo came over to join them. So did Miss Torres.

"Amado, remember women are weak and men aren't made of sweet bread," Miss Arroyo said.

This embarrassed me but it wasn't altogether unpleasant. Miss Sandoval winked at Miss de la Rosa, then looked back at me.

"Don't go too fast with the Americana, Amado," she said. "Remember the procession is long and the candles are small."

They laughed and slapped me on the back. They all wanted to know when I was going to take Miss Rosas to the movies. "She didn't say," I blurted out without thinking.

This brought another burst of laughter. It drove me back up to the window ledge where I got out my package of Faros and thought about the wonderful thing that had happened. But I was too nervous to stay there. So I went to the men's room and looked at myself in the mirror again, wondering why Miss Rosas liked me so well. The mirror made it brutally clear that my looks hadn't influenced her. So it must have been something else, perhaps character. But that didn't seem likely either. Joe Apple had told me I didn't have much of that. And other store officials had bulwarked his opinion. Still, I had seen homely men walking the streets of El Paso's Little Chihuahua quarter with beautiful Mexican women and no one could explain that either. Anyway it was time for another walk. So I took one.

This time I trudged through Little Chihuahua, where both Miss Rosas and I lived. Little Chihuahua looked different to me that day. It was a broken-down Mexican quarter honeycombed with tenements, Mom and Pop groceries, herb shops, cafes, and spindly salt-cedar trees; with howling children running its streets and old Mexican revolutionaries sunning themselves on its curbs like iguanas. But on that clear frosty day it was the world's most romantic place because Cecilia Rosas lived there.

While walking, I reasoned that Miss Rosas might want to go dancing after the movies. So I went to Professor Toribio Ortega's dance studio and made arrangements to take my first lesson. Some neighborhood boys saw me when I came out. They bawled "Mariquita" and made flutteringly effeminate motions, all vulgar if not obscene. It didn't matter. On my lunch hour I went back and took my first lesson anyway. Professor Ortega danced with me. Softened by weeks of dreaming, I went limp in his arms imagining he was Miss Rosas.

The rest of the day was the same as many others before it. As usual I spent most of it stealing glances at Miss Rosas and slipping up to the window ledge. She looked busy, efficient, not like a woman in love. Her many other admirers trooped to the water fountain to look at the way her black silk dress fitted her curves. Their profane admiration made me scowl even more than I usually did at such times.

When the day's work was done, I plodded home from the store just as dreamily as I had gone to it. Since I had no one else to confide in, I invited my oldest sister, Dulce Nombre de María, to go to the movies with me. They were showing Jorge Negrete and María Felix in *El Rapto* at the Colon Theater. It was a romantic movie, just the kind I wanted to see.

After it was over, I bought Dulce Nombre *churros* and hot *champurrado* at the Golden Taco Cafe. And I told my sister all about what had happened to me. She looked at me thoughtfully, then combed my hair back with her fingertips as though trying to soothe me. "Manito," she said, softly. "I wouldn't. . . ." Then she looked away and shrugged her shoulders.

On Monday I borrowed three dollars from my Uncle Rodolfo without telling him what it was for. Miss Rosas hadn't told me what night she wanted me to take her to the movies. But the way she had looked at me made me think that almost any night would do. So I decided on Friday. Waiting for it to come was hard. But I had to keep my mind occupied. So I went to Zamora's newsstand to get the Alma Norteña songbook. Pouring through it for the most romantic song I could find, I decided on *La Cecilia.*

All week long I practiced singing it on my way to school and in the shower after basketball practice with the Little Chihuahua Tigers at the Sagrado Corazón gym. But, except for singing this song, I tried not to speak Spanish at all. At home I made my mother mad by saying in English. "Please pass the sugar."

My mother looked at me as though she couldn't believe what she had heard. Since my Uncle Rodolfo couldn't say anything more than "hello" and "goodbye" in English, he couldn't tell what I had said. So my sister Consuelo did.

"May the Dark Virgin with the benign look make this boy well enough to speak Christian again," my mother whispered.

This I refused to do. I went on speaking English even though my mother and uncle didn't understand it. This shocked my sisters as well. When they asked me to explain my behavior, I parroted Miss Rosas, saying, "We're living in the United States now."

My rebellion against being a Mexican created an uproar. Such conduct was unorthodox, if not scandalous, in a neighborhood where names like Burciaga, Rodríguez, and Castillo predominated. But it wasn't only the Spanish language that I lashed out against.

"Mother, why do we always have to eat *sopa, frijoles, refritos, mondongo,* and *pozole?*" I complained. "Can't we ever eat roast beef or ham and eggs like Americans do?"

My mother didn't speak to me for two days after that. My Uncle Rodolfo grimaced and mumbled something about renegade Mexicans who want to eat ham and eggs even though the Montes Packing Company turned out the best *chorizo* this side of Toluca. My sister Consuelo giggled and called me a Rio Grande Irishman, an American Mister, a gringo, and a *bolillo.* Dulce Nombre looked at me worriedly.

Life at home was almost intolerable. Cruel jokes and mocking laughter made it so. I moped around looking sad as a day without bread. My sister Consuelo suggested I go to the courthouse and change my name to Beloved Wall which is English for Amado Muro. My mother didn't agree. "If *Nuestro Señor* had meant for Amadito to be an American he would have given him a name like Smeeth or Jonesy," she said. My family was unsympathetic. With a family like mine, how could I ever hope to become an American and win Miss Rosas?

Friday came at last. I put on my only suit, slicked my hair down with liquid vaseline, and doused myself with Dulce Nombre's perfume.

"Amado's going to serenade that pretty girl everyone calls La Americana," my sister Consuelo told my mother and uncle when I sat down to eat. "Then he's going to take her to the movies."

This made my uncle laugh and my mother scowl.

"*Qué pantalones tiene* (what nerve that boy's got)," my uncle said, "to serenade a twenty-year-old woman."

"La Americana," my mother said derisively. "That one's Mexican as pulque cured with celery."

They made me so nervous I forgot to take off my cap when I sat down to eat.

"Amado, take off your cap," my mother said. "You're not in La Lagunilla Market."

My uncle frowned. "All this boy thinks about is kissing girls," he said gruffly.

"But my boy's never kissed one," my mother said proudly.

My sister Consuelo laughed. "That's because they won't let him," she said.

This wasn't true. But I couldn't say so in front of my mother. I had already kissed Emalina Uribe from Porfirio Díaz Street not once but twice. Both times I'd kissed her in a darkened doorway less than a block from her home. But the kisses were over so soon we hardly had time to enjoy them. This was because Ema was afraid of her big brother, the husky one nicknamed Toro, would see us. But if we'd had more time it would have been better, I knew.

Along about six o'clock the three musicians who called themselves the Mariachis of Tecalitlán came by and whistled for me, just as they had said they would do. They never looked better than they did on that night. They had on black and silver charro uniforms and big, black, Zapata sombreros.

My mother shook her head when she saw them. "Son, who ever heard of serenading a girl at six o'clock in the evening," she said. "When your father had the mariachis sing for me it was always at two o'clock in the morning—the only proper time for a six-song *gallo*."

But I got out my Ramírez guitar anyway. I put on my cap and rushed out to give the mariachis the money without even kissing my mother's hand or waiting for her to bless me. Then we headed for Miss Rosas' home. Some boys and girls I knew were out in the street.

This made me uncomfortable. They looked at me wonderingly as I led the mariachi band to Miss Rosas' home.

A block away from Miss Rosas' home I could see her father, a grizzled veteran who fought for Pancho Villa, sitting on the curb reading the Juárez newspaper, *El Fronterizo.*

The sight of him made me slow down for a moment. But I got back in stride when I saw Miss Rosas herself.

She smiled and waved at me. "Hello, Amadito," she said.

"Hello, Señorita Cecilia," I said.

She looked at the mariachis, then back at me.

"Ay, Amado, you're going to serenade your girl," she said. I didn't reply right away. Then when I was getting ready to say "Señorita Cecilia, I came to serenade you," I saw the American man sitting in the sports roadster at the curb.

Miss Rosas turned to him. "I'll be right there, Johnny," she said.

She patted my cheek. "I've got to run now, Amado," she said. "Have a real nice time, darling."

I looked at her silken legs as she got into the car. Everything had happened so fast I was dazed. Broken dreams made my head spin. The contrast between myself and the poised American in the sports roadster was so cruel it made me wince.

She was happy with him. That was obvious. She was smiling and laughing, looking forward to a good time. Why had she asked me to take her to the movies if she already had a boyfriend? Then I remembered how the other salesladies had laughed, how I had wondered why they were laughing when they couldn't even hear what we were saying. And I realized it had all been a joke, everyone had known it but me. Neither Miss Rosas nor the other salesladies had ever dreamed I would think she was serious about wanting me to take her to the movies.

The American and Miss Rosas drove off. Gloomy thoughts oppressed me. They made me want to cry. To get rid of them I thought of going to one of the "bad death" cantinas in Juárez where tequila starts fights and knives finish them—to one of the cantinas where the panders, whom Mexicans call *burros,* stand outside shouting "It's just like Paris, only not so many people" was where I wanted to go. There I could forget her in Jalisco-state style with mariachis, tequila, and night-life women. Then I remembered I was so young that night-life women would shun me and *cantineros* wouldn't serve me tequila.

So I thought some more. Emalina Uribe was the only other alternative. If we went over to Porfirio Díaz Street and serenaded her I could go back to being a Mexican again. She was just as Mexican as I was, Mexican as *chicharrones*. I thought about smiling, freckle-faced Ema.

Ema wasn't like the Americana at all. She wore wash dresses that fitted loosely and even ate the *melocha* candies Mexicans like so well on the street. On Sundays she wore a Zamora shawl to church and her mother wouldn't let her use lipstick or let her put on high heels.

But with a brother like Toro who didn't like me anyway, such a serenade might be more dangerous than romantic. Besides that, my faith in my looks, my character, or whatever it was that made women fall in love with men, was so undermined I could already picture her getting into a car with a handsome American just like Miss Rosas had done.

The Mariachis of Tecalitlán were getting impatient. They had been paid to sing six songs and they wanted to sing them. But they were all sympathetic. None of them laughed at me.

"Amado, don't look sad as I did the day I learned I'd never be a millionaire," the mariachi captain said, putting his arm around me. "If not that girl, then another."

But without Miss Rosas there was no one we could sing *La Cecilia* to. The street seemed bleak and empty now that she was gone. And I didn't want to serenade Ema Uribe even though she hadn't been faithless as Miss Rosas had been. It was true she hadn't been faithless, but only lack of opportunity would keep her from getting into a car with an American, I reasoned cynically.

Just about then Miss Rosas' father looked up from his newspaper. He asked the mariachis if they knew how to sing *Cananea Jail*. They told him they did. Then they looked at me. I thought it over for a moment. Then I nodded and started strumming the bass strings of my guitar. What had happened made it only too plain I could never trust Miss Rosas again. So we serenaded her father instead.

## Study Guide

1. An adolescent boy's infatuation with an older woman is a popular theme in literature. Compare Amado Muro's "Cecilia Rosas" with other stories dealing with adolescent infatuations. (James Joyce's "Araby" is an excellent example.) Is Amado Muro's primary concern depicting the central character's infatuation, or does the infatuation of Amado for Cecilia have a larger thematic significance?

2. Many of the feelings Amado describes in the story are characteristic of adolescents. To what extent is his response to Cecilia individualized? Does the sense of individuality depend on the narrator's being a Mexican-American?

3. How does the narrator view himself? How does he view his job? His family? His future? Do these attitudes add a dimension to his infatuation with Cecilia Rosas? Is she a particularly appropriate object for his adoration because she rejects her Mexican heritage?

4. What ironies are involved in the boy's decision to serenade Cecilia?

5. To what extent is the conflict in the story one that reflects the conflict between majority and minority cultures?

6. Does the boy's attempt to adopt Anglo language and customs tell us anything about the nature of his "love" for Cecilia? Does his adoration of Cecilia tell us anything about his attitude toward himself?

7. "Cecilia Rosas" is in part concerned with a boy torn between two cultures, that of his family and that represented by Cecilia Rosas. Similar conflicts occur in all of our lives. For instance, when a student goes away to college, he sometimes must choose between a way of life that his family finds acceptable and one that his college friends approve of. Select such an experience in your own life and use it as the basis for a narrative. Try to show why you made the choice in favor of one or another of the cultures.

8. In an essay, explore some problem that minority-group members might have when they enter a society dominated by another group. You might, for instance, explore the problems that black or Spanish-American students would encounter on a middle-class college campus with a student body that is predominantly white.

What difficulties involving language, dress, dating habits, etc. might such a student have? In your essay, try to consider the manner in which one evaluates himself and his culture when he finds himself in an environment strikingly different from that he is accustomed to.

# 11. To Endure

ROBERT GRANAT

*Who speaks of conquering? To endure is everything.*—Rilke.

I just come home from school when Anastasio die. "Queeeh!" he say, and that was all.

Right away I go to the picture Mama cut from the calendar where Jesus is pulling open his chest for to show us his beautiful heart and I cross myself. Then I go tell everybody—Daddy, Franque (that is Francisco, my brother) and Arcelia (that is Arcelia, my sister). And we all begin to cry for the old man but really we was pretty happy. We like Anastasio OK but he take too long to die.

Anastasio was the uncle of my mother and he live with us since I can remember. But he been sick three months and he take all the kitchen for himself, because Mama didn't want for none of us to sleep in the room with Anastasio when he was sick, so Franque and me and Arcelia all got to sleep together in one bed in the other room with Daddy and Mama in another bed and Ubaldo in the basket. And one thing, I sure don't like to sleep with nobody else in the bed, especially Franque and Arcelia, and that was the real reason I was pretty happy when Anastasio die. He make too many people sleep in one place.

Mama and the other ladies put the wedding suit of Anastasio on him and we put him on the long bench Carlos Trujillo loan us and after supper everybody come to make the *velorio* and we cry and sing *alabados* and drink coffee and eat bizcochitos. Arcelia got to go to bed all by herself but I stay up all night, I think.

Next morning we didn't go to school on account Anastasio was dead. Carlos Trujillo and Daddy and Franque and me take the tarpaulin off the pickup and we make I guess you call it a tent right outside the window and we carry Anastasio on the bench and put him under so Mama can fix the kitchen and look out to see if Anastasio OK.

"He gonna be cold out here," Arcelia say. She don't know nothing; she only six.

*"Está muerto,"* I tell her. "He's dead. He don't feel nothing."

Mama and Mrs. Trujillo and my Aunt Manuelita and Arcelia and Ubaldo was going to stay home and take care of everything because all the men—me and Franque and Daddy and Carlos Trujillo —got to take the pickup to Sandoval to buy a box to bury Anastasio with. Sandoval is the biggest town in Madera County, about a hundred miles from Piñoncito and I never been there but Franque been two times with Daddy. I help Franque kick the mud off the pickup and put in water . . . was cold, almost winter, and we let out the water every night so it don't freeze and bust the motor. I put on my clean levis, I was always saving for something like this, and I was happy I didn't have no school today and was going to Sandoval.

Then Arcelia—big cry-baby—start to cry she want to go with us, and she make me cry too because I didn't want no girls with us, especially Arcelia. But Mama say why not, and Daddy get mad and say "Shut your mouth or ain't nobody going to go." So Arcelia get in and she stick her tongue at me and I was going to hit her only everybody was there and I couldn't. So Daddy and Franque and Carlos Trujillo get inside and Franque drive. Arcelia and me ride in the back with the rope and the chains and the shovel and the boards for if we get stuck. She stand in one corner and me in the other one.

Is about forty-five miles to the black-top road the other side Mesa Quemada. The farther I ever go before was to Peña's Cash Store in Rio Seco where my cousin live. But Franque didn't stop. He keep right on going. The roads was pretty bad. The grader ain't been through and some places got pretty lot of mud. But we didn't get stuck. Franque, he's fifteen. He's a pretty good driver.

Then I fall asleep. I was trying not to but I couldn't help it. To sit all night with Anastasio make me too tired. And I was ashamed too, because I ain't no kid like Arcelia. I already have eleven years.

I feel Arcelia shake me. *"Pendejo, pendejo, levántate!"*

I shake my head fast. *" 'Onde 'stamos?"* I say. "Where are we?"

"Sandoval, *tonto!"* she say.

"Don't call me no *tonto*, you monkey!" I say, that's *chongo* in Mexican. But I was ashamed anyway to be sleeping when we got to Sandoval.

We was already at the funeral company. Daddy get out. "We going inside to buy the box for Anastasio. You want to come with us or wait out here?"

I want to come and see the funeral company, and Arcelia do too, but Daddy say no, she too little, she got to wait outside in the pickup.

"Varoz Brothers Mortuary" I say when I read the big sign they got there. I can read pretty good English, better than Franque and better than Daddy too. Inside was Mr. Varoz. I think he was going to be Americano but he was Spanish like us, only got Anglo clothes with a tie on. He talk in Mexican with Daddy and Carlos Trujillo and they tell him Anastasio die and they want a nice box to bury him with. So Mr. Varoz take us in the back where they keep the boxes. "Ah *qué!"* . . . how many they got there! Big ones, brown ones, black ones, all colors, shiny like a new car. They even got little white ones for little kids. They got enough boxes to put everybody in Piñoncito, I think.

"What kind you want?" say Mr. Varoz.

"Well, we want a pretty good one," say Daddy, "maybe the Welfare going to help pay."

Mr. Varoz pick a nice box, grey color like the pickup, only shiny with gold things to carry it with. I tell Franque maybe was too big for Anastasio but Franque say no, Anastasio going to fit good inside. Mr. Varoz call some other men—maybe they was his brothers—and everybody carry the box out and put it on the pickup. I help. Ah *qué!* was heavy, more heavy than Anastasio on Carlos Trujillo's bench.

"Arcelia, get out the way!" I say and we throw the box in back of the pickup. Franque and Carlos Trujillo tie it on with the rope.

"That rope going to hold OK?" say Mr. Varoz in English and he push it with his hands. "I guess it's OK if you take it easy."

*"Está bien,"* Daddy say. My Daddy know only few words in English, maybe twenty.

Daddy and Carlos Trujillo got to buy some things and so we drive back to where the stores was. We all get inside the pickup because was not far. "Nice man, that Varoz," say Carlos Trujillo. Daddy say yes, only make him pay twenty dollars down-payment.

Franque park in front of a bar and he go in there for a drink with Daddy and Carlos Trujillo. Daddy give me fifty cents and say for me and Arcelia to buy something. I go in a store and get some change and I keep thirty cents and give Arcelia twenty cents. That was fair. She only six and don't know what is money. For me I buy two comic books and two Milky Way. Milky Way only cost a nickel in Sandoval. Arcelia look at everything and don't know what she want, so I take her out the store. "OK, you ain't going to get nothing," I say, "and Daddy going to get mad we taking so long."

We was almost back at the pickup and then Arcelia start yelling. "That . . . *eso quiero* . . . I want that!"

I look and seen she was pointing her finger at something in the window of a store. Inside the window was shoes and stockings and ribbons and levis and things like that. "What you want?" I tell her. I was wishing Daddy let me go with him and not stay with Arcelia. She don't know nothing. "You make everything always bad," I tell her.

But she was yelling and everybody in the street was starting to look at me like I was hitting her.

"*Qué quieres?*" I say again, "What you want?"

"The dress," she say, "I want that dress!"

I look and seen what she want was a white dress like girls wear for First Communion.

"Arcelia—*pendeja!*—you think the man going to give you that dress for twenty cents?"

"*Sí, sí, ese quiero, lo quiero!*" she yell. So I take her inside the store so she will shut her mouth.

"How much cost the white dress in the window?" I say to the man. He was Americano.

"Three eighty-nine," he say, "you got the money?"

"See, *tonta!* Cost more than three dollars!" I say, but Arcelia keep crying so I pull her outside again, "Is not my fault," I tell the Americano. "She don't understand nothing."

Daddy and Carlos Trujillo and Franque was coming out of the bar. They smell like whisky. They look at Arcelia crying.

"What's the matter with Arcelia? You hit her?" Daddy say.

"No, I didn't do nothing. She want to buy that dress, cost three dollars." I was feeling mad and bad and was starting to cry too because I didn't do nothing bad.

"What dress?" say Carlos Trujillo.

"The white one in the window."

"It's a dress for First Communion."

"Arcelia's too little for that dress," Daddy say. "*Vamos*, is getting dark. Franque, you feel OK to drive?"

"Yah," say Franque and he open his mouth like when you tired. I know he was tired like me from the *velorio,* and Daddy let him drink whisky, too.

Arcelia and me get in the back of the pickup with the box of Anastasio. It made like a little wall for us, because was getting pretty cold. Arcelia was still crying in the corner and I feel bad too. Poor kid, she didn't know what is three dollars.

"Anyway, you still got twenty cents. I don't got nothing," I say to her. "Tomorrow you can buy two Milky Way at Mr. Bond." Mr. Bond cost ten cents for a Milky Way.

But Arcelia was still crying. Better for her to stay home.

"Here." I break one of my Milky Way in half and I give the biggest one to her. She didn't say nothing but she take it.

*Hiii-jolá,* was cold! I stand up and look at the road. Franque was going pretty fast. We pass a big trailer truck. I think almost he was going to hit it. "Take it easy, Franque, take it easy," I hear Carlos Trujillo say inside.

I sit down again. I seen Arcelia was sleeping under the blanket Mama give her to keep warm, behind the box of Anastasio. Was like a hole there where the wind can't come in. I make myself little and put my nose inside my shirt so I feel warm and I was ashamed because again I fall asleep.

*Hijo,* was terrible! When that happen was dark. I was sleeping so I didn't know what it was. But was terrible. Everything come in one minute. Daddy yell "Franque! Franque!" and then was a big noise and the pickup hit something and something hit me and then everything stop. I didn't know nothing till was finished. But was terrible, I tell you that much.

Then I hear Daddy yell in the front. "*Tonto! Imbécil! Animal!*" and I hear he was hitting Franque. Franque jump out with his hands on his head and making a noise like a dog when somebody kick him.

Then Daddy come out with Carlos Trujillo.

"Abrán! Arcelia! *Qué pasó!* You OK? You not hurt?"

"I'm OK, Daddy," I say. But then they turn on the flashlight and everybody see was sure terrible thing that happen. Was the box of Anastasio.

When the pickup hit, the rope break and the box come on us, and was sure big. Now I feel it. Was on my leg.

"Abrán! Where's Arcelia?"

"She was sleeping."

"*Apúrense,* quick, pull away the box!" Carlos Trujillo say. They pull it off my leg. I get up. It hurt, but not too bad. "I'm OK, Daddy," I say.

But nobody listen to me. They was all looking at Arcelia. Carlos turn the light on her.

"*Ay Dios!* No! Arcelia, Arcelia! *Hijita mía!*" Daddy was saying. He try to wake her up.

"Don't shake her, . . . that's bad," say Carlos Trujillo. Carlos is pretty smart. His mother is the *médica,* and she knows about sick people and babies. Poor Franque, he just stand there shaking and crying and like eating his lips.

"Maybe she just knock out, Daddy," I say.

"Look, her mouth!" Daddy say.

"No, is just Milky Way," I say.

Carlos wipe her mouth with his handkerchief. It was candy, except a little bit on the corner. That was blood, only not much, like when you cut your lip. Carlos pick up Arcelia. "May be bad," he say, "we got to go back and see the doctor."

Carlos tell Franque to go see how was the truck. But Franque seem like he can't move so I go. I seen we run into a place where they cut out the hill to make the road. Not rock, just sand. The front of the pickup look pretty bad, but the tires was OK and the lights was still on.

The motor start OK and Carlos get the pickup back on the road and drive back to Sandoval. Daddy was holding Arcelia wrapped up in the blanket. I hear him talking to Arcelia but she didn't say nothing to him. Franque and me ride in the back with the box of Anastasio, and we didn't say nothing either.

Only got two doctors in Madera County and my teacher say it's not enough for all those thousand people. The doctor's house was full of people waiting when we get there. The lady who work for the doctor didn't understand Mexican so good, so I tell her in English what happen with Franque and the pickup and the box of Anastasio. She look scared.

"*Es malo? Qué tiene mi hijita?*" Daddy say in Mexican.

"My Daddy want to know if it's bad," I tell the lady in English.

The lady say she don't know, she not the nurse, only secretary, and the doctor is out on "emergency call" but he was coming right back.

I tell this to my Daddy but he didn't understand what was an emergency call so he sit down with Arcelia and try to make her speak. Was funny. Was some ladies there sitting holding little babies like Ubaldo, and Daddy with his levis and black leather jacket was sitting holding Arcelia. No, was terrible. Daddy was crying and I like it better when he is mad.

We wait and wait and the doctor was still on emergency call. Then Carlos Trujillo bend down and put his ear on Arcelia's chest and feel her neck.

"*Está muerta, tu hijita,*" he say to Daddy, "your little girl is dead."

Carlos Trujillo was driving very slow and careful and it take a long time to get back to Piñoncito. But this time I didn't fall asleep. I wasn't tired. I was thinking.

Poor Franque, he was crying in the back of the pickup with me. He tell me he was going to run away to the Army, but he was too young and Daddy need him to take care the sheep. Carlos Trujillo was sure nice to him. He tell Franque was not his fault. They let him drink whisky and he was tired from the *velorio.* It was wrong to let him drive.

And was sure nice what Carlos do for Arcelia too. He go back to the store and buy the white First Communion dress Arcelia want with his own three dollars.

And Mr. Varoz from the funeral company sure was nice too. He didn't believe it till he seen Arcelia. Then he give Daddy a big *abrazo,* that means like a kiss, and he tell us to wait in the front room. In a little while he bring Arcelia back in a little white box special for children. He make her look pretty, all clean and with her hair brushed and he put the white dress on her. Inside the box was soft like a sheep only more white and shiny. The dress was too big for her but Mr. Varoz fix it so she look like a fairy in the second-grade reader. And he didn't cost us nothing for it.

But when we get past Peña's Cash Store in Rio Seco I think only one thing. What was we going to tell Mama? And I think everybody was thinking that like me.

Mama was sitting with Ubaldo when we come in. She got her

dress open and Ubaldo was sucking his milk. "It's late," she say and she go to put beans and coffee on the fire. Everybody stand there waiting. " '*Onde 'stá la Arcelia?*" she say and I seen her eyes get big. Then Carlos Trujillo come and grab her tight and tell her. Mama make a terrible scream like a goat when you going to cut his neck. Worse than that. I was scared and I run outside to the pickup. I call to Franque but he was gone. I wait and I was shivering because was cold. I hear Mama crying worse than everybody together at the *velorio* for Anastasio. And I hear Ubaldo screaming too because he didn't get no more milk. Then everything was quiet.

Mama come to the door. "Abrán, hurry, eat your supper," she say and I come. I want to kiss Mama but I was scared. The beans was in the plates. Mama sit down in the corner under the picture of the Virgin next to the one of Jesus opening his chest to show us his beautiful heart. She was talking to the Virgin.

"*Ay María Santísima . . . Madre Purísima de Dios . . . óyemeóyeme . . . perdí mi hijita, mi hijita perdí . . . Ay . . . Ay . . . Ay . . . Ay . . . Ay . . .*"

And underneath she hold Ubaldo up so he could suck his milk.

## Study Guide

1.  From whose point of view is the narrative recounted?

2.  How old is the narrator? What is his nationality? What elements in the narrative reveal the answers to these questions?

3.  Is the author consistent in maintaining this point of view? How is he limited by the nature of the person who narrates the story?

4.  What relationship does the quotation from Rilke that prefaces the story have to its contents?

5.  The story, which is recounted by Abrán, an 11-year-old rural Mexican boy, begins and ends with a death. Does the narrator's awareness of death change in any way during the course of the story? Does he respond to the death of his sister in a different manner than he had responded to the death of his great uncle? How do you account for the nature of the two responses?

6.  Is the poverty of Abrán's family a central factor in the story? If so what role does it play?

7.  What emotional reaction do you have toward the central characters in the story? Does that reaction change? If so, when and why does it change?

8.  What response does the author want us to have toward Daddy, Franque, and Carlos after the death of Arcelia? How is our response to them governed by the response of the narrator? How would you describe the narrator's response to his sister's death? When does he fully comprehend its impact?

9.  Reread the last three paragraphs in the story. In what way do they clarify the title?

10. Are the characters in "To Endure" victimized by any of the forces described by Stan Steiner in "The Man Who Worked for Thirty Years Without Pay"?

11. To what extent is this story a story of rural Mexican-Americans? To what extent is it a story concerned with a universal experience?

12. In "To Endure," Robert Granat describes an extremely moving experience from the point of view of a child. Select some

equally emotional experience which you have had and write an essay in which you describe it from the point of view of an adult. Then write a second essay dealing with the experience recounted from the perspective of a child. In what ways must you change the essay to convey a sense of a child's perception?

# 12. On the Warpath at Alcatraz

## KEN MICHAELS

An old Sioux treaty provides that unused government land be returned to the Indians. To take Alcatraz Island under provisions of that treaty had been an Indian plan since 1963, when the prison there was closed and the convicts removed. Occasional stillborn attempts were made by students thru the years, but late last year the mood was right. At Thanksgiving time 89 Indians made an invasion, and the Indians have been on Alcatraz since. They intend to stay forever.

You know nothing about the Alcatraz situation except what you see in the papers and on TV, but from a warm bed you go into the rain and out to the Indian center—a second floor office space above a store front on San Francisco's California avenue. A quiet Indian woman types in the corner. She nods you to the front office. Inside there is a bale of hay. Two Indians are having a word battle, one asking the other for his clothing allowance, the other asking him if he's too proud to wear donated clothes like everybody else. Judy Scraper, Shawnee, is behind a desk in a purple sweatshirt and denim jeans, paying no attention to the battle. Judy makes out your boat pass as the argument rages, and you stand by the bale of hay

"On the Warpath at Alcatraz" by Ken Michaels. Reprinted, courtesy of the *Chicago Tribune*.

and read a placard pinned on the wall behind Judy's desk: THE TROUBLE WITH THIS PLACE IS . . . THERE'S TOO MANY CHIEFS AND NOT ENOUGH INDIANS.

The door to the next office opens, and inside is another bale of hay and people sitting around on the floor on blankets. One guy is sleepy-eyed; he just got up, and he's tucking white shirttails into khaki trousers.

Leaving, you catch a color postcard taped to the door: Alcatraz with the face of Geronimo printed over it and red letters at the top proclaiming: THIS LAND IS MY LAND.

At 8:30 you arrive at Fisherman's Wharf. Sun strains from the rain clouds, and occasional warm rays slant across the wet piers. Fishermen swab morning decks, and waiters hustle to work, yelling in Italian to the boatmen.

At the end of a long, wet pier three Indians huddle waiting for the boat. One is in army fatigues, another is in denim, the third has a poncho on his back. It's wet and cold, but they're all feeling good after being three days and nights on the town.

The kid in denim is 19. He's Navajo. He came at Christmas time from a reservation in Arizona.

"Got a nice freight all the way. I didn't want the reservation any more and heard about this on the radio and came out. I like it. On the reservation there's not much to do. You hang around, go into town once in a while. I did bootlegging. You get wine in town for 60 cents and sell it on the reservation for $2. I took off when I was 17 and went to L.A., but they picked me up for vagrancy, and the judge he was a nice guy, he sent me back to the reservation."

The kid's eyes are debauched-looking. He pulls a crumpled blue-and-red-striped envelope out of his denim breast pocket. "From my folks. They wonder how it is out here." It's funny. He laughs. "Sure, man. It's O.K. I'm staying. Need sleep. Got to get back on the island, sleep. Been in town too long."

More Indians arrive on the pier, and we stand close and wait in silence. It starts to rain again. At the next pier beneath the coast guard house the clean white cutter lolls in the bay.

The boat that will take us to the island chugs in, carrying a dozen Indian passengers. Standing tall at the helm is the skipper, a black man in a bright yellow poncho and a pale blue captain's hat. He's charging them too much, and they're wrecking the boat, he claims, and there's a lot of trouble, and they're going to get rid of him pretty soon and get their own boat with their own skippers.

As the Ino docks, there is much exaggerated rope-throwing and tying and people helping each other off. There's a great camaraderie you can't mistake. The people love each other.

A Cadillac pulls up on the pier, out steps the Indians' lawyer, Mr. Grossman. We all sign the ledger and climb aboard the Ino.

You're sitting on a bench on the bow, feeling the watery wind on your face as the boat churns toward the island. Grossman joins you. "Do you know Indians? I didn't either until I took the case. The Indians you read about, the ones high up in government, the so-called spokesmen—they don't represent the Indian people. The real Indians call them Uncle Tomahawks."

Grossman points to Alcatraz. "This is the first time all tribes have gotten together on something. They want to be in charge of themselves, left alone to work out their own way. They're not begging, they're not against society, they're not militant, they don't want to change the world. They're wonderful people trying to get along."

Back of the island we drift softly to the dock. High against a cliff, a sign which used to identify the island as government property is streaked with bright Indian red; painted in large red letters is the message that it's now United Indian Property and Indian Land. INDIANS WELCOME.

Before the boat even ties up, everybody piles out and takes off. Suddenly you're alone. Sheer rock walls rise all around. A broken road leads nowhere. An old guard shack is falling down. Weeds tangle thru the motor pool. Faded blue government trucks rust away like junk.

After trudging up a long, crooked stairway you emerge onto a plateau of asphalt caged in by cyclone fence. Beyond the asphalt is a wall of government-looking housing, and beyond that the finest view of San Francisco anywhere. The city floats out there: You can't resist: from a guard rail you watch the city for a long time, feeling for the cons who used to stay here and put up with the view day and night, year in, year out.

You see Grossman and the Indian leaders grouped on the next plateau, discussing today's 10 a.m. meeting with the government guys. Robert Robertson, executive director of the National Council on Indian Opportunity, is here from Washington and all morning they'll sit around the table of the main cell block's dining hall, and it'll be quiet and orderly, but nobody will budge.

You cross a muddy court and meet Dickie in front of the block. She wears a headband and cloth coat and comes from Auburn, Cal., where she owned a beauty shop. Dickie shows you into the block, a rotten, sinister place filled with infamy and charisma. It's 18th-century animals-in-cages, but it draws. Everybody who comes onto the island wants to see the block first; they run up the hill to get at it and live it for a while.

Rain beats on the skylight while you and Dickie walk the long rows of concrete and bars and emptiness. Dickie tells you how some of the Indians slept in the cells when they first came here but moved out because the cells were too cold and small. "They're tiny." Dickie edges into one and demonstrates, spreading her arms to show you that even a little person like herself can reach from side to side and touch. Pathetically, she stands proud: being able to touch is a feat. Dickie in her Indian headband standing proud like that, spreading her arms in the tight cell, hits you as sadly symbolic.

We cross to Al Capone's—a double cell with pink walls, with all the bars and plumbing stripped out for souvenirs. Then Dickie shows you the dungeon and tells you they used to throw the prisoners down in the hole.

"I'm in cosmetology," Dickie says. "I have two shops. I don't need this. I got a degree. Both my daughters are cosmetologists, too. We got a big house, nine rooms with washer, dryer, air conditioning —everything. I heard about this and came here. We're Indians, and that's what we want to be. At a meeting I made a suggestion that we wear Indian clothes on the island; it would have been *right,* but they didn't do it."

You and Dickie keep passing groups of Indians in the rows and halls who smile and nod but never say anything. In the Indian Land office, formerly the vestry room of the block's chapel, six Indians with a guitar are having a meeting, and nobody is saying anything. Thru the windows you see an Indian man and his wife and their five kids having a picnic cook-out on the block's concrete landing. Nobody is talking.

Nobody wears glasses, either. On the whole island, all day, you don't see one pair of glasses.

"The radio station is locked, but you can peek in the window." Dickie pulls away a corner of blanket, and inside on a Masonite tabletop are two mikes, an amplifier, and wires. The area is roped off with clothesline hung with orange and red blankets. Every night they go on the air for 15 minutes over FM. One night you listened at home, and their message was soft songs and poetry filled with destiny. Alien, but determined and quietly optimistic.

"Want to see our turkey?" Dickie leads you down the block to a kind of handball court with high bars and anchor fencing. Chicken-wired off in a corner is a black turkey. Behind him waddles a skinny duck. When we come up, they both scoot, and some kids have to go chasing them down by solitary confinement.

You ask Dickie if there is pestilence. She says that they don't have any rats, they're lucky. You ask about roaches. She answers no, they're lucky, no roaches, either. Dickie tells you they're very careful about disposal and that a private scavenger from the city comes out and carts away the garbage for free.

How about power?

"The regular wires are all crystallized. We use an emergency generator. I don't know who pays for it. And there's only cold water."

You and Dickie leave the block and stand outside. The breeze is wet and fresh after the stink of the cells. From the city you hear a faint traffic din and see the automobile haze pressing down.

"Maybe we can grow vegetables here." Dickie points out a small clearing below. "We'll try next summer. Did you see the tepee? The boys built it to sleep in because it's cold in the buildings at night. The tepee sleeps 15; it's real warm in there." Dickie guides you to where the tepee is, then we shake hands, and Dickie treads uphill and into the trees.

The rain blows stronger as you tread down a concrete ramp. You discover yourself pulling up your collar, worrying about the wind and rain and your appearance. But around here it doesn't matter if your hair is all funny or your pants unpressed or shoes soggy. The Indians aren't worried about that.

Above a rock cliff which drops to the bay, the tepee lies on a plateau facing the Golden Gate and the sea. From there you can't see the cell block or other prison buildings; you wouldn't know you are on Alcatraz. It's grass and trees and sea and the cross members of the bark-colored tepee rising against the gray sky. Only the sounds of wind and rain, birds and trees.

A kid named Ray has on an Indian derby with a feather in it and walks you to the kitchen as he holds his transistor to his ear. Ray is from the Walla Walla tribe and hitchhiked down a month ago with his family from Olympia, Wash. He's in 7th grade in the mornings and in the afternoons helps in the kitchen.

The kitchen used to be in the main cell block, but recently they moved it down near the caretaker's place where they're all staying.

It's filled with provisions—cartons of canned goods, sacks of grain —and on the stove bubble two big tubs of spaghetti. The cook—Ted Jake, a Paiute—is back on the job now after a stay in the hospital: Christmas day he had too much of his own sauce and took a header off the block's third tier onto the concrete.

Where does it all come from, you ask Ted, and he says, "from the people," throwing his arm to the world. "The people send it to us." Then Ted takes you out into Dining and shows you how he's going to knock out another wall and give himself space to feed twice as many at a sitting and how they're going to rearrange the tables to accommodate more as the population increases.

Jennie Rose Joe, R.N., is Navajo and she comes on week-ends to help out nurse Stella Leach, Colville Sioux, in the clinic. The clinic is one of the apartments in the caretaker's place, where most of the women and children stay. "We have sick call every day," says Jennie, "and the kids get examined three times a week. Doctors from the mainland donate their time."

You ask if they are Indian doctors, and Jennie Rose laughs out loud. "Are you kidding? There are only about two Indian doctors in the whole United States."

In the next apartment is the nursery school. Carlos Lavender is painting some cabinets saffron, and his wife Maria is at the stove cooking Spam and eggs for 19 pre-schoolers who sit at tables in the dinette watching Sesame Street.

Upstairs in Arts and Crafts, Francis Allen, Sac and Fox tribe, sits at a table of looms, beads, and leatherwork. It's quiet. The kids won't be in until the afternoon. Francis tells you about plans for a permanent Indian educational and cultural center on the island. You ask about support.

"We'll get it supported. There are grants and funds. Maybe we'll do Indian art on a voluntary basis and sell it outside. Bead and leather goods. We could put 'Alcatraz' on it. People would buy it."

After discussing the hardships of setting up a new independent society, you ask Francis about justice on the island. How do they handle law and order?

"We have special meetings. We elect a council and make rules. You follow the rules or you can't stay."

Is there ever trouble? Fights?

"Only Indian fights: Couple of the boys push each other, then back off, then go push each other again, then walk away again, then shake hands."

What will you do if they kick you off the island?

Francis shakes his head indignantly. "No. No. You kick Communists or somebody off islands. You don't kick Indians off any American island. No."

Big Rock Elementary school is in the sunny apartment across the hall from Arts and Crafts. It has 24 students in grades 1 thru 7 and two Indian teachers fully qualified with state credentials. State curriculum guides are followed strictly, and the teacher-pupil ratio is superb: 1 to 12.

Leaving the upper tier you look over the banister rail where 12-year-old Yvonne Oakes fell four stories to the concrete and her death. It happened in early January, and everybody said it was ominous, that they *knew* something tragic would happen to the Indians on Alcatraz sooner or later. After the funeral, Yvonne's father and mother and the remaining four children left the island and never came back.

The rains started heavy then, provision boats were delayed, and only the determined stayed. Whereas the population generally had been 150 and had swelled to 700 at times over the holidays, after the tragedy the number diminished to 50 and stayed there.

The government closed in, hitting away with the argument that they wanted the island vacated for the health and safety of the women and children.

But the Indians stay. Resident population is up over 100 again, and another 100 come on week-ends. So far there have been about 15,000 tribal visitors.

The government accuses the Indians of vandalism, of climbing into the lighthouse tower and breaking expensive mirrors. The Indians deny it. The government threatens to discontinue the water barge. The Indians answer that they'll bring water on in five-gallon cans. The government says it will shut off the electricity. The Indians say go ahead. The government tries health and safety again. The Indians grin.

The meeting breaks, and down the cliff from the block climb the government guys and the Indians. The government guys are white raincoats and pork pie hats. The Indians are headbands and blankets. One Indian carries a Sony recorder under his arm and tapes of the meeting. Together they stand, the government guys waiting for the coast guard cutter, the Indians waiting for the Ino. They're talking to each other, but they're not saying anything.

The boats arrive. The cutter takes its passengers; the Ino takes the Indians. Clambering on, the Indians make it loud and clear in front of the government guys that they're not abandoning the island for good, that they're just going to the mainland for something and will be back on the next boat. One shouts to his friends on the dock that he'll see them at the pow-wow tonight, the dance they're going to have in the main rec yard.

Across the bay we churn, the skipper above in his yellow poncho and blue captain's hat. To starboard the sleek white cutter begins to outdistance us. It hurts. "Come on, come *on*," an Indian yells half-kidding, half-serious up to the black man at the helm, "pour it on."

The cutter slides away from us even more, making us look sick. You can barely see the government guys now as they stand forward in their long, white windbreaker raincoats.

"Man the torpedoes!" an Indian calls out, and we all start laughing.

"Fire one! Fire two! Fire them all!"

We laugh a while and talk a while, and a guy tells you if they ever try to come and get them off the island, they'll scatter in all directions and dig in and hold out, if it comes to that, with bows and arrows; the rain comes down, the Ino coughs along, the white cutter far out of sight now, and when we finally reach the mainland, just before we disembark an Indian with some wine in him wanders over and touches you and says: "Tell them we're nice people. Out on that island you could meet another Indian and it don't matter where he's from—from North Dakota or from Oklahoma or from anywhere—and right away you get along: he's a friend, and you know. Tell them we're good people and we love each other, will you do that for me?"

## Study Guide

1. In his article, Ken Michaels describes conditions at Alcatraz shortly after the abandoned prison was invaded by Indians in 1969. What was the ultimate result of the Indians' attempt to reclaim this unused federal land?

2. What emotional response does the author have toward Alcatraz? How is this response conveyed? Is there anything unexpected in the Indians' response to the "Rock"? How do you account for this response?

3. How would you describe the society the Indians have attempted to establish at Alcatraz? Is it like any other attempts to establish countercultural societies with which you are familiar?

4. Michaels' article is primarily descriptive, and he is concerned with the conditions he discovered in the Indian settlement on Alcatraz. Are there any explicit criticisms of America's treatment of the Indian contained in the article? Are there any implicit criticisms?

5. What uses does Michaels make of humor in the article?

6. Discuss the author's point of view. What is gained by his use of the second person in the article?

7. What organizing structure has Michaels used in the article?

8. Visit a ghetto, a commune, or an Indian reservation and write an informal narrative in which you describe your impressions of the people you meet and the life they lead.

9. One of the Indians Michaels meets complains that "The Indians you read about, the ones high up in government, the so-called spokesmen—they don't represent the Indian people. The real Indians call them Uncle Tomahawks." His statement suggests that a few influential Indians have misrepresented the majority of Indian Americans. Is there an Indian establishment that preys upon other, less fortunate Indians? Investigate Indian society in America and present your findings in a research paper.

10. The Indians Michaels met on Alcatraz describe the government's efforts to evict them from the abandoned prison. Is the government's action in this case typical of the official reaction to the needs of minority groups?

# 13. *Slant-Eyed Americans*

## TOSHIO MORI

My mother was commenting on the fine California weather. It was Sunday noon, December 7. We were having our lunch, and I had the radio going. "Let's take the afternoon off and go to the city," I said to Mother.

"All right. We shall go," she said dreamily. "Ah, four months ago my boy left Hayward to join the army, and a fine send-off he had. Our good friends—ah, I shall never forget the day of his departure."

"We'll visit some of our friends in Oakland and then take in a movie," I said. "Care to come along, Papa?"

Father shook his head. "No, I'll stay home and take it easy."

"That's his heaven," Mother commented. "To stay home, read the papers over and over, and smoke his Bull Durham."

I laughed. Suddenly the musical program was cut off as a special announcement came over the air: At 7:25 a.m. this morning a squadron of Japanese bombing planes attacked Pearl Harbor. The battle is still in progress.

"What's this? Listen to the announcement," I cried, going to the radio.

Abruptly the announcement stopped and the musicale continued.

From *Yokohama California* by Toshio Mori. Published by The CAXTON PRINTERS, Ltd., Caldwell, Idaho, and used by permission.

"What is it?" Mother asked. "What has happened?"

"The radio reports that the Japanese planes attacked Hawaii this morning," I said incredulously. "It couldn't be true."

"It must be a mistake. Couldn't it have been a part of a play?" asked Mother.

I dialed other stations. Several minutes later one of the stations confirmed the bulletin.

"It must be true," Father said quietly.

I said, "Japan has declared war on the United States and Great Britain."

The room became quiet but for the special bulletin coming in every now and then.

"It cannot be true, yet it must be so," Father said over and over.

"Can it be one of those programs scaring the people about invasion?" Mother asked me.

"No, I'm sure this is a news report," I replied.

Mother's last ray of hope paled and her eyes became dull. "Why did it have to happen? The common people in Japan don't want war, and we don't want war. Here the people are peace-loving. Why cannot the peoples of the earth live together peacefully?"

"Since Japan declared war on the United States it'll mean that you parents of American citizens have become enemy aliens," I said.

"Enemy aliens," my mother whispered.

Night came but sleep did not come. We sat up late in the night hoping against hope that some good news would come, retracting the news of vicious attack and open hostilities.

"This is very bad for the people with Japanese faces," I said.

Father slowly shook his head.

"What shall we do?" asked Mother.

"What can we do?" Father said helplessly.

At the flower market next morning the growers were present but the buyers were scarce. The place looked empty and deserted. "Our business is shot to pieces," one of the boys said.

"Who'll buy flowers now?" another called.

Don Haley, the seedsman, came over looking bewildered. "I suppose you don't need seeds now."

We shook our heads.

"It looks bad," I said. "Will it affect your business?"

"Flower seed sale will drop but the vegetable seeds will move quicker," Don said. "I think I'll have to put more time on the vegetable seeds."

Nobu Hiramatsu who had been thinking of building another greenhouse joined us. He had plans to grow more carnations and expand his business.

"What's going to happen to your plans, Nobu?" asked one of the boys.

"Nothing. I'm going to sit tight and see how the things turn out," he said.

"Flowers and war don't go together," Don said. "You cannot concentrate too much on beauty when destruction is going about you."

"Sure, pretty soon we'll raise vegetables instead of flowers," Grasselli said.

A moment later the market opened and we went back to the tables to sell our flowers. Several buyers came in and purchased a little. The flowers didn't move at all. Just as I was about to leave the place I met Tom Yamashita, the Nisei gardener with a future.

"What are you doing here, Tom? What's the matter with your work?" I asked as I noticed his pale face.

"I was too sick with yesterday's news so I didn't work," he said. "This is the end. I am done for."

"No, you're not. Buck up, Tom," I cried. "You have a good future, don't lose hope."

"Sometimes I feel all right. You are an American, I tell myself. Devote your energy and life to the American way of life. Long before this my mind was made up to become a true American. This morning my Caucasian American friends sympathized with me. I felt good and was grateful. Our opportunity has come to express ourselves and act. We are Americans in thought and action. I felt like leaping to work. Then I got sick again because I got to thinking that Japan was the country that attacked the United States. I wanted to bury myself for shame."

I put my hand on his shoulder. "We all feel the same way, Tom. We're human so we flounder around awhile when an unexpected and big problem confronts us, but now that situation has to be passed by. We can't live in the same stage long. We have to move along, face the reality no matter what's in store for us."

Tom stood silently.

"Let's go to my house and take the afternoon off," I suggested. "We'll face a new world tomorrow morning with boldness and strength. What do you say, Tom?"

"All right," Tom agreed.

At home Mother was anxiously waiting for me. When she saw Tom with me her eyes brightened. Tom Yamashita was a favorite of my mother's.

"Look, a telegram from Kazuo!" she cried to me, holding up an envelope. "Read it and tell me what he says."

I tore it open and read. "He wants us to send $45 for train fare. He has a good chance for a furlough."

Mother fairly leaped in the air with the news. She had not seen my brother for four months. "How wonderful! This can happen only in America."

Suddenly she noticed Tom looking glum, and pushed him in the house. "Cheer up, Tom. This is no time for young folks to despair. Roll up your sleeves and get to work. America needs you."

Tom smiled for the first time and looked at me.

"See, Tom?" I said. "She's quick to recover. Yesterday she was wilted, and she's seventy-three."

"Tom, did you go to your gardens today?" she asked him.

"No."

"Why not?" she asked, and then added quickly. "You young men should work hard all the more, keeping up the normal routine of life. You ought to know, Tom, that if everybody dropped their work everything would go to seed. Who's going to take care of the gardens if you won't?"

Tom kept still.

Mother poured tea and brought the cookies. "Don't worry about your old folks. We have stayed here to belong to the American way of life. Time will tell our true purpose. We remained in America for permanence—not for temporary convenience. We common people need not fear."

"I guess you are right," Tom agreed.

"And America is right. She cannot fail. Her principles will stand the test of time and tyranny. Someday aggression will be outlawed by all nations."

Mother left the room to prepare the dinner. Tom got up and began to walk up and down the room. Several times he looked out the window and watched the wind blow over the field.

"Yes, if the gardens are ruined I'll rebuild them," he said. "I'll take charge of every garden in the city. All the gardens of America for that matter. I'll rebuild them as fast as the enemies wreck them. We'll have nature on our side and you cannot crush nature."

I smiled and nodded. "Good for you! Tomorrow we'll get up early in the morning and work, sweat, and create. Let's shake on it."

We solemnly shook hands, and by the grip of his fingers I knew he was ready to lay down his life for America and for his gardens.

"No word from him yet," Mother said worriedly. "He should have arrived yesterday. What's happened to him?"

It was eight in the evening, and we had had no word from my brother for several days.

"He's not coming home tonight. It's too late now," I said. "He should have arrived in Oakland this morning at the latest."

Our work had piled up and we had to work late into the night. There were still some pompons to bunch. Faintly the phone rang in the house.

"The phone!" cried Mother excitedly. "It's Kazuo, sure enough."

In the flurry of several minutes I answered the phone, greeted my brother, and was on my way to San Leandro to drive him home. On the way I tried to think of the many things I wanted to say. From the moment I spotted him waiting on the corner I could not say the thing I wanted to. I took his bag and he got in the car, and for some time we did not say anything. Then I asked him how the weather had been in Texas and how he had been.

"We were waiting for you since yesterday," I said. "Mother is home getting the supper ready. You haven't eaten yet, have you?"

He shook his head. "The train was late getting into Los Angeles. We were eight hours behind time and I should have reached San Francisco this morning around eight."

Reaching home it was the same way. Mother could not say anything. "We have nothing special tonight, wish we had something good."

"Anything would do, Mama," my brother said.

Father sat in the room reading the papers but his eyes were over the sheet and his hands were trembling. Mother scurried about getting his supper ready. I sat across the table from my brother, and in the silence which was action I watched the wave of emotions in the room. My brother was aware of it too. He sat there without a word, but I knew he understood. Not many years ago he was the baby of the family, having never been away from home. Now he was on his own, his quiet confidence actually making him appear larger. Keep up the fire, that was his company's motto. It was evident that he was a soldier. He had gone beyond life and death matter, where the true soldiers of war or peace must travel, and had returned.

For five short days we went about our daily task, picking and bunching the flowers for Christmas, eating heavy meals, and visiting the intimates. It was as if we were waiting for the hour of his departure, the time being so short. Every minute was crowded with privacy, friends, and nursery work. Too soon the time for his train came but the family had little to talk.

"Kazuo, don't worry about home or me," Mother said as we rode into town.

"Take care of yourself," my brother told her.

At the 16th Street Station Mother's close friend was waiting for us. She came to bid my brother good-bye. We had fifteen minutes to wait. My brother bought a copy of *The Coast* to see if his cartoons were in.

"Are you in this month's issue?" I asked.

"I haven't seen it yet," he said, leafing the pages. "Yes, I'm in. Here it is."

"Good!" I said. "Keep trying hard. Someday peace will come, and when you return laughter will reign once again."

My mother showed his cartoon to her friend. The train came in and we got up. It was a long one. We rushed to the Los Angeles-bound coach.

Mother's friend shook hands with my brother. "Give your best to America. Our people's honor depend on you Nisei soldiers."

My brother nodded and then glanced at Mother. For a moment her eyes twinkled and she nodded. He waved good-bye from the platform. Once inside the train we lost him. When the train began to move my mother cried, "Why doesn't he pull up the shades and look out? Others are doing it."

We stood and watched until the last of the train was lost in the night of darkness.

*Study Guide*

1. "Slant-Eyed Americans" describes the reactions of a Nisei family to the bombing of Pearl Harbor by the Japanese. At what point in the story do you become aware of the fact that the characters are not white, middle-class Americans?

2. With what typically American concerns is the family occupied?

3. How do the characters' reactions to the events of the story differ from those you might expect a Japanese family to have?

4. How were the Nisei treated during World War II? Does a knowledge of their treatment enhance your appreciation of this story?

5. Toshio Mori treats a well-known historical event from the perspective of an unusual audience. Select some other important event and describe it from the point of view of one of the minority groups described in this text.

6. Throughout his story, Mori emphasizes the patriotism and Americanism of his characters. Why do you feel he places so much emphasis on these qualities? What assumptions do you suppose Caucasian Americans may have had about their Japanese neighbors in the early 1940's? How does this story contradict them?

7. Write a brief definition of prejudice.

8. To what extent does the author attempt to contradict a prejudiced opinion of Oriental Americans in this selection? Present your ideas in a brief critical essay.

9. Investigate the migration of Chinese and Japanese groups to America. To what extent have these groups faced problems comparable to those of other minorities discussed in this text? To what extent have Oriental Americans become assimilated into the Caucasian population? To what extent have they retained an independent culture? Present your findings in a documented essay.

# 14. Coming of Age in Nueva York

## PETE HAMILL

Here, examine the baggage, with the great jets screaming in behind us and the glossy girls staring from the counters of the San Juan airport and the signs blinking at us from every space and the horde of strange cold faces coming through the arrival gates and the cold wind of New York starting to blow within them across the darkened airfield. Quickly: while the children run to the candy machines and the girl from Trans Caribbean argues with the passengers on the outgoing flights and the cop lolls against the wall swinging the bat of authority and you check the ticket again and hope that nobody knows that you have some pages of La Prensa in your shoes and some yames for your aunt in Brooklyn. Quickly: it is getting cold.

The luggage: new undershirts bought in the Pueblo supermarket on the road to Bayamón. Some slacks, and shirts, and the suit bought for Belen's wedding two years ago to that guy from Caguas who left her later. That luggage, and the other kind. The way the flags of the Popular party blow in the sea breeze in spring over the tarpaper roofs of La Perla; children playing in those mud streets; tourists with peeling faces gawking over the walls of the old city; the sea beyond, *foaming at the shore, and then green, and then turning dark blue away out where the Atlantic conquers the Caribbean. Up in the hills, the road turning, chickens cawing in the damp morning, an old* jibaro *with a lined face walking on homemade sandals with a machete on his hip, the flamboyant trees exploding against the hillsides, a flock of white birds against the blue roof of the sky. That luggage: nuns in white habits walking along the Avenida Ponce de Leon, and the tourist ladies in bikinis on the beaches of the Condado, and the Cuban whores along the waterfront in San Juan Antiguo, and the way the sidewalks in El Fanguito were made with rubber tires and there was no electricity and no toilets and you drank water from a common pump. One summer the ticks came like a plague and attached themselves to the skins of children, and the public health people sprayed and made everyone sicker. That luggage: the yellow eyes of old men, women gone crazy with the spirits, the man who used to wear silk suits in the afternoons and play piano in the bands and who was found dead one morning with a needle in his arm. That luggage: but the sweet part more than the bad, with the sun climbing in the sky, and the sound of laughter, and the distant swelling roar of the sea, and music.*

*New York, mon. Check the luggage. I've got some Don Q in the overcoat, and when I sit down, I'm going to start drinking. It's dark out, but I've made this trip before. I don't want to see the swells around El Morro, or the lights of fishing boats, or the garish light-blinking spread of San Juan. I don't want to see it vanish behind me. I might never see it again.*

The Puerto Ricans came to New York to live better. It was as simple as that. It was a trickle at first, in the 1920s and 1930s, because the ticket on the Bull Line cost more than a man could earn in a year, and the trip was long and dangerous and the city was a mean, hard place then, if your skin was dark and your language was Spanish. Some of the earliest worked on the Brooklyn piers, unloading bananas, with the spiders large enough to play baseball with and the old Bull Line captains keeping the men in line. A few drifted into the South Bronx and the Lower East Side, to the places that were being abandoned by the Jews and the Irish who were starting to make it. But most went to East Harlem, El Barrio, where 110th and Lex was the center of the world, and you could buy *plátanos* at the Park Avenue market and rice and beans from people you knew.

They came here because the island they left behind was the sinkhole of the Caribbean, with a life expectancy of 32, a place where the American rulers would sit around the palace in white duck while *jíbaros* died in the mountains from yaws and parasites. Even today, with conditions changed radically from the dark years of the 1920s and 1930s, the population density of Puerto Rico is 11 times that of the United States, unemployment runs at a constant 13 per cent, and the per capita income is still only about $1,000 a year. New York might have been a strange and alien place to those early arrivals, but it was better than dying young.

And then the migration started to build. Puerto Ricans were different from others who had come to New York from the slums of Europe. Most importantly, they were citizens and had been so by act of Congress since 1917. So they were not immigrants, they were migrants. They fought in the First World War and all the wars after, and if there were large numbers of Puerto Ricans then who wanted independence from the United States, it was only because the United States had treated them so shabbily. The *independentistas* followed in the footsteps of Muñoz Rivera, and later followed a brilliant man named Albizu Campos, who died finally of heartache and insanity. Muñoz' son, Luis Muñoz-Marín, made the journey in those years, and sat around the Village writing poetry and Socialist tracts and enjoying himself more than he ever would again.

And through all those years, before the explosions of the years after the Second World War, the dream remained the same: to come to New York, make money, learn a trade, and go home to Puerto Rico. Muñoz-Marín went back and became the most important politician in the history of the island. For others it wasn't so easy. I remember once, a few years ago, sitting around one afternoon in Luis Cora's barbershop in East Harlem, talking to a man who had settled in New York in 1921. He was a seaman who had given up the sea because his wife was lonely, and who had come to New York because he had no job back in Puerto Rico.

"I always thought I would go back," the old man said. "But it was too expensive, too long a trip. I finally went in 1958, with my son, who paid for the airplane ticket. In three days I was ready to come home. I had been away too long and I was a New Yorker, not a real Puerto Rican anymore. It was sad."

A Puerto Rican was something strange and exotic in those days. There weren't enough of them to be a threat to anybody, not enough of them to be identified as a group. The word "spic" came later (most common theory: from the phrase "No spik Inglis"). It came with the wave after the war. It came with the airplane.

And it was the airplane that changed everything. The ships started shifting to freight (and I knew a woman who had been torpedoed in one off the Bahamas during the war and lived to put double locks on her home in Williamsburg and lose a husband to alcohol). The airplane changed it all. The hustlers moved in with the charter flights and created a kind of airborne steerage, with shaking aircraft, packed with women and screaming children, skimming out over the Atlantic, pushing against the headwinds of the North, moving on, leaving it all behind, heading for New York. A lot of the planes never made it, falling into the sea with their cargoes of people doomed to hope, until the charter flights were banned and the big lines took over.

Every day the planes unloaded, and the people were pathetic to look at. Their suitcases were cardboard, tied with rope, holding everything they possessed. They did not understand the cold; they had seen snow only in the movies; they arrived in January in sports shirts, with vague addresses scribbled in pencil on the backs of envelopes, and hardly any money. The cold overwhelmed a lot of them. "After that first winter," a friend told me, "I was never warm." Somehow they would make it from the airports to town, and there were jokes among them later, when they had the luxury of laughter, that the Puerto Ricans were the only people in New York who knew how to get to Idlewild by public transportation.

There was no place to go except to the slums, of course: to the dark spiky landscapes of fire escapes and mean streets and doors covered with metal. There was never enough heat, and they plugged towels into the cracked windows to keep out winter, and bought a hundred thousand miles of felt tape to tack around doors, and made blankets from leftover clothes, and carried drums of kerosene up to the stoves in the parlor, and kept the gas ovens going at night. It was never warm enough, and every time you picked up a paper then and saw a headline that said SEVEN PERISH IN TENEMENT BLAZE, you knew it was Puerto Ricans and that they had died of the cold.

That New York cold killed a lot of them. The cold that made a man a "spic" instead of a man. The cold that sent women off to work in sweatshops for more money than their husbands were making cleaning the slops in the cellar of the Waldorf. Myths were growing up then, in the late '40s and early '50s, especially after the outbreak of the Korean War brought jobs and the Puerto Rican trickle became a flood. They were here to go on welfare. They had come here because Vito Marcantonio, the old leftist congressman, had bought their votes. It didn't seem to matter that the Puerto Rican migration coincided almost exactly with the increase or decrease in jobs or that the Puerto Ricans had arrived at a time when automation was starting to eliminate the jobs which were traditionally the first rung on the immigrants' ladder. The myths grew up, part of the New York cold, part of everything that is mean-spirited and ungenerous in us.

The cold broke things apart among those who were not prepared to resist it. I remember one man I knew in East Harlem, sitting alone in his kitchen, while platoons of roaches scurried across the walls, his wife gone off, the house smelling of feet and long-burnt bacon, talking quietly over a can of Schaefer about how it had all gone wrong. "We should not have come here," he said. "This is an evil place. There is no respect, not for people, not for fathers." His daughter had not been home for two nights. She was 15 and he didn't know what to do about her. He talked about her, and about how he would like to go back to Puerto Rico, and how if he could find his wife he would bring her back with him and they could put the thing together again. His tone said that his mouth was lying. The city had broken him, and he sat there while a parakeet he had bought for his wife's birthday whistled in the other room. It was August and the cold came through the rooms, damp and threatening and triumphant.

But the Puerto Ricans have done what all the immigrants did. They have endured. They turned out to be long-distance runners, not sprinters, and now they are a very important part of this town. There are, to begin with, their numbers. The latest count shows that there are 1,586,397 Puerto Ricans in the United States (up from 855,724 in the 1960 census), with 977,832 of them in New York (up from 629,430 in 1960). In 1950, Puerto Ricans were only 3 per cent of the city's population; today they are almost 11 per cent. About one-third are second generation. One recent set of figures showed that there are 244,458 Puerto Rican students in the public school system, an increase of 75 per cent over a 10-year period.

The Puerto Ricans have spread to all parts of the city (although Richmond still does not have any sizable population). Brooklyn now has the most—a symbol, I suppose, of the trend of migration; in this town a lot of the old immigrants went from the Manhattan slums to the Bronx and on to Brooklyn. The Puerto Ricans, who once were most heavily concentrated in East Harlem, were forced into the slums of the South Bronx by the swinging ball of urban renewal, and are now making it into the greener glades of Brooklyn. In addition, the number of Puerto Ricans outside the city has increased from 30,000 to 51,200, a 70 per cent jump. Suffolk County, with its Puerto Rican population increase of 4,700, leads the other 62 counties in the state.

More important is the fact that the Puerto Ricans have been accepted. It has been a long time since I have heard the word "spic" around this town. (The Spanish-language papers continue to use the word *boricua,* which derives from the pre-Spanish name for the island, Borinquen. A lot of the second-generation kids just refer to each other as "P.R.s.") In my white-middle-class neighborhood, the Puerto Ricans open grocery stores and put starched collars on their children in the mornings before sending them off to school.

The Puerto Ricans have followed the old routes: some 10,000 of them run small businesses in this town, and some are expanding into larger things. There are people like José Rojas, who is now the president of Puerto Rican Steel Products Incorporated at 4 Whale Square in Brooklyn. He and eight others have started their own steel plant, with the help of private business interests and the United Puerto Rican and Spanish Organizations of Sunset Park. Or someone like Pablo Morales, who got a $2,000 loan from the Banco de Ponce several years ago to buy a truck, and now owns five trucks in his own garage on Westchester Avenue and Southern Boulevard in El Bronx. The Puerto Rican banks themselves are an important part of the story, ever since they were allowed to operate in New York after changes in the state banking laws in 1961; Banco de Ponce now has four branches in the city, as has the Banco Popular, and the Banco Crédito is now breaking into this lucrative market.

The Puerto Rican Homeowners Association has plans to build a $2.7 million low- and middle-income housing development in Brooklyn, and the Puerto Rican Community Development Project has instituted programs which in one year led to 402 members of the community's receiving high school equivalency diplomas. Everywhere the mood is one of energy and movement; it is a long way from the desperate days of the early arrivals, when you would see thin, shivering girls in spring coats in winter walking 14th Street with guys in plastic-visored yacht caps, going to S. Klein on Christmas Eve to buy their kids the scraps. The great Puerto Rican neighborhoods are still solid blocks in the town: East Harlem, the South Bronx, Williamsburg, Red Hook, the Lower East Side. But there are Puerto Ricans scattered now throughout the city, in Bay Ridge and Corona and Inwood and out into the suburbs. They've purchased through grief and work and endurance that special thing which the sociologists work so hard at dehumanizing: mobility.

That mobility has freed the first brigades of the emerging Puerto Rican middle class in this town (with the same set of conflicts over loyalties to those left behind which afflicts the black middle class). But there are still hundreds of thousands living in desperate situations, and the Puerto Ricans are in fact still at the bottom of the city's economic ladder. One recent study (by Leonard S. Kogan and Morey J. Wantman) estimated that the median annual income for all city families was $6,684. The Puerto Ricans earned $3,949, non-whites $4,754, and whites $7,635. The Puerto Ricans had gained only $49 in two years, while whites gained $927. Puerto Ricans receiving relief rose more in percentage than any other group—from 29.5 per cent of the welfare rolls in 1959 to 33 per cent in 1967—they are now about 35 to 40 per cent. Some estimates state that some 40 per cent of the city's Puerto Ricans are receiving some form of public assistance, most of it supplementing the low wages paid to Puerto Rican fathers.

In East Harlem last year, according to Herbert Bienstock, the regional director of the Bureau of Labor Statistics, 36.9 per cent of Puerto Rican workers were unemployed or sub-employed. The general rate was 33.1, indicating that blacks there fared slightly better. In Bedford-Stuyvesant, 29.7 per cent of Puerto Ricans were unemployed, compared to 27.6 per cent of the blacks. In Harlem itself, 12 per cent of the Puerto Ricans are unemployed, and 8 per cent of the blacks.

In some respects, the situation is not encouraging at all. White-collar employment of Puerto Rican men actually declined from 17 to 12 per cent from 1960 to 1965, according to Richard Lewisohn of the Economic Development Administration, while—in the familiar pattern—white-collar employment of Puerto Rican women increased (from 18.7 per cent to 24.9 per cent). In a report released last year by the federal government's Equal Employment Opportunity Commission, we learned that only .9 per cent of these employed in radio-TV and newspaper white-collar jobs were Puerto Ricans. (On the three major New York dailies, only 2.5 per cent of *all* employees were Puerto Rican or of Latin background.) In the banking industry, only 5.1 per cent of white-collar employees were Puerto Rican. The government queried 4,239 firms with 100 employees or more, or with more than $50,000 in federal contracts; some 1,926 firms did not employ a single Puerto Rican in a white-collar job. A survey by the State Human Rights Commission showed that of 25 of the city's 41 major advertising agencies, only 1.6 of their 18,000 employees were Puerto Rican.

Some of this can be attributed to the problem of education. An analysis by the Puerto Rican Forum shows that of those Puerto Ricans who finish high school, 90 per cent have been getting a general diploma, 8 per cent a vocational degree, and only 1.2 per cent the academic diploma leading to college. In the elementary schools, there is still an insistence on teaching kids in English, which they sometimes do not know, with the result that ordinarily bright kids are stunned and humiliated before they have much of a chance to learn anything at all.

Another factor is that the Puerto Ricans are the youngest people in the city, with a median age (according to a 1966 City University study) of 19.1, compared to 38.6 for whites and 26.1 for nonwhites. This indicates a group in flux, and the educational statistics at present might be quite misleading; there might be an explosion of academic diplomas any year now. It is one indication of the way the Board of Education sees the students, however, that despite the fact that blacks and Puerto Ricans make up more than one-half of the city's public school population, only 30 of the more than 900 schools are named after distinguished blacks and only five after Puerto Ricans.

And yet, just because the Puerto Ricans are so young, and just because they are starting to make their move, we have to deal with their presence in a rational way. Anyone who understands New York will understand that their presence is a good thing for us, perhaps the most fortunate piece of luck we have had since the end of the Second World War.

To begin with, the Puerto Ricans have brought an element of stability to New York. When the white middle class started its mass stampede to the suburbs, lamming like units of a defeated army across the frontier, the Puerto Ricans stayed on. They stayed on because they had to stay on. You simply do not have a choice if you can't ever imagine yourself having $2,000 for a down payment on a house. They stayed on, too, because they wanted to. More than the white-middle-class refugees, the Puerto Ricans understood early that this could be a mean and nasty and vicious town, but it was also a great one.

"I tried living in the country," my friend José Torres, the former light-heavyweight champion of the world, once told me. "It was beautiful. There was grass and trees and clean air and birds. People were friendly. It was healthy. The schools were not crowded. The trouble was that I started going crazy. I needed noise."

Noise. Not the noise of jackhammers and ripped sidewalks and coughing trucks. What Torres means is the noise of streets, to be able to walk along Smith Street in Brooklyn and hear people shouting back and forth at each other in greeting and guys coming out of saloons on Saturday afternoons to stop friends and whisper *piropos* to girls ("Ah, *mi vida,* it must have been a fine and splendid mother to have produced such a beauty as you"). The noise is at a party in my friend Cocolo's house on Dean Street, the bathtub packed with ice and beer, babies crying in the kitchen, the table groaning with *pulpo,* and arguments in English and Spanish over the Mets and Mario Procaccino and the cost of cigars and Fidel Castro and the best way to seduce a Swedish girl. Cocolo has hit the number for the third time that year, and all his friends are there, and his relatives. "Hey, you better eat all this stup, mon, because you doan hit the number three times in a year every year." Cocolo is beaming, and on his wall he has a picture of Jack Kennedy and a poster from the O'Dwyer campaign and a smaller picture of Robert Kennedy, and later in the night, all of us slowed by beer and food, and the children asleep, and not much more to travel to daylight, Cocolo points up at the picture of Bob Kennedy and says, "Hey mon, you explain this goddam country. What kine of a sum-of-a-bitch would shoot that guy? Huh? You explain that to me, mon." And the other three guys start to sing, because they've seen this happen before, and they don't want Cocolo, who is 38 years old and weighs 240 pounds, to start crying all over again.

That kind of noise: and nights in Otero's on Smith Street, eating *pernil* in the back room, and talking boxing at the bar, and how one night we all came in late and the place was empty and Junior, the bartender, had a big bandage on his face. "What the hell happened?" someone said. "You get in a fight with your girl?" And Junior said, no, it wasn't a fight, it was a car accident. Pedro Ortiz, the meanest-looking man in Brooklyn, leers: "Hey, Junior, you don't have to lie to us." And Junior gets mad and goes into the back room and comes back with the door from his car, the whole goddam door, smashed and crumpled, and everyone starts to laugh, and Pedro Ortiz falls off the stool, and we order another round.

That's what José Torres means by noise. Noise and life. Travel around a little and look at it: the Jefferson Theatre, with the children crying in the audience and guys selling ice cream right in the middle of the movie, and a great comic like Johnny El Men making jokes on the stage about being a Puerto Rican in New York. Move around: to the Broadway Casino, or Carlos Ortiz' place in the South Bronx, or the Club Caborrojeño, and make a Saturday night. Who's on? La Playa, or Tito Puente, or El Gran Combo, with the music thundering down, the musicians making bad jokes, the lights sly and romantic, the girl singers with impossibly narrow waists above implacable swelling hips. And on the dance floor, girls with soft fleshy faces doing hammering mambos with their shoes off, series after series, the guys weaving baroque steps around them, the floor itself starting to groan from the pounding, the single guys lined against the walls, the people from the community clubs sitting in private parties at the tables, an occasional older woman chaperoning her daughter or niece. Ten years ago, Torres and I spent a lot of time in those places, and maybe he would have been a better fighter and I would have been a better writer if we had stayed home. I doubt it. We certainly wouldn't have had as much laughter.

The problems remain terrible. Nine out of 10 Puerto Ricans over the age of 25 have never finished high school. There are still large sections of the community which do not read or speak English, which depend for news and information on the Spanish radio and TV (UHF) stations and upon *El Diario-La Prensa* (the other Spanish-language paper, *El Tiempo,* is a right-wing sheet directed to the community of Cuban exiles and other non-Puerto Rican Spanish-speaking people in the city: *El Tiempo* supported Mario Procaccino over Herman Badillo in the Democratic primary). There are still many Puerto Ricans working for unconscionably low salaries in sweatshops and factories run by gangster unions; a union like the International Ladies Garment Workers Union still does not have real representation of Puerto Ricans at its highest level despite the overwhelming number of Puerto Ricans in its rank and file. Narcotics remains a poison, with some communities, like Hunts Point in the Bronx, practically devastated by the problem. Heroin addicts were practically unknown in Puerto Rico itself until those who were contaminated started coming home from New York. The Puerto Rican street gangs, which were so prominent in the 1950s (the Enchanters, the Dragons, the Latin

Gents, etc.), have largely disappeared, not because of especially enlightened social workers, but because a junkie doesn't have much time for gangbusting. ("It's not cool anymore to be in the hitter's bag, man," one kid told me last year.)

In the 1950s and early 1960s, there were still so many broken marriages that they seemed to a casual outsider to be almost a majority. Every day's issue of *El Diario* carried stories of guys who would visit their estranged wives and throw wives, kids and selves out the fourth floors of tenements. The pressures were intolerable: women who worked and made more money than men offended the Puerto Rican male's occasionally exaggerated sense of *machismo;* the resort to welfare was humiliating; the disgraceful conditions of the tenements themselves did not exactly make for the most encouraging belief in a happy and rich future. But that seems to have lessened with the breakthrough the Puerto Rican men made into the town itself. If a man does not feel he is being supported by his wife he can find it a lot easier to live with her, whether he is a Puerto Rican or not.

The younger generation of Puerto Ricans are also making the whole thing move in another way. They don't feel sorry for themselves, they have been here all their lives, they have a sense of what must be done and how to go after it. Some are starting militant Puerto Rican organizations, like Barrio Nuevo in East Harlem. Others are going the college route. Many of them have been made aware of the obscene distortions in American life which let blacks, Puerto Ricans and poor whites fight unjust wars while the children of the middle class have the luxury of protesting it from the sanctity of the college campus. Some have gone into a rather romantic, nostalgic Puerto Rican independence bag, which might work if the Puerto Rican in Puerto Rico could only believe it was the best thing for him. (The various independence parties have never fared well at the polls in Puerto Rico, which, if it ever gives up its present semi-colonial commonwealth status, would more likely opt for becoming a state.) Increasingly, the younger generation is political, and if that has set up a generation gap of sorts, it is only because the Puerto Ricans are finally part of something larger. For one thing, they have a sense of laughter now that just wasn't there 15 years ago; I think of the group of Puerto Rican high school girls on the F train, coming back from Coney Island singing: "We all live in a yellow submarine, eating rice and beans, eating rice and beans . . ."

The young people are throwing over some of the things their

parents believed in. The ones I've talked to are not terrified of Communists (despite all the horror stories passed on to them about Fidel). They certainly don't listen much to the spiritist heresy, in which *brujas* (witches) can be hired to cast spells, or win women, or whatever else one might want, at a price and with the purchase of the right herbs at the *botánica*. Religion itself doesn't seem very strong anymore, either. Some 85 per cent of the Puerto Ricans in Puerto Rico are Catholics, but until very recently the church there was run by outsiders, by Irish bishops or Spanish bishops, by anyone but Puerto Rican bishops. In New York this meant that not many Puerto Ricans ever went to church, and those that "got religion" generally ended up in a more lively, less authoritarian, but somewhat more puritanical form of Christianity like the Pentecostal.

The younger people seem more interested in specifics. I remember going to a meeting in East Harlem the day after the 1967 riots took place. Ted Velez and Andrew Segarra and Torres and a lot of others had worked long into the night trying to cool the riots, and this meeting, in a school auditorium, was held to try to make sure that that trouble would not flare up again. There were representatives from the city and from the police to listen to the grievances of the young people who had done most of the fighting and bottle-throwing. Their initial grievance, as it had been in other circumstances in other sections of the city, was with the Tactical Patrol Force. The TPF, these kids felt, was an armed guard of cops from outside the district, cops who could not possibly know who was who in East Harlem, who probably did not know much about Puerto Ricans, and who had reacted brutally and without sensitivity to the first outbreak of trouble. That was predictable. But when that had been cleared out of the way, they got down to the real issues. One kid got up, his voice laden with emotion, and said very loudly: "All right, to hell with that for a minute. I want to know *why* in the goddam hell you can't get the garbage off 112th Street? Just get the garbage and we'll believe you." It is a measure of how the bureaucracy cannot seem to unwind itself that in August of this year there was almost a second East Harlem riot. It was over the failure of the Sanitation Department to pick up the garbage on 112th Street.

When there was trouble on the Lower East Side the year before last, I went down there to talk to the people on the streets. One guy ran up to his apartment. "I got to get our demands, mon." The demands were again familiar: get the TPF out of the neighborhood, clean the garbage more frequently ("We got big families, mon, and we make more garbage"). But the demands that interested me were the ones that seemed most Puerto Rican. One was "a place to play dominoes." The other: "dancing once in a while."

Politically, the Puerto Ricans are certainly on the move. The near victory of Herman Badillo in the Democratic primary has probably removed "the Puerto Rican thing" the way John F. Kennedy's 1960 victory changed the myth about Catholics running for President. This was not supposed to be the year for a Puerto Rican, and Badillo was supposed to have been better off running for the controller's office or as president of the City Council on somebody else's ticket. When he almost won (he lost by 38,000 votes), he established himself *and* the Puerto Ricans as an important political force in New York. On the other hand, there still remains a problem of apathy to be overcome. The Puerto Ricans are still the hardest people in the city to get registered, because of a combination of factors (distrust of politicians, uneasiness about the language, and fear of anything resembling an agent of the government are some of the factors; among older Puerto Ricans, there is still some feeling that they aren't from New York, that their political candidates are an airplane ride away).

The streak of conservatism in the Puerto Ricans also seems to be widening as more of them make it into the middle class. Many of them join regular Democratic clubs, because they see those clubs as the safest way to make it politically; a man like Tony Mendez, the regular boss of East Harlem, remains a powerful man politically, and some of the less radical or adventurous younger Puerto Ricans don't want to take any chances on blowing a career by playing Don Quixote. Rivalry among Puerto Rican politicians is rather strong, and sometimes leads to bizarre situations: next year there will not be a single Puerto Rican serving on the City Council, despite the fact that there are more Puerto Ricans here than in San Juan. In those councilmanic districts where a Puerto Rican might have been elected, Puerto Ricans ran against each other and non-Puerto Ricans slipped through the seams.

Despite that, the Puerto Rican community seems more together now than it has ever been. "Up until a couple of years ago," a pretty young schoolteacher from the Two Bridges district told me, "I was ashamed to say I was a Puerto Rican. I would say I was Spanish, or something like that. Today I'm ashamed for being ashamed. We P.R.s are really going to take this town."

They might just do that—politically, at least—and it might not be such a bad thing. They have already added things to New York which have made it a better place: their music and their food and their sense of the outrageous. No matter where you want to go, if you travel with a Puerto Rican cabdriver, he'll take you there; he'll say: "Hey, I don't know where it is, but you show me, mon, and I take you." The rocky decade with the marriages seems over, and the stable family unit is there again, the way it is in Puerto Rico. There is still a feeling among those who came here from Puerto Rico that they don't really belong to this town, but in that sense they belong nowhere. My friend Johnny Manzanet, who is a boxing commissioner now, once said to me: "You know, I sit here in New York, and I'm homesick for Salinas; I go home to Salinas and I'm homesick for New York. I don't know what the hell I am."

What seems to be forming is a special breed: the New York Puerto Rican. One who listens to La Lupe and the Beatles, who reads the *Times* and *El Diario,* who can move around the East Side pubs and still make it up to the Broadway Casino. He is a baseball fan, because of Orlando Cepeda and Roberto Clemente and a dozen other stars who came up from the island; but he probably does not look for the score of the Ponce-Caguas game anymore; he more than likely roots for the Mets (I have yet to meet a Puerto Rican who cared for pro football or rooted for the Yankees). But he no longer needs to go to prizefights to identify vicariously with heroes. He seems to be breaking down between two New York cultural traditions, with a touch of the third: the Puerto Rican with the can of beer in a paper bag playing dominoes on the street is the Irish Puerto Rican; the guy selling the beer in the *bodega* is the Jewish Puerto Rican; the guy starting to move into numbers and narcotics in East Harlem is the Mafia Puerto Rican. Ah, give me your tired, your poor . . .

*Here, compadre, put the luggage in the rack. I'll be in the bar having a Scotch and soda. It will be warm soon enough. I have to tell my friends about snow, and the lights of Broadway, and the way the kids wear their hair in the East Village, and that crazy night I spent at the Electric Circus with the newspapermen. That, and hard afternoons looking for work, and the time we had to grab the landlord and push his face against the wall to make him listen to the rats scratching behind us. That, but the good things too: theatres, and the Big A, and fight night at the Garden, and hanging around the corner on Degraw Street, and playing ball in the weekend leagues in Central Park, and the great shows coming through at the San Juan and the*

*Puerto Rico. That, and how the skyline looks coming across from Jersey at night, and the way the girls swagger down Fifth Avenue on the first warm day of spring. It will be warm soon enough, and I want to see the pastel houses in the sun and the palms blowing in the breeze and the dead calm before the hurricanes. And music.*

## Study Guide

1. Hamill begins his essay with a long description of a Puerto Rican's departure for New York from San Juan. How does this passage function in the essay? Does it serve to establish the attitude which the author wishes the reader to have toward the Puerto Rican?

2. The author traces the migration of Puerto Ricans to New York City over a fifty-year period. Write a brief summary of this migratory movement.

3. What factors does Hamill feel distinguish the Puerto Ricans from other migrants? How are their lives like and/or unlike those of other minority groups discussed in this text?

4. What problems did the Puerto Rican migrants encounter when they arrived in New York City?

5. Hamill states: "But the Puerto Ricans have done what all the immigrants did. They have endured . . . and now they are a very important part of this town [New York City]." He goes on to describe the gradual assimilation of the Puerto Ricans into the native population of New York. Investigate the assimilation of other migratory groups into the population of a large metropolitan area. How does the emergence of the Puerto Rican middle class in New York resemble that of other groups of immigrants in American history? How is it different? Present your findings in a documented essay.

6. What unsolved problems does Hamill find still confronting the Puerto Ricans?

7. Hamill states that the Puerto Ricans have emerged as a significant political force in New York City. Paraphrase Hamill's discussion of the political emergence of this group. Then investigate the political activities of some minority group in your own community. Write an essay in which you compare the success or failure of this group in politics with that of the Puerto Ricans in New York.

8. Near the conclusion of his essay, Hamill compares elements of the Puerto Rican population to Jewish, Irish, and Italian immigrants of an earlier era. Does this comparison suggest anything to you

concerning the nature of the process of assimilation which he has discussed earlier?

9.   Select a prominent minority group in your own community. Then write an essay tracing its history from the group's original entry into your community to the present time.

# 15. The White Negro: Superficial Reflections on the Hipster

## NORMAN MAILER

*Our search for the rebels of the generation led us to the hipster.*
*The hipster is an* enfant terrible *turned inside out. In character*
*with his time, he is trying to get back at the conformists by*
*lying low . . . You can't interview a hipster because his main goal*
*is to keep out of a society which, he thinks, is trying to make*
*everyone over in its own image. He takes marijuana because it*
*supplies him with experiences that can't be shared with "squares."*
*He may affect a broad-brimmed hat or a zoot suit, but usually he*
*prefers to skulk unmarked. The hipster may be a jazz musician;*
*he is rarely an artist, almost never a writer. He may earn his*
*living as a petty criminal, a hobo, a carnival roustabout or a*
*freelance moving man in Greenwich Village, but some hipsters*
*have found a safe refuge in the upper income brackets as*
*television comics or movie actors. (The late James Dean, for one,*
*was a hipster hero.) . . . It is tempting to describe the hipster in*
*psychiatric terms as infantile, but the style of his infantilism*
*is a sign of the times. He does not try to enforce his will on others,*
*Napoleon-fashion, but contents himself with a magical omni-*
*potence never disproved because never tested. . . . As the only*
*extreme nonconformist of his generation, he exercises a*

Reprinted by permission of G. P. Putman's Sons from *Advertisements for Myself,* by
Norman Mailer. Copyright © 1959 by Norman Mailer.

*powerful if underground appeal for conformists, through*
*newspaper accounts of his delinquencies, his structureless jazz,*
*and his emotive grunt words.*

—"Born 1930: The Unlost Generation"
by Caroline Bird
*Harper's Bazaar,* Feb. 1957

Probably, we will never be able to determine the psychic havoc of the concentration camps and the atom bomb upon the unconscious mind of almost everyone alive in these years. For the first time in civilized history, perhaps for the first time in all of history, we have been forced to live with the suppressed knowledge that the smallest facets of our personality or the most minor projection of our ideas, or indeed the absence of ideas and the absence of personality could mean equally well that we might still be doomed to die as a cipher in some vast statistical operation in which our teeth would be counted, and our hair would be saved, but our death itself would be unknown, un-honored, and unremarked, a death which could not follow with dignity as a possible consequence to serious actions we had chosen, but rather a death by *deus ex machina* in a gas chamber or a radio-active city; and so if in the midst of civilization—that civilization founded upon the Faustian urge to dominate nature by mastering time, mastering the links of social cause and effect—in the middle of an economic civilization founded upon the confidence that time could indeed be subjected to our will, our psyche was subjected itself to the intolerable anxiety that death being causeless, life was causeless as well, and time deprived of cause and effect had come to a stop.

The Second World War presented a mirror to the human con-dition which blinded anyone who looked into it. For if tens of mil-lions were killed in concentration camps out of the inexorable agonies and contractions of super-states founded upon the always insoluble contradictions of injustice, one was then obliged also to see that no matter how crippled and perverted an image of man was the society he had created, it was nonetheless his creation, his collective creation (at least his collective creation from the past) and if society was so murderous, then who could ignore the most hideous of questions about his own nature?

Worse. One could hardly maintain the courage to be individual, to speak with one's own voice, for the years in which one could complacently accept oneself as part of an elite by being a radical were forever gone. A man knew that when he dissented, he gave a note upon his life which could be called in any year of overt crisis. No wonder then that these have been the years of conformity and depression. A stench of fear has come out of every pore of American life, and we suffer from a collective failure of nerve. The only courage, with rare exceptions, that we have been witness to, has been the isolated courage of isolated people.

## 2

It is on this bleak scene that a phenomenon has appeared: the American existentialist—the hipster, the man who knows that if our collective condition is to live with instant death by atomic war, relatively quick death by the State as *l'univers concentrationnaire,* or with a slow death by conformity with every creative and rebellious instinct stifled (at what damage to the mind and the heart and the liver and the nerves no research foundation for cancer will discover in a hurry), if the fate of twentieth-century man is to live with death from adolescence to premature senescence, why then the only life-giving answer is to accept the terms of death, to live with death as immediate danger, to divorce oneself from society, to exist without roots, to set out on that uncharted journey with the rebellious imperatives of the self. In short, whether the life is criminal or not, the decision is to encourage the psychopath in oneself, to explore that domain of experience where security is boredom and therefore sickness, and one exists in the present, in that enormous present which is without past or future, memory or planned intention, the life where a man must go until he is beat, where he must gamble with his energies through all those small or large crises of courage and unforeseen situations which beset his day, where he must be with it or doomed not to swing. The unstated essence of Hip, its psychopathic brilliance, quivers with the knowledge that new kinds of victories increase one's power for new kinds of perception; and defeats, the wrong kind of defeats, attack the body and imprison one's energy until one is jailed in the prison air of other people's habits, other people's defeats, boredom, quiet desperation, and muted icy self-destroying rage. One is Hip or one is Square (the alternative which each new generation coming into American life is beginning to feel), one is a rebel or one conforms, one is a frontiersman in the Wild West of American night life, or else a Square cell, trapped in the totalitarian tissues of American society, doomed willy-nilly to conform if one is to succeed.

A totalitarian society makes enormous demands on the courage of men, and a partially totalitarian society makes even greater demands, for the general anxiety is greater. Indeed if one is to be a man, almost any kind of unconventional action often takes disproportionate courage. So it is no accident that the source of Hip is the Negro for he has been living on the margin between totalitarianism and democracy for two centuries. But the presence of Hip as a working philosophy in the sub-worlds of American life is probably due to jazz, and its knifelike entrance into culture, its subtle but so penetrating influence on an avant-garde generation—that postwar generation of adventurers who (some consciously, some by osmosis) had absorbed the lessons of disillusionment and disgust of the twenties, the depression, and the war. Sharing a collective disbelief in the words of men who had too much money and controlled too many things, they knew almost as powerful a disbelief in the socially monolithic ideas of the single mate, the solid family and the respectable love life. If the intellectual antecedents of this generation can be traced to such separate influences as D. H. Lawrence, Henry Miller, and Wilhelm Reich, the viable philosophy of Hemingway fit most of their facts: in a bad world, as he was to say over and over again (while taking time out from his parvenu snobbery and dedicated gourmandize), in a bad world there is no love nor mercy nor charity nor justice unless a man can keep his courage, and this indeed fitted some of the facts. What fitted the need of the adventurer even more precisely was Hemingway's categorical imperative that what made him feel good became therefore The Good.

So no wonder that in certain cities of America, in New York of course, and New Orleans, in Chicago and San Francisco and Los Angeles, in such American cities as Paris and Mexico, D.F., this particular part of a generation was attracted to what the Negro had to offer. In such places as Greenwich Village, a ménage-à-trois was completed—the bohemian and the juvenile delinquent came face-to-face with the Negro, and the hipster was a fact in American life. If marijuana was the wedding ring, the child was the language of Hip for its argot gave expression to abstract states of feeling which all could share, at least all who were Hip. And in this wedding of the white and the black it was the Negro who brought the cultural dowry. Any Negro who wishes to live must live with danger from his first day, and no experience can ever be casual to him, no Negro can saunter down a street with any real certainty that violence will not visit him on his walk. The cameos of security for the average white:

mother and the home, job and the family, are not even a mockery to millions of Negroes; they are impossible. The Negro has the simplest of alternatives: live a life of constant humility or ever-threatening danger. In such a pass where paranoia is as vital to survival as blood, the Negro has stayed alive and begun to grow by following the need of his body where he could. Knowing in the cells of his existence that life was war, nothing but war, the Negro (all exceptions admitted) could rarely afford the sophisticated inhibitions of civilization, and so he kept for his survival the art of the primitive, he lived in the enormous present, he subsisted for his Saturday night kicks, relinquishing the pleasures of the mind for the more obligatory pleasures of the body, and in his music he gave voice to the character and quality of his existence, to his rage and the infinite variations of joy, lust, languor, growl, cramp, pinch, scream and despair of his orgasm. For jazz is orgasm, it is the music of orgasm, good orgasm and bad, and so it spoke across a nation, it had the communication of art even where it was watered, perverted, corrupted, and almost killed, it spoke in no matter what laundered popular way of instantaneous existential states to which some whites could respond, it was indeed a communication by art because it said, "I feel this, and now you do too."

So there was a new breed of adventurers, urban adventurers who drifted out at night looking for action with a black man's code to fit their facts. The hipster had absorbed the existentialist synapses of the Negro, and for practical purposes could be considered a white Negro.

To be an existentialist, one must be able to feel oneself—one must know one's desires, one's rages, one's anguish, one must be aware of the character of one's frustration and know what would satisfy it. The overcivilized man can be an existentialist only if it is chic, and deserts it quickly for the next chic. To be a real existentialist (Sartre admittedly to the contrary) one must be religious, one must have one's sense of the "purpose"—whatever the purpose may be—but a life which is directed by one's faith in the necessity of action is a life committed to the notion that the substratum of existence is the search, the end meaningful but mysterious; it is impossible to live such a life unless one's emotions provide their profound conviction. Only the French, alienated beyond alienation from their unconscious could welcome an existential philosophy without ever feeling it at all; indeed only a Frenchman by declaring that the unconscious did not exist could then proceed to explore the delicate involutions of consciousness, the microscopically senuous and all but ineffable *frissons* of mental becoming, in order finally to create the theology of atheism and so submit that in a world of absurdities the existential absurdity is most coherent.

In the dialogue between the atheist and the mystic, the atheist is on the side of life, rational life, undialectical life—since he conceives of death as emptiness, he can, no matter how weary or despairing, wish for nothing but more life; his pride is that he does not transpose his weakness and spiritual fatigue into a romantic longing for death, for such appreciation of death is then all too capable of being elaborated by his imagination into a universe of meaningful structure and moral orchestration.

Yet this masculine argument can mean very little for the mystic. The mystic can accept the atheist's description of his weakness, he can agree that his mysticism was a response to despair. And yet . . . and yet his argument is that he, the mystic, is the one finally who has chosen to live with death, and so death is his experience and not the atheist's, and the atheist by eschewing the limitless dimensions of profound despair has rendered himself incapable to judge the experience. The real argument which the mystic must always advance is the very intensity of his private vision—his argument depends from the vision precisely because what was felt in the vision is so extraordinary that no rational argument, no hypotheses of "oceanic feelings" and certainly no skeptical reductions can explain away what has become for him the reality more real than the reality of closely reasoned logic. His inner experience of the possibilities within death is his logic. So, too, for the existentialist. And the psychopath. And the saint and the bullfighter and the lover. The common denominator for all of them is their burning consciousness of the present, exactly that incandescent consciousness which the possibilities within death has opened for them. There is a depth of desperation to the condition which enables one to remain in life only by engaging death, but the reward is their knowledge that what is happening at each instant of the electric present is good or bad for them, good or bad for their cause, their love, their action, their need.

It is this knowledge which provides the curious community of feeling in the world of the hipster, a muted cool religious revival to be sure, but the element which is exciting, disturbing, nightmarish perhaps, is that incompatibles have come to bed, the inner life and the violent life, the orgy and the dream of love, the desire to murder and the desire to create, a dialectical conception of existence with a lust for power, a dark, romantic, and yet undeniably dynamic view of existence for it sees every man and woman as moving individually through each moment of life forward into growth or backward into death.

## 3

It may be fruitful to consider the hipster a philosophical psychopath, a man interested not only in the dangerous imperatives of his psychopathy but in codifying, at least for himself, the suppositions on which his inner universe is constructed. By this premise the hipster is a psychopath, and yet not a psychopath but the negation of the psychopath, for he possesses the narcissistic detachment of the philosopher, that absorption in the recessive nuances of one's own motive which is so alien to the unreasoning drive of the psychopath. In this country where new millions of psychopaths are developed each year, stamped with the mint of our contradictory popular culture (where sex is sin and yet sex is paradise), it is as if there has been room already for the development of the antithetical psychopath who extrapolates from his own condition, from the inner certainty that his rebellion is just, a radical vision of the universe which thus separates him from the general ignorance, reactionary prejudice, and self-doubt of the more conventional psychopath. Having converted his unconscious experience into much conscious knowledge, the hipster has shifted the focus of his desire from immediate gratification toward that wider passion for future power which is the mark of civilized man. Yet with an irreducible difference. For Hip is the sophistication of the wise primitive in a giant jungle, and so its appeal is still beyond the civilized man. If there are ten million Americans who are more or less psychopathic (and the figure is most modest), there are probably not more than one hundred thousand men and women who consciously see themselves as hipsters, but their importance is that they are an elite with the potential ruthlessness of an elite, and a language most adolescents can understand instinctively, for the hipster's intense view of existence matches their experience and their desire to rebel.

Before one can say more about the hipster, there is obviously much to be said about the psychic state of the psychopath—or, clinically, the psychopathic personality. Now, for reasons which may be more curious than the similarity of the words, even many people with a psychoanalytical orientation often confuse the psychopath with the psychotic. Yet the terms are polar. The psychotic is legally insane, the psychopath is not; the psychotic is almost always incapable of discharging in physical acts the rage of his frustration, while the psychopath at his extreme is virtually as incapable of restraining his violence. The psychotic lives in so misty a world that what is happening at each moment of his life is not very real to him whereas the psychopath seldom knows any reality greater than the face, the voice, the being of the particular people among whom he may find himself at any moment. Sheldon and Eleanor Glueck describe him as follows:

*The psychopath . . . can be distinguished from the person sliding into or clambering out of a "true psychotic" state by the long tough persistence of his anti-social attitude and behaviour and the absence of hallucinations, delusions, manic flight of ideas, confusion, disorientation, and other dramatic signs of psychosis.*

The late Robert Lindner, one of the few experts on the subject, in his book *Rebel Without a Cause—The Hypnoanalysis of a Criminal Psychopath* presented part of his definition in this way:

*. . . the psychopath is a rebel without a cause, an agitator without a slogan, a revolutionary without a program: in other words, his rebelliousness is aimed to achieve goals satisfactory to himself alone; he is incapable of exertions for the sake of others. All his efforts, hidden under no matter what disguise, represent investments designed to satisfy his immediate wishes and desires. . . . The psychopath, like the child, cannot delay the pleasures of gratification; and this trait is one of his underlying, universal characteristics. He cannot wait upon erotic gratification which convention demands should be preceded by the chase before the kill: he must rape. He cannot wait upon the development of prestige in society: his egoistic ambitions lead him to leap into headlines by daring performances. Like a red thread the predominance of this mechanism for immediate satisfaction runs through the history of every psychopath. It explains not only his behaviour but also the violent nature of his acts.*

Yet even Lindner who was the most imaginative and most sympathetic of the psychoanalysts who have studied the psychopathic personality was not ready to project himself into the essential sympathy—which is that the psychopath may indeed be the perverted and dangerous front-runner of a new kind of personality which could become the central expression of human nature before the twentieth century is over. For the psychopath is better adapted to dominate those mutually contradictory inhibitions upon violence and love which civilization has exacted of us, and if it be remembered that not every psychopath is an extreme case, and that the condition of psychopathy is present in a host of people including many politicians, professional soldiers, newspaper columnists, entertainers, artists, jazz musicians, call-girls, promiscuous homosexuals and half the executives of Hollywood, television, and advertising, it can be seen that there are aspects of psychopathy which already exert considerable cultural influence.

What characterizes almost every psychopath and part-psychopath is that they are trying to create a new nervous system for themselves. Generally we are obliged to act with a nervous system which has been formed from infancy, and which carries in the style of its circuits the very contradictions of our parents and our early milieu. Therefore, we are obliged, most of us, to meet the tempo of the present and the future with reflexes and rhythms which come from the past. It is not only the "dead weight of the institutions of the past" but indeed the inefficient and often antiquated nervous circuits of the past which strangle our potentiality for responding to new possibilities which might be exciting for our individual growth.

Through most of modern history, "sublimation" was possible: at the expense of expressing only a small portion of oneself, that small portion could be expressed intensely. But sublimation depends on a reasonable tempo to history. If the collective life of a generation has moved too quickly, the "past" by which particular men and women of that generation may function is not, let us say, thirty years old, but relatively a hundred or two hundred years old. And so the nervous system is overstressed beyond the possibility of such compromises as sublimation, especially since the stable middle-class values so prerequisite to sublimation have been virtually destroyed in our time, at least as nourishing values free of confusion or doubt. In such a crisis of accelerated historical tempo and deteriorated values, neurosis tends to be replaced by psychopathy, and the success of psychoanalysis (which even ten years ago gave promise of becoming a direct major force) diminishes because of its inbuilt and characteristic incapacity to handle patients more complex, more experienced, or more adventurous than the analyst himself. In practice, psychoanalysis has by now become all too often no more than a psychic blood-letting. The patient is not so much changed as aged, and the infantile fantasies which he is encouraged to express are condemned to exhaust themselves against the analyst's nonresponsive reactions. The result for all too many patients is a diminution, a "tranquilizing" of their most interesting qualities and vices. The patient is indeed not so much altered as worn out—less bad, less good, less bright, less willful, less destructive, less creative. He is thus able to conform to that contradictory and unbearable society which first created his neurosis. He can conform to what he loathes because he no longer has the passion to feel loathing so intensely.

The psychopath is notoriously difficult to analyze because the fundamental decision of his nature is to try to live the infantile fantasy, and in this decision (given the dreary alternative of psychoanalysis) there may be a certain instinctive wisdom. For there is a dialectic to changing one's nature, the dialectic which underlies all psychoanalytic method: it is the knowledge that if one is to change one's habits, one must go back to the source of their creation, and so the psychopath exploring backward along the road of the homosexual, the orgiast, the drug-addict, the rapist, the robber and the murderer seeks to find those violent parallels to the violent and often hopeless contradictions he knew as an infant and as a child. For if he has the courage to meet the parallel situation at the moment when he is ready, then he has a chance to act as he has never acted before, and in satisfying the frustration—if he can succeed—he may then pass by symbolic substitute through the locks of incest. In thus giving expression to the buried infant in himself, he can lessen the tension of those infantile desires and so free himself to remake a bit of his nervous system. Like the neurotic he is looking for the opportunity to grow up a second time, but the psychopath knows instinctively that to express a forbidden impulse actively is far more beneficial to him than merely to confess the desire in the safety of a doctor's room. The psychopath is ordinately ambitious, too ambitious ever to trade his warped brilliant conception of his possible victories in life for the grim if peaceful attrition of the analyst's couch. So his associational journey into the past is lived out in the theatre of the present, and he exists for those charged situations where his senses are so alive that he can be aware actively (as the analysand is aware passively) of what his habits are, and how he can change them. The strength of the psychopath is that he knows (where most of us can only guess) what is good for him and what is bad for him at exactly those instants when an old crippling habit has become so attacked by experience that the potentiality exists to change it, to replace a negative and empty fear with an outward action, even if—and here I obey the logic of the extreme psychopath —even if the fear is of himself, and the action is to murder. The psychopath murders—if he has the courage—out of the necessity to purge his violence, for if he cannot empty his hatred then he cannot love, his being is frozen with implacable self-hatred for his cowardice. (It can of course be suggested that it takes little courage for two strong eighteen-year-old hoodlums, let us say, to beat in the brains of a candy-store keeper, and indeed the act—even by the logic of the psychopath—is not likely to prove very therapeutic, for the victim is not an immediate equal. Still, courage of a sort is necessary, for one murders not only a weak fifty-year-old man but an institution as well, one violates private property, one enters into a new relation with the police and introduces a dangerous element into one's life. The hoodlum is therefore daring the unknown, and so no matter how brutal the act, it is not altogether cowardly.)

At bottom, the drama of the psychopath is that he seeks love. Not love as the search for a mate, but love as the search for an orgasm more apocalyptic than the one which preceded it. Orgasm is his therapy—he knows at the seed of his being that good orgasm opens his possibilities and bad orgasm imprisons him. But in this search, the psychopath becomes an embodiment of the extreme contradictions of the society which formed his character, and the apocalyptic orgasm often remains as remote as the Holy Grail, for there are clusters and nests and ambushes of violence in his own necessities and in the imperatives and retaliations of the men and women among whom he lives his life, so that even as he drains his hatred in one act or another, so the conditions of his life create it anew in him until the drama of his movements bears a sardonic resemblance to the frog who climbed a few feet in the well only to drop back again.

Yet there is this to be said for the search after the good orgasm: when one lives in a civilized world, and still can enjoy none of the cultural nectar of such a world because the paradoxes on which civilization is built demand that there remain a cultureless and alienated bottom of exploitable human material, then the logic of becoming a sexual outlaw (if one's psychological roots are bedded in the bottom) is that one has at least a running competitive chance to be physically healthy so long as one stays alive. It is therefore no accident that psychopathy is most prevalent with the Negro. Hated from outside and therefore hating himself, the Negro was forced into the position of exploring all those moral wildernesses of civilized life which the Square automatically condemns as delinquent or evil or immature or morbid or self-destructive or corrupt. (Actually the terms have equal weight. Depending on the telescope of the cultural clique from which the Square surveys the universe, "evil" or "immature" are equally strong terms of condemnation.) But the Negro, not being privileged to gratify his self-esteem with the heady satisfactions of categorical condemnation, chose to move instead in that other direction where all situations are equally valid, and in the worst of perversion, promiscuity, pimpery, drug addiction, rape, razor-slash, bottle-break, what-have-you, the Negro discovered and elaborated a morality of the bottom, an ethical differentiation between the good and the bad in every human activity from the go-getter pimp (as opposed to the lazy one) to the relatively dependable pusher or prostitute. Add to this, the cunning of their language, the abstract ambiguous alternatives in which from the danger of their oppression they learned to speak ("Well, now, man, like I'm looking for a cat to turn me on . . ."), add even more the profound sensitivity of the Negro jazzman who was the cultural mentor of a people, and it is not too difficult to believe that the language of Hip which evolved was an artful language, tested and shaped by an intense experience and therefore different in kind from white slang, as different as the special obscenity of the soldier, which in its emphasis upon "ass" as the soul and "shit" as circumstance, was able to express the existential states of the enlisted man. What makes Hip a special language is that it cannot really be taught—if one shares none of the experiences of elation and exhaustion which it is equipped to describe, then it seems merely arch or vulgar or irritating. It is a pictorial language, but pictorial like non-objective art, imbued with the dialectic of small but intense change, a language for the microcosm, in this case, man, for it takes the immediate experiences of any passing man and magnifies the dynamic of his movements, not specifically but abstractly so that he is seen more as a vector in a network of forces than as a static character in a crystallized field. (Which latter is the practical view of the snob.) For example, there is real difficulty in trying to find a Hip substitute for "stubborn." The best possibility I can come up with is: "That cat will never come off his groove, dad." But groove implies movement, narrow move-

ment but motion nonetheless. There is really no way to describe someone who does not move at all. Even a creep does move—if at a pace
exasperatingly more slow than the pace of the cool cats.

## 4

Like children, hipsters are fighting for the sweet, and their language is a set of subtle indications of their success or failure in the
competition for pleasure. Unstated but obvious is the social sense
that there is not nearly enough sweet for everyone. And so the sweet
goes only to the victor, the best, the most, the man who knows the
most about how to find his energy and how not to lose it. The emphasis is on energy because the psychopath and the hipster are nothing without it since they do not have the protection of a position or
a class to rely on when they have overextended themselves. So the
language of Hip is a language of energy, how it is found, how it is
lost.

But let us see. I have jotted down perhaps a dozen words, the
Hip perhaps most in use and most likely to last with the minimum
of variation. The words are man, go, put down, make, beat, cool,
swing, with it, crazy, dig, flip, creep, hip, square. They serve a variety of purposes and the nuance of the voice uses the nuance of the
situation to convey the subtle contextual difference. If the hipster
moves through his life on a constant search with glimpses of Mecca
in many a turn of his experience (Mecca being the apocalyptic orgasm) and if everyone in the civilized world is at least in some small
degree a sexual cripple, the hipster lives with the knowledge of how
he is sexually crippled and where he is sexually alive, and the faces
of experience which life presents to him each day are engaged, dismissed or avoided as his need directs and his lifemanship makes possible. For life is a contest between people in which the victor
generally recuperates quickly and the loser takes long to mend, a
perpetual competition of colliding explorers in which one must grow
or else pay more for remaining the same (pay in sickness, or depression, or anguish for the lost opportunity), but pay or grow.

Therefore one finds words like go, and make it, and with it,
and swing: "Go" with its sense that after hours or days or months
or years of monotony, boredom, and depression one has finally had
one's chance, one has amassed enough energy to meet an exciting
opportunity with all one's present talents for the flip (up or down)
and so one is ready to go, ready to gamble. Movement is always to

be preferred to inaction. In motion a man has a chance, his body is warm, his instincts are quick, and when the crisis comes, whether of love or violence, he can make it, he can win, he can release a little more energy for himself since he hates himself a little less, he can make a little better nervous system, make it a little more possible to go again, to go faster next time and so make more and thus find more people with whom he can swing. For to swing is to communicate, is to convey the rhythms of one's own being to a lover, a friend, or an audience, and—equally necessary—be able to feel the rhythms of their response. To swing with the rhythms of another is to enrich oneself—the conception of the learning process as dug by Hip is that one cannot really learn until one contains within oneself the implicit rhythm of the subject or the person. As an example, I remember once hearing a Negro friend have an intellectual discussion at a party for half an hour with a white girl who was a few years out of college. The Negro literally could not read or write, but he had an extraordinary ear and a fine sense of mimicry. So as the girl spoke, he would detect the particular formal uncertainties in her argument, and in a pleasant (if slightly Southern) English accent, he would respond to one or another facet of her doubts. When she would finish what she felt was a particularly well-articulated idea, he would smile privately and say, "Other-direction . . . do you really believe in that?"

"Well . . . No," the girl would stammer, "now that you get down to it, there is something disgusting about it to me," and she would be off again for five more minutes.

Of course the Negro was not learning anything about the merits and demerits of the argument, but he was learning a great deal about a type of girl he had never met before, and that was what he wanted. Being unable to read or write, he could hardly be interested in ideas nearly as much as in lifemanship, and so he eschewed any attempt to obey the precision or lack of precision in the girl's language, and instead sensed her character (and the values of her social type) by swinging with the nuances of her voice.

So to swing is to be able to learn, and by learning take a step toward making it, toward creating. What is to be created is not nearly so important as the hipster's belief that when he really makes it, he will be able to turn his hand to anything, even to self-discipline. What he must do before that is find his courage at the moment of violence, or equally make it in the act of love, find a little more between his woman and himself, or indeed between his mate and himself (since many hipsters are bisexual), but paramount, imperative, is the necessity to make it because in making it, one is making the new habit, unearthing the new talent which the old frustration denied.

Whereas if you goof (the ugliest word in Hip), if you lapse back into being a frightened stupid child, or if you flip, if you lose your control, reveal the buried weaker more feminine part of your nature, then it is more difficult to swing the next time, your ear is less alive, your bad and energy-wasting habits are further confirmed, you are farther away from being with it. But to be with it is to have grace, is to be closer to the secrets of that inner unconscious life which will nourish you if you can hear it, for you are then nearer to that God which every hipster believes is located in the senses of his body, that trapped, mutilated and nonetheless megalomaniacal God who is It, who is energy, life, sex, force, the Yoga's *prana*, the Reichian's orgone, Lawrence's "blood," Hemingway's "good," the Shavian life-force; "It"; God; not the God of the churches but the unachievable whisper of mystery within the sex, the paradise of limitless energy and perception just beyond the next wave of the next orgasm.

To which a cool cat might reply, "Crazy, man!"

Because, after all, what I have offered above is an hypothesis, no more, and there is not the hipster alive who is not absorbed in his own tumultuous hypotheses. Mine is interesting, mine is way out (on the avenue of the mystery along the road to "It") but still I am just one cat in a world of cool cats, and everything interesting is crazy, or at least so the Squares who do not know how to swing would say.

(And yet crazy is also the self-protective irony of the hipster. Living with questions and not with answers, he is so different in his isolation and in the far reach of his imagination from almost everyone with whom he deals in the outer world of the Square, and meets generally so much enmity, competition, and hatred in the world of Hip, that his isolation is always in danger of turning upon itself, and leaving him indeed just that, crazy.)

If, however, you agree with my hypothesis, if you as a cat are way out too, and we are in the same groove (the universe now being glimpsed as a series of ever-extending radii from the center), why then you say simply, "I dig," because neither knowledge nor imagination comes easily, it is buried in the pain of one's forgotten experience, and so one must work to find it, one must occasionally exhaust oneself by digging into the self in order to perceive the outside. And indeed it is essential to dig the most, for if you do not dig you lose your superiority over the Square, and so you are less likely to be cool (to be in control of a situation because you have swung where the Square has not, or because you have allowed to come to consciousness a pain, a guilt, a shame or a desire which the other has not had the courage to face). To be cool is to be equipped, and if you are equipped it is more difficult for the next cat who comes along to put you down. And of course one can hardly afford to be put down too often, or one is beat, one has lost one's confidence, one has lost one's will, one is impotent in the world of action and so closer to the demeaning flip of becoming a queer, or indeed closer to dying, and therefore it is even more difficult to recover enough energy to try to make it again, because once a cat is beat he has nothing to give, and no one is interested any longer in making it with him. This is the terror of the hipster—to be beat—because once the sweet of sex has deserted him, he still cannot give up the search. It is not granted to the hipster to grow old gracefully—he has been captured too early by the oldest dream of power, the gold fountain of Ponce de León, the fountain of youth where the gold is in the orgasm.

To be beat is therefore a flip, it is a situation beyond one's experience, impossible to anticipate—which indeed in the circular vocabulary of Hip is still another meaning for flip, but then I have given just a few of the connotations of these words. Like most primitive vocabularies each word is a prime symbol and serves a dozen or a hundred functions of communication in the instinctive dialectic through which the hipster perceives his experience, that dialectic of the instantaneous differentials of existence in which one is forever moving forward into more or retreating into less.

5

It is impossible to conceive a new philosophy until one creates a new language, but a new popular language (while it must implicitly contain a new philosophy) does not necessarily present its philosophy overtly. It can be asked then what really is unique in the life-view of Hip which raises its argot above the passing verbal whimsies of the bohemian or the lumpenproletariat.

The answer would be in the psychopathic element of Hip which has almost no interest in viewing human nature, or better, in judging human nature, from a set of standards conceived a priori to the experience, standards inherited from the past. Since Hip sees every answer as posing immediately a new alternative, a new question, its emphasis is on complexity rather than simplicity (such complexity that its language without the illumination of the voice and the articulation of the face and body remains hopelessly incommunicative). Given its emphasis on complexity, Hip abdicates from any conventional moral responsibility because it would argue that the results of our actions are unforeseeable, and so we cannot know if we do good or bad, we cannot even know (in the Joycean sense of the good and the bad) whether we have given energy to another, and indeed if we could, there would still be no idea of what ultimately the other would do with it.

Therefore, men are not seen as good or bad (that they are good-and-bad is taken for granted) but rather each man is glimpsed as a collection of possibilities, some more possible than others (the view of character implicit in Hip) and some humans are considered more capable than others of reaching more possibilities within themselves in less time, provided, and this is the dynamic, provided the particular character can swing at the right time. And here arises the sense of context which differentiates Hip from a Square view of character. Hip sees the context as generally dominating the man, dominating him because his character is less significant than the context in which he must function. Since it is arbitrarily five times more demanding of one's energy to accomplish even an inconsequential action in an unfavorable context than a favorable one, man is then not only his character but his context, since the success or failure of an action in a given context reacts upon the character and therefore affects what the character will be in the next context. What dominates both character and context is the energy available at the moment of intense context.

Character being thus seen as perpetually ambivalent and dynamic enters then into an absolute relativity where there are no truths other than the isolated truths of what each observer feels at each instant of his existence. To take a perhaps unjustified metaphysical extrapolation, it is as if the universe which has usually existed conceptually as a Fact (even if the Fact were Berkeley's God) but a Fact which it was the aim of all science and philosophy to reveal, becomes instead a changing reality whose laws are remade at each instant by everything living, but most particularly man, man raised to a neo-medieval summit where the truth is not what one has felt yesterday or what one expects to feel tomorrow but rather truth is no more nor less than what one feels at each instant in the perpetual climax of the present.

What is consequent therefore is the divorce of man from his values, the liberation of the self from the Super-Ego of society. The only Hip morality (but of course it is an ever-present morality) is to do what one feels whenever and wherever it is possible, and—this is how the war of the Hip and the Square begins—to be engaged in one primal battle: to open the limits of the possible for oneself, for oneself alone, because that is one's need. Yet in widening the arena of the possible, one widens it reciprocally for others as well, so that the nihilistic fulfillment of each man's desire contains its antithesis of human co-operation.

If the ethic reduces to Know Thyself and Be Thyself, what makes it radically different from Socratic moderation with its stern conservative respect for the experience of the past is that the Hip ethic is immoderation, childlike in its adoration of the present (and indeed to respect the past means that one must also respect such ugly consequences of the past as the collective murders of the State). It is this adoration of the present which contains the affirmation of Hip, because its ultimate logic surpasses even the unforgettable solution of the Marquis de Sade to sex, private property, and the family, that all men and women have absolute but temporary rights over the bodies of all other men and women—the nihilism of Hip proposes as its final tendency that every social restraint and category be removed, and the affirmation implicit in the proposal is that man would then prove to be more creative than murderous and so would not destroy himself. Which is exactly what separates Hip from the authoritarian philosophies which now appeal to the conservative and liberal temper—what haunts the middle of the twentieth century is that faith in man has been lost, and the appeal of authority has been that it would restrain us from ourselves. Hip, which would return us to ourselves, at no matter what price in individual violence, is the affirmation of the barbarian, for it requires a primitive passion about human nature to believe that individual acts of violence are always to be preferred to the collective violence of the State; it takes literal faith in the creative possibilities of the human being to envisage acts of violence as the catharsis which prepares growth.

Whether the hipster's desire for absolute sexual freedom contains any genuinely radical conception of a different world is of course another matter, and it is possible, since the hipster lives with his hatred, that many of them are the material for an elite of storm troopers ready to follow the first truly magnetic leader whose view of mass murder is phrased in a language which reaches their emotions. But given the desperation of his condition as a psychic outlaw, the hipster is equally a candidate for the most reactionary and most radical of movements, and so it is just as possible that many hipsters will come—if the crisis deepens—to a radical comprehension of the horror of society, for even as the radical has had his incommunicable dissent confirmed in his experience by precisely the frustration, the denied opportunities, and the bitter years which his ideas have cost him, so the sexual adventurer deflected from his goal by the implacable animosity of a society constructed to deny the sexual radical as well, may yet come to an equally bitter comprehension of the slow relentless inhumanity of the conservative power which controls him from without and from within. And in being so controlled, denied, and starved into the attrition of conformity, indeed the hipster may come to see that his condition is no more than an exaggeration of the human condition, and if he would be free, then everyone must be free. Yes, this is possible too, for the heart of Hip is its emphasis upon courage at the moment of crisis, and it is pleasant to think that courage contains within itself (as the explanation of its existence) some glimpse of the necessity of life to become more than it has been.

It is obviously not very possible to speculate with sharp focus on the future of the hipster. Certain possibilities must be evident, however, and the most central is that the organic growth of Hip depends on whether the Negro emerges as a dominating force in American life. Since the Negro knows more about the ugliness and danger of life than the white, it is probable that if the Negro can win his equality, he will possess a potential superiority, a superiority so feared that the fear itself has become the underground drama of domestic politics. Like all conservative political fear it is the fear of unforeseeable consequences, for the Negro's equality would tear a profound shift into the psychology, the sexuality, and the moral imagination of every white alive.

With this possible emergence of the Negro, Hip may erupt as a psychically armed rebellion whose sexual impetus may rebound against the antisexual foundation of every organized power in America, and bring into the air such animosities, antipathies, and new conflicts of interest that the mean empty hypocrisies of mass conformity will no longer work. A time of violence, new hysteria, confusion and rebellion will then be likely to replace the time of conformity. At that time, if the liberal should prove realistic in his belief that there is peaceful room for every tendency in American life, then Hip would end by being absorbed as a colorful figure in the tapestry. But if this is not the reality, and the economic, the social, the psychological, and finally the moral crises accompanying the rise of the Negro should prove insupportable, then a time is coming when every political guidepost will be gone, and millions of liberals will be faced with political dilemmas they have so far succeeded in evading, and with a view of human nature they do not wish to accept. To take the desegregation of the schools in the South as an example, it is quite likely that the reactionary sees the reality more closely than the liberal when he argues that the deeper issue is not desegregation but miscegenation. (As a radical I am of course facing in the opposite direction from the White Citizen's Councils—obviously I believe it is the absolute human right of the Negro to mate with the white, and matings there will undoubtedly be, for there will be Negro high school boys brave enough to chance their lives.) But for the average liberal whose mind has been dulled by the committee-ish cant of the professional liberal, miscegenation is not an issue because he has been told that the Negro does not desire it. So, when it comes, miscegenation will be a terror, comparable perhaps to the derangement of the American Communists when the icons to Stalin came tumbling down. The average American Communist held to the myth of Stalin for reasons which had little to do with the political evidence and everything to do with their psychic necessities. In this sense it is equally a psychic necessity for the liberal to believe that the Negro and even the reactionary Southern white are eventually and fundamentally people like himself, capable of becoming good liberals too if only they can be reached by good liberal reason. What the liberal cannot bear to admit is the hatred beneath the skin of a society so unjust that the amount of collective violence buried in the people is perhaps incapable of being contained, and therefore if one wants a better world one does well to hold one's breath, for a worse world is bound to come first, and the dilemma may well be this: given such hatred, it must either vent itself nihilistically or become turned into the cold murderous liquidations of the totalitarian state.

# 6

No matter what its horrors the twentieth century is a vastly exciting century for its tendency is to reduce all of life to its ultimate alternatives. One can well wonder if the last war of them all will be between the black and the whites, or between the women and the men, or between the beautiful and ugly, the pillagers and managers, or the rebels and the regulators. Which of course is carrying speculation beyond the point where speculation is still serious, and yet despair at the monotony and bleakness of the future have become so engrained in the radical temper that the radical is in danger of abdicating from all imagination. What a man feels is the impulse for his creative effort, and if an alien but nonetheless passionate instinct about the meaning of life has come so unexpectedly from a virtually illiterate people, come out of the most intense conditions of exploitation, cruelty, violence, frustration, and lust, and yet has succeeded as an instinct in keeping this tortured people alive, then it is perhaps possible that the Negro holds more of the tail of the expanding elephant of truth than the radical, and if this is so, the radical humanist could do worse than to brood upon the phenomenon. For if a revolutionary time should come again, there would be a crucial difference if someone had already delineated a neo-Marxian calculus aimed at comprehending every circuit and process of society from ukase to kiss as the communications of human energy—a calculus capable of translating the economic relations of man into his psychological relations and then back again, his productive relations thereby embracing his sexual relation as well, until the crises of capitalism in the twentieth century would yet be understood as the unconscious adaptations of a society to solve its economic imbalance at the expense of a new mass psychological imbalance. It is almost beyond the imagination to conceive of a work in which the drama of human energy is engaged, and a theory of its social currents and dissipations, its imprisonments, expressions, and tragic wastes are fitted into some gigantic synthesis of human action where the body of Marxist thought, and particularly the epic grandeur of *Das Kapital* (that first of the major *psychologies* to approach the mystery of social cruelty so simply and practically as to say that we are a collective body of humans whose life-energy is wasted, displaced, and procedurally stolen as it passes from one of us to another)—where particularly the epic grandeur of *Das Kapital* would find its place in an even more God-like view of human justice and injustice, in some more excruciating vision of those intimate and institutional processes which lead to our creation and disasters, our growth, our attrition, and our rebellion.

## Study Guide

1. Long before today's so-called hippies appeared on the scene, Mailer analyzed hip culture. To what extent do today's hippies reflect the attitudes Mailer wrote about? To what extent are these attitudes reflected in the popular arts? In politics?

2. To what historical events does Mailer suggest the hipster is responding? How does he feel these events have changed the quality of human life?

3. Mailer writes that when men live with death as an "immediate danger" they accept its terms. What do you think he means by this statement? How does Mailer link the hipster's life style with the immediate danger of death?

4. How does Mailer relate the hipster to the American Negro? What qualities of Negro life are reflected in the hipster's life style?

5. How are the life styles of the hipster and the Negro linked to existential philosophy?

6. Mailer describes the hipster as a philosophic psychopath. What psychopathic qualities does hip culture exhibit?

7. The psychopath, according to Mailer, tries to create a new nervous system for himself. Is this idea reflected in today's youth culture? You might consider the qualities of its music and its art as well as the emphasis it places upon drugs.

8. Consider Mailer's remarks on the psychopath and his use of violence. Do these remarks clarify the activities of any violent elements in today's youth culture? If so, how?

9. Why does Mailer use sexual terms to describe the nature of the hipster's quest? Is he trying to shock his reader? Do his sexual metaphors truly clarify his ideas?

10. Mailer describes hip language. Has this language lost any of its originality since he wrote this essay?

11. Does Mailer feel that hipsters have any particular ethical code? How would you describe it?

12. Examine the essays of Rubin and Harris in this volume. What hip attitudes do they reflect?

13. Does Mailer have an accurate view of the philosophic and political position of the black man in America?

14. Mailer suggests that the hipster has exchanged his identity for one closely resembling that of the American Negro. In a research paper, try to determine the extent to which the music, language, or life style of today's youth culture reflects that of the Negro in America.

15. Does Mailer's "White Negro" seem to be struggling against any social forces described by Fromm and MacLeish?

16. Mailer suggests that in exchanging his identity for one similar to that of the American Negro, the hipster finds a greater degree of individuality and freedom than he might have otherwise. In an essay, compare and contrast the hipster's concept of freedom with that of the Afro-American.

17. Using visual media, try to illustrate the correspondence between black and hip culture. Seek to point out the similarities and striking differences through a collage or a montage of photographs.

# 16. Reality

DAVID HARRIS

One of the tools we use to locate ourselves is Reality.

Out of innumerable experiences, insights, and conditions, we isolate those comparative few we find to be *real*. Out of innumerable possible actions to reach an object, we choose the *realistic* one.

With our notion of Reality we construct a means of being.

Our lives are an effort at making *realities*. When we make something real, we concretize ourselves in the world around us. For example, America has made the *threat of international communism* a reality. For the Yaqui Indians, living in the same hemisphere, it is decidedly unreal. Their reality is bound up in the worship of the forest.

A society produces and distributes Reality. It provides common mechanisms and processes for making things *real*. Societies are distinctive according to how they *realize* the world around them. I am concerned with that *how*. It is what we live with and, in the end, is synonymous with the *how* of our daily living.

I call the process of making something real a *logic*.

America has a logic. When we want something, America is, among other things, the way we go about getting it. It is not so much *what* we want, as *how* we get it. The *what* seems to flow from the *how*.

The logic of America reflected around us is an instrumental one. Most simply, it is the logic of "if A, then B." The easiest way to picture it is to visualize a machine. If you engage cog A, then spindle B turns. In this logic, the actor and the realization of his action are separate. The action is not contained in the framework of the actor. He and his act are instigators of a process which is beyond their control or involvement. For example: soldiers make war in the pursuit of peace; businessmen make profits under the rationale of common democracy. In each of these examples men act, but the intention of the act is in no way carried in the act itself. The actor and the act are a force designed to activate a distant process which supposedly produces the intended reality.

A man's act is an instrument in a process located beyond his existence. He is an input. A's leading to B is never left up to A. Since the act in itself does not lead to the desired result (A, in itself, is not B) this logic presupposes an overriding, qualitatively different entity which will actually make A into B. When activated in a society, such a logic necessitates the paternal and authoritarian state to make the needed translations. The state must be responsible for making acts of war into peace and capitalism into democracy, for they obviously are incapable of such changes in themselves. The first result of this process is the dispossession of a man from his actions. His actions are a function of the process that will supposedly *realize* them.

In this instrumental logic, the man who acts does not have a direct relationship to the things he wishes to come from his action. If he wishes B, he must instead do A. If he wishes peace, he must first do war. His actions have a direct relationship to an overseeing intermediary. He feeds the state, which in turn is supposed to satisfy his intention. His action then is an extension of the state. Reality ceases to be a function of those who compose it. Reality becomes a product of the state.

Looking for a moment at ourselves, we can see our intentions, our actions, and their results. Following the instrumental American logic, the three exist in complete disconnection. The act realizes neither the intention nor the supposed end. The act realizes the mechanism it is being done for and with. Instead of making our realities, the established reality of the state begins to make us in its image. We no longer carry out our intentions but make our actions a tool of the state in hopes it will realize them. In letting A take the place of the B we want, we become supplicants. We are the recipients of reality rather than its source. We become strangers in a strange land.

Whether or not this instrumental process leads eventually from A to B may be a secondary or an irrelevant consideration. (Although evidence seems to witness that it does not, five thousand years of war being the most obvious example.) What is primary is that despite rationalization and ideology, we experience and are shaped by the immediacy of A, not the promised resultant B—it is A we must live with. Whatever else comes of the process, those of us involved in it have been made powerless. In it, we are stripped of our rightful construction of reality. We are *unreal*. Our presence is that of dependence and servitude, not freedom and creation. Our doing ceases to spring from ourselves, and our lives become merely instruments in a process that grants us reality only as tools of things we neither create nor find ourselves reflected in.

In this logic, which leaves the actual fact of reality to a Great Other that we faithfully serve in return for morsels that help hide our pain, we cease to exist. We become an impotent pause.

## Study Guide

1. Harris suggests that the logic of America separates the actor from the realization of his action. "The action," he states, "is not contained in the framework of the actor. He and his act are instigators of a process which is beyond their control or involvement." Explain these statements in your own language. Do they have any relationship to ideas in the essays of Baldwin, Fromm, and MacLeish?

2. What paradox results from the sort of logic Harris describes?

3. Harris uses the example of men making war to achieve peace as an illustration of his idea. Can you think of any parallel examples where this same sort of logic is involved? (You might consider the creation of unemployment to create prosperity.)

4. What ethical problems confronting Americans grow out of the distinction between intention and action?

5. What metaphors does Harris use to describe this logical process? To describe man's relationship to the state?

6. Harris says the result of the logic he describes makes men the recipients of reality rather than the source of it. Does this reflect any ideas you have encountered elsewhere in this book?

7. What is the ultimate effect on the individual of this logical process?

8. Harris points out the apparent illogicality in using war as an instrument for achieving peace. Develop an essay in which you discuss some other way in which the actions of society seem to contradict its stated intentions.

9. Harris concludes his essay by saying that when we lose control of "the actual fact of reality . . . we become an impotent pause." Try to express this idea through a visual medium.

10. Harris is critical of the American government because its intentions are contradicted by its actions. Might a similar criticism be leveled against many radical protest groups? Explore the activities of such organizations as S.D.S. Present your findings in a documented essay.

# 17. *Long Hair, Aunt Sadie, Is a Communist Plot*

JERRY RUBIN

My earliest introduction to Communism involved family intrigue and outasight chicken soup. Every family has a black sheep. Mine was Aunt Sadie in New York.

"She went to Russia to meet Stalin," members of the family used to gossip to each other.

When I was a kid, my family often visited Aunt Sadie, and she served the best chicken soup in the whole world. She used to say to me, "**Jerry**, you must still be hungry. Please eat some more, **Jerry darling**. Eat some more good chicken soup."

And as she ladled more chicken soup into my already overflowing bowl, she'd whisper into my ear, "The capitalists need unemployment to keep wages down."

I lost contact with Aunt Sadie and meanwhile became a family misfit myself. Then one unexpected afternoon Aunt Sadie knocked on the door of my Lower East Side apartment. I hadn't seen her in ten years.

"Aunt Sadie," I shouted, hugging her. "I'm a commie, too!"

She didn't even smile.

Maybe she was no longer a Communist?

"Aunt Sadie, what's the matter?"

She hesitated. "**Jerry**, why don't you cut your hair?"

So I gave her a big bowl of Nancy's outasight chicken soup and began:

"Aunt Sadie, long hair is a commie plot! Long hair gets people uptight—more uptight than ideology, cause long hair is communication. We are a new minority group, a nationwide community of longhairs, a new identity, new loyalties. We longhairs recognize each other as brothers in the street.

"Young kids identify short hair with authority, discipline, unhappiness, boredom, rigidity, hatred of life—and long hair with letting go, letting your hair down, being free, being open.

"Our strategy is to steal the children of the bourgeoisie right away from the parents. Dig it! Yesterday I was walking down the street. A car passed by, parents in the front seat and a young kid, about eight, in the back seat. The kid flashed me the clenched fist sign."

"**But, Jerry** . . ." Aunt Sadie stammered.

"Aunt Sadie, *long hair is our black skin*. Long hair turns white middle-class youth into niggers. Amerika is a different country when you have long hair. We're outcasts. We, the children of the white middle class, feel like Indians, blacks, Vietnamese, the outsiders in Amerikan history."

"**But, Jerry**," Aunt Sadie interrupted, "the Negroes in the ghettoes, they're only hurting themselves. I mean, all of the vandalism and everything . . ."

"Long hair polarizes every scene, Aunt Sadie. It's instant confrontation. Everyone is forced to become an actor, and that's revolutionary in a society of passive consumers.

"Having long hair is like saying hello to everybody you see. A few people automatically say 'Hi' right back; most people get furious that you disturbed their environment."

"**Jerry**, *you have so much to offer*. If only you'd cut your hair. People laugh at you. They don't take you seriously."

"Listen, Aunt Sadie, *long hair* is what makes them take us seriously! Wherever we go, our hair tells people where we stand on Vietnam, Wallace, campus disruption, dope. We've living **TV** commercials for the revolution. We're walking picket signs.

"Every response to longhairs creates a moral crisis for straights. We force adults to bring all their repressions to the surface, to expose their real feelings."

"**Feelings, schmeelings, Jerry**," Aunt Sadie said. "I'm telling you that in my time we were radicals. We were invited to a convention in the Soviet Union to meet Stalin. And who did they pick to represent us? Who did they pick? I'm telling you who they picked.

"They picked the people who were down-to-earth, who were clean and nice. I didn't have long hair. I didn't smell. . . ."

"Aunt Sadie, I don't want to go to any fucking conventions," I said.

"That doesn't matter," she replied, suddenly pushing aside untasted her bowl full of Nancy's good chicken soup. "But you should be clean and nice. Did your mother teach you to smell bad, maybe?"

"Aunt Sadie, you won't believe this, but you're uptight about your body. Man was born to let his hair grow long and to smell like a man. We are descended from the apes, and we're proud of our ancestry. We're natural men lost in this world of machines and computers. Long hair is more beautiful than short hair. We love our bodies. We even smell our armpits once in a while.

"Grownups used to tell us kids that black people smelled bad. We asked, 'What's wrong with Negroes?' and they said, 'Did you ever get close enough to smell them?' If middle-class people say that now about blacks, they'll get a good black-power punch across their fucking mouths, so they say it about longhairs. We ask them, 'Did you ever get close enough to smell a longhair?' and they shout back at us, 'Go take a bath.'

"Amerikans are puritans. Amerikans are afraid of sex. Amerika creates a sexual prison in which men think they have to be supermen and have to see sensitivity as weakness. Women are taught that self-assertion is unfeminine. *So Marines go to Vietnam and get their asses kicked by Viet Kong women.*

"Long hair is the beginning of our liberation from the sexual oppression that underlies this whole military society. Through long hair we're engaged in a sexual assault that's going to destroy the political-economic structure of Amerikan society!"

"God help you destroy it, **Jerry**," Aunt Sadie wailed, chicken-soup tears dribbling down her cheeks. "But you'd be so much more effective if you would cut your hair and dress nicely."

Aunt Sadie and I weren't getting very far. It was sad that the two black sheep in the family couldn't identify with each other.

"**Jerry**," Aunt Sadie said, getting up to leave. "Just remember one thing: there are two classes in the world, the bourgeoisie and the working class. You're either on one side or the other. It has nothing to do with hair.

"If you'd only get a haircut. You're only hurting yourself. . . ."

I embraced her, took the $20 she gave me to buy "some nice new clothes," and waved good-bye.

*"Watch out, Aunt Sadie!" I shouted as she left. "Some of the most longhaired people I know are bald."*

## Study Guide

1.  Two central conflicts are united in Rubin's essay; the conflict between the Old Left and the New Left, and the conflict separating the generations. Which predominates? What effect does their combination have? What statement is Rubin trying to make about the Old Left?

2.  Aunt Sadie is mentioned first as the communist black sheep of Rubin's family. What kind of person do you expect her to be? Are your expectations fulfilled?

3.  Two life styles come into conflict here. Do you think the life style of the young has the political significance that Rubin ascribes to it?

4.  Develop an essay on (1) the symbolic value of clothing or hair, or (2) the conflict between the generations.

5.  Use the essay you have written as the basis for a film or collage.

6.  Retell the episode described in Rubin's narrative from the point of view of Aunt Sadie.

# 18. Rex Reed Talks to the Jefferson Airplane's Grace Slick

REX REED

A few blocks from San Francisco's poorest low-rent district, in a run-down neighborhood that once knew elegance, stands a seedy white three-story mausoleum supported by four decaying ionic columns. Ancient white lace curtains blow lazily in the breeze behind its open cut-glass windows. Its paint is dappled with age, like an enormous pastry crust that has been too lightly dusted with confectioner's sugar. A tiny patch of dead zinnias nuzzles the walk that leads to a sagging front porch where a broken toilet seat leans, cracked and peeling, against the door jamb. Enrico Caruso once stayed there, but now its former glory has fallen into a state of disrepair, like a noble countess violated by an army of callous invaders. This is the home of the Jefferson Airplane.

I pressed the bell next to a red heart that said "Stop the War." An upstairs window slammed open, and a girl with a scrubbed Ivory-soap face and long curly hair leaned out. "Yeah? What do you want?"

"Is Grace Slick in?"

"I'm Grace. I'll be right down."

I had only seconds to recover. She doesn't look anything like

Rex Reed, "Rex Reed talks to the Jefferson Airplane's Grace Slick," from *Stereo Review,* November, 1970. Copyright © 1970 by Rex Reed. No portion of this article can be reprinted without written consent of the author.

her photographs. There she is, on the album covers and in the rock magazines and underground newspapers, looking like a dark purple menace—long straight hair falling seductively about her face and shoulders like ravens' wings, deep pools of darkness signaling world-weary indifference from eyes like ripe olives. And here was this girl in neatly tailored slacks and a Mexican poncho (I later learned she was pregnant), cautiously opening the bead-curtained glass doors for a stranger, like a fourteen-year-old kid whose mother was gone for the day.

"I just wanted to make sure you weren't the FBI. They're always hassling us, trying to run us in for dope. I guess they think because we're rock musicians we have some kind of orgy going on here all the time. The FBI is always phoning us up and threatening to come over and talk to us, and we just say 'Yeah, well, call our lawyer first —he's Mayor Alioto's lawyer and he'll have something to say about that,' and they leave us alone. Crosby, Stills and Nash live here when they're in town, and the Grateful Dead, so there's always some kind of hassle going on with the cops. Everybody in the group has been busted for dope except Jorma Kaukonen, who plays guitar." (Jack Casady, the Airplane's bassist, had recently been picked up by the San Francisco police while sitting in a mud puddle, stoned on pot.) "And me," she added. "I've been lucky. The last time the group was busted down in New Orleans I had just left the room to go wash my hair. Come in."

Inside, it was about as cheerful as the interior of an Egyptian sarcophagus. Dark mahogany walls rose twenty feet high in a room the size of a dance hall. Light filtered through stained-glass windows above a massive winding staircase, like a Barbary Coast brothel in an old Marlene Dietrich movie. There was no furniture except a pool table over which hung the dangling mock skeleton of a dinosaur. Through a carved rosewood doorway, we entered the living room. The walls were covered with velvet the color of raspberry sherbet. White columns supported raspberry ceilings inlaid with gilt-edged cupids who grinned dopily down on huge marble walk-in fireplaces that hadn't been used since the San Francisco earthquake. We walked through this room quietly, which is about the only way you can walk through a room like that, as if not to disturb the seance that seemed certain to commence at any moment. Beyond was another enormous room that was also empty, except for a statue of St. Teresa with a San Francisco police badge on her bosom. "She was kicked out of the church or something, so we like her," Grace explained. "We used to eat all our meals down here like a family, but it's hard to keep heated in the winter, so now we just sort of go out for pizzas and stuff."

She led the way into the Jefferson Airplane's kitchen at the back of the house, also empty except for a king-size stainless-steel freezer with pornographic comic strips pasted on the door and walls of cupboards full of cat food and underground newspapers. A dirty window overlooked the back yard, where I could see the rotting hull of a fishing boat. "Let's go up to my room," she said. "We can talk better up there." I followed up the turn-of-the-century staircase, dodging model airplanes hanging from Tiffany lamps. David Crosby (of Crosby, Stills, and Nash) came bounding down the stairs, almost knocking over a treetop-tall antique replica of Nipper, the old RCA "His Master's Voice" trademark, with an arrow through its head and a sign reading "Keep the Indians on Alcatraz." "See ya later," waved Crosby. "Later," said Grace. "Dave's been sleeping in my bed the past week and the place is a mess."

The second floor contains the Airplane's office and Grace's bedroom, and the third floor is devoted to all the pads of the other members of the group, their friends and girls. In the office, Jack Casady was talking on one of a myriad of phones while an admiring circle of teen-age Groupies sat on a sofa (covered with an American flag) sipping organic apple juice. There were rows of filing cabinets and junk-shop furniture; I counted forty psychedelic posters on the walls. "You gotta see this," laughed Grace, pointing to a gallery of high-fashion photographs and magazine covers of beautiful girls in elaborate Adolfo hats and Dior gowns, beautiful girls smoking mentholated cigarettes, all looking as though they had just stepped out of *Harper's Bazaar*. "Who are they?" I asked, doubtful that they could be friends of the Airplane. She roared. "They're all *me!* That was my modeling period. Boy, was I freaked out then. That's before I found out where my head was at."

The rest of the house is a blur to me now. I remember only a sensual assault of strobe lights, burning incense, psychedelic revolving sculptures, half-naked men with long hair roaming in and out of bedrooms, a room in which the entire floor consisted of a water bed pumped full of water that shook and revolved when I sat on it until I was seasick ("We all lie on it stoned and listen to music," said Grace), ceilings hung with parachute silk, cash registers, a floor-to-ceiling poster of Trotsky with a dart in his forehead, old Christmas trees, modern canvases filled with nails, airplane propellers, and tree trunks.

Grace's pad is like Norma Shearer's bedroom in *Marie Antoinette:* Tad's Steak House wallpaper, Victorian satin drapes, flowered carpets and flowered ceilings, cupids and roses and cornucopias, gilt-edged chairs with the bottoms falling out, purses made of pheasant feathers hanging on wall sconces with melted candles, musical instruments, and suitcases everywhere with clothes hanging out. We sat on box springs covered with red velvet, and when I looked up at the ceiling over her bed, I found myself staring into the horror-filled eyes of a battalion of naked women being plunged to some unspeakable destination in a chariot drawn by rabid wolves with fangs dripping blood. It's the last thing Grace Slick sees when she goes to bed at night.

A mortician's pall cloaked the room. She was waiting for the interview to begin; I was waiting for Banquo's ghost to appear. The surroundings didn't faze her. She was as cheerful as a bluejay. "Why are you looking at me so strangely?" she asked, puffing on a True.

"I guess it's just that you surprise me. I was wondering what an all-American girl-next-door is doing in a place like this."

She made a funny face, half-smile, half-yecch. "Black people say *'we,'* meaning their black brothers and sisters. I say *'we,'* meaning hippies, because I'm thirty years old and I've been in this freaky-clothes and long-hair scene for twelve years. I may not look like a hippie, but I do identify with these people because the musicians, writers, and painters of today are all called hippies by a stupid society that doesn't understand them. I'm one of the nonconformists, so I'm a hippie too, I guess. I never get hassled, but those guys out there in their crew cuts and their button-down shirts never leave the guys in the group alone. They can't stand to see these guys with long hair and all these beautiful chicks on their arms making more money in ten minutes than they can do in ten years. So they call them faggots and they won't cash their checks and we have a terrible time finding hotels to stay in. People come up to us in airports and sniff at us and say 'What a smell!' and it is so incredibly stupid because we bathe every day. But it's a life style, not the length of the hair or the clothes, and we have fun and I'm much happier now than I ever was working in a department store. So I don't mind being called a hippie because it gives me an identity with a group of people I dig, and then after we get the hippie label, we get more attention and more people listen to our beliefs. Right now rock musicians think the same way about the Vietnam situation as a lot of other people, but *we're* the ones the kids listen to. The whole point of the rock revolution is to take care of business in the time we live in. Rock musicians get into the blood stream of more young people than anyone else in this time, man, so they have more influence and power over them than even the politicians or the clergy."

I put down my list of prepared questions. Grace Slick is not into forms and formality; formal interviews are out. One does not *interview* her; one *raps*. So we rapped. "Then you think rock has turned into something more meaningful than casual entertainment with a beat for dancing? A more serious social comment on our times?"

"Well, you can't hear the lyrics anyway, so I suppose it's dance music to some people. But it's never impersonal. I mean, that's what killed opera. Opera should've been more *current* if it was to survive. It should've gotten to the people faster. As it is, those guys just told stories. Every century's got that stuff happening. People got tired of trying to *relate* to something that wasn't saying anything. Crosby, Stills and Nash are now doing a song about Kent State. It's *now*. I think of rock musicians as journalists, as musical reporters. The better the journalist the more fandangos he can pull off. The cake's always there, it's how you put the junk on it. In order for people to warm to something, it has to hit them *now*, and that's what rock does. *Scientific American* says the female fruitfly needs to hear the male fruitfly at 150 decibels to make it with him. If he sings any lower, she won't listen. That's approximately the volume we play in. That's out-front sex. You can just enjoy it for that and that's okay, too. It's all groovy. Sometimes we get audiences that are uptight and don't respond. We just play for ourselves. It's like guys who come up against a chick—or another guy, or a *dog,* I don't care—and they get no sexual response and they keep working at it. Leave it alone is the Airplane's motto. I remember a town we played once called Grinnell, Iowa. All these kids came, man. The girls had on 1950's dresses and corsages and the guys had crew cuts to prove their masculinity, and it brought them down to see their way threatened. They couldn't believe what they were *seeing!* They just sat there and didn't move or applaud or *anything*. So two years later we went back and they were naked in the mud, totally freaked out on LSD. The whole country is changing, becoming more involved, and rock is the music that is changing them."

"Have you deliberately tried to inject social comment into the songs you write?"

"Not really. Your music has to come from your own experience. Mine was not a ghetto experience. I guess the closest I came was on the recording of *White Rabbit*. I read *Alice in Wonderland* as a child, and it wasn't until later, after I had tried drugs, that I began to get into it. I like Lewis Carroll because it was obvious he was into opium."

"Lewis Carroll was into opium? Hmmm. . . ."

"Oh, sure. *Alice* has never been for kids, it's for adults. But I know adults read it to their kids, so the point of the song was to warn parents that Carroll was into the drug scene, so don't put your kids down because they're into it. It was snide, I suppose, but I've always had a sarcastic mouth."

"But what I don't understand is why the kids need drugs to dig rock. It seems to me that if you need to get stoned to appreciate something, it must be flawed in the first place."

"Well, it's like if you had the dough and the custard but no chocolate, you'd be missing part of the eclair. Drugs help the way aspirin helps get rid of a headache. Since we're still killing people, we haven't figured out a way to love each other, so drugs help. Pot is a very peaceful drug. The Airplane condones the judicious use of drugs, but that doesn't mean we want people to harm themselves physically or blow the tops of their heads off with LSD. It's up to the individual to decide whether he should or shouldn't. I used to take acid myself because it was a wonderful, groovy experience, but I haven't been on a trip in a long time. I can't take drugs while working. One joint puts me to sleep, then I've gotta take speed to wake up and then that's like rotting your brain out too early. I can't handle fifty things at once. The only time I get stoned now is when I'm writing music. It depends on the individual needs. I know people who don't take *anything* and they're more stoned than I am. Van Gogh, Salvador Dali, people like that. They're crazy already, so they don't need it. I tried peyote and I was amazed at the amount of concentration I could put into or get out of a leaf. I sat in a room for four hours and I got more interested in textures and fibers than ever before. But I've never seen telephone poles turn into snakes, or anything like that. My main advice to kids about acid is don't drive, because you won't notice when the lights change. The steering wheel starts waving, and you stare at it and everybody starts honking behind you.

The only time acid is really harmful is when it is preceded by fear. If you are afraid you are going to have a bad trip, you probably will."

"I guess I'm not convinced."

"That's cool. You're not into that scene. I don't put that down. The best thing about the rock-drug scene is that nobody tries to force anything on anybody. That's why Peter Townshend of the Who hit Abbie Hoffman over the head with his guitar onstage at Woodstock. It wasn't the time to try to force anybody into politics. I don't think I'm narrow-minded about music just because I sing rock. Listen, the only two records I owned for eight years were Grieg's *Peer Gynt Suite* and Irving Berlin's *Say It with Music*. On my recording of *Rejoyce* I even patterned one horn section after Gil Evans. I used to play all the arrangements he did for Miles Davis over and over. I nearly drove the Airplane crazy when *Sketches of Spain* came out. I played it about eighty times a day. Now I don't listen to much of anything. I don't own a TV set, a telephone, or a record player. The group usually buys a good record as a business expense, so I know I'll get to hear it somehow. Crosby, Stills and Nash are around the house singing everything anyway, so who needs to buy records? I like every kind of music, except country-and-western. I wasn't always into rock, you know."

True. She comes from a very straight, middle-class background that would probably consider her music noise. Her real name is Grace Wing. She was born in Evanston, Illinois, in 1939, her mother was "a pop singer—very square—sang *Tea for Two* a lot," and her father was an investment banker. She attended high school in Palo Alto, then spent a year at New York's fashionable and exclusive Finch College studying costume design and merchandising, and a year at the University of Miami majoring in art. The revolt against formality and the Establishment was beginning about that time. "I hated all those rich debutantes at Finch," she says. "What a weird scene. Tricia Nixon is a good example of what they turn out. I was invited to her birthday party at the White House. They sent out these little engraved invitations to the alumni and accepted unbiasedly the first ones who responded. So I called Abbie Hoffman, and he slicked down his hair and put on a blue suit. He looked like a karate-chopping pimp. It was a gas. So we showed up at the White House and got thrown out as 'security risks.' Boy, were they right, because I had 600 micro-milligrams of LSD in my purse that we were going to put into the tea. Can you hear them now? 'Wow, the President's daughter is freaked out drawing dirty pictures on the White House walls!' The security guards were criticized in the press. People wrote, 'How ridiculous—not letting someone in because she's a rock singer.' Well, it's not ridiculous because I really would have done it. I figured the worst thing a little acid could do to Tricia Nixon is turn her into a merely delightful person instead of a grinning robot. But we were aiming for the Old Dad, hoping he might come down to the party and have a cup of tea. Far out. I figure if they can shoot us down, we can get them high, right?"

After two years of college, Grace dropped out and returned to San Francisco "to find out where my head was at." She had already studied classical guitar and found it a bore, so she started hanging around the hippie folk singers in Haight-Ashbury and learned how to accompany herself on the guitar and sing ballads like *Barbara Allen.* She hadn't yet broken entirely with the Establishment. She married a photographer named Jerry Slick and helped put him through school at San Francisco State College by modeling designer clothes at I. Magnin. "I was nowhere. My old man was very square, I hated my job. I made extra money by growing pot in our backyard. We had a next-door neighbor who used to hang over the fence and say 'Hey, Gracie, how's your plants?' She watered them for us when we were away. She never knew what she was watering. Haight-Ashbury was a friendly place when I lived there. That was before it got overcrowded and violence broke out and the hippies started killing each other. It's dead now, a terrible scene. You cram a lot of rats in one place and they panic and start fighting each other."

Eventually she quit her modeling job, tried LSD, bought a steel-string guitar and some cheap sound equipment at Sears Roebuck, and started singing with a group called the Great Society. "I looked around and saw how bad the competition was, so I decided what the hell." She heard the Jefferson Airplane in some of the places she sang and they heard her, and in October 1966, when their lead singer left to get married, Grace joined the group. The Airplane had made a small dent in the rock world already, but it was the addition of the little broad with the go-to-hell grind in her voice that put them on the map. In less than six months after she climbed aboard, they were making $10,000 a night and more, depending on the gig. Their albums and singles sold in the millions, and Grace became a celebrity. She insists that although rock has become big business, she is not in it for the money. "Everybody thinks we're rich and I suppose some of the rock groups are, but although they tell me the Airplane has made millions of dollars, we're all broke. We have never been businessmen, so none of our earnings have ever been invested, and all of our money has been tied up in legal hassles for years. We have no idea how much money has been stolen from us by bad managers, insensitive managers, crooks. Each member of the band gets $250 a week to live on, and everything else we make goes back into the group for expenses, sound equipment, lawyers. Nobody has any money in the bank. This house is all we own. The money from royalties and publishing and all that is tied up in an old contract, and we never get a dime from any of it. We are always in trouble with the government over taxes. We're fighting it out in court to get some of our money, but we've lost four times already. The only extravagance I've noticed is cars. Paul has a Porsche and some of the other guys have Cadillacs."

Grace owns an Aston-Martin DB-4, which she bought with the royalty money paid to her from an old contract with the Great Society before she joined the Airplane. "I was walking down Van Ness Avenue, where the foreign car agencies are, and I walked into the showroom with my hippie clothes on, and suddenly all the salesmen started running away. I thought 'Gee, I don't look that awful,' so I followed them all into the back room and said, 'What's happening, baby?' and this salesman stared at my hippie clothes and my bare feet and sniffed, 'It's the new DB-4 just arrived,' and I said, 'How much is it?' and he just smiled like he was really into putting me down, man, and I said, 'Like, how much *is* it, man? again, and he said it was $18,592 plus tax, and I said, 'Far out, I'll take it.' Then I took two ten-thousand-dollar bills out of my pocket and paid him. I think he's still lying on the floor. It's a groovy car, but it's been in the shop four weeks now. It takes like two years to get a part. I don't miss it. Material things are unimportant."

She has been married to Jerry Slick for ten years, but they seldom see each other. "I don't think my marriage is odd. What I think is weird is when people stay together all the time. I'm in love with Paul Kantner, who plays rhythm guitar with the Airplane. I love him, I live with him, and I sleep with him. My husband digs it. It's cool with him. We're still married because we don't have the energy to go through all the paper work. I can't see telling some fifty-year-old judge I want a divorce because—why? Because I don't like my old man any more? I like him fine. He's one of my best friends. He's one of the few people I know who can be totally objective. He's very amusing. He'll nail up a newspaper headline '4,000 Frogs in Thailand Go Mad!' or something wacky, and when all his friends read it, he takes it down. I just outgrew him and got into something else. We'll get around to getting a divorce some day if our tax situation gets messed up any more than it already is. But I could let it slide on forever. I'm not into legal papers and documents and contracts. That's not where my head is at. I let people like my family worry about the stupid things in life."

She has said some harsh things about her family in interviews, so I asked her if she was still on friendly terms with them. "They think I'm nuts. They've lived for sixty years now assuming that a certain method of conduct will net you certain rewards—the rewards being a house, a freezer, a mortgage, an electric kitchen, the Episcopal church. Those don't happen to be *my* rewards or the needs of my generation, but you can't wake these people up to that. What my parents don't understand is that all that junk I was taught has nothing to do with my life. I used to fight with them but I don't anymore. My little brother's in jail for smoking dope. He used to be their only hope—'Well, the chick is nuts, but maybe the kid'll be O.K.'—well, now they know they can't hassle his life either."

So what are you into now, Grace Slick, with this new freedom? Ecology? "I would've been into it fifty years ago, but it's too late now. Nobody's going to give up their cars. Space is the only thing left, and there's not much of it. That's why Haight-Ashbury's dead. One cantaloupe rind doesn't smell as bad as forty rotten cantaloupe rinds. All the hippies are moving into the mountains now."

Women's Lib? "It's pretty dumb. I mean, in the face of other things that are more important, it's flippant. It's like a lotta chicks suddenly decided 'Hey, I don't like to cook!' and they're making a lotta noise about it. Well, there's a lotta things chicks can do that won't force them into a home. I been around a lotta guys, not one of them ever asked me to *cook!* I say, 'Hey, I don't cook, man, I do *this!*' and they say 'Cool.' I've never had some guy come up to me and say, 'Hey, how come you can't tell me how to tear apart a car?' I don't care if they can't sew, either."

Religion? "I believe there's a lotta stuff going on out there, whether it's molecules or mud or whatever. But I don't believe in all that God junk. I've never talked to spirits, either. Never had any flashes. Man is the only animal that knows he's going to die, so we invent a Heaven to keep from going crazy. Most people are hypnotized by organized religion from childhood; only a few really have the stuff. I don't think it's Billy Graham who has the stuff, though."

I asked her if rock had taken the place of religion in the society of the young. With drugs to keep it going, wasn't it creating a new style of worship through the same hypnotic effect on the minds of the young that she had just accused organized religion of doing? "I don't want to get philosophical about rock. It's just entertainment. Thirty years ago they went to the Copacabana with their drug, which was cocktails, and they turned on for a few hours. We're doing the same thing. The one thing rock does is promote peace. The Airplane is doing the same thing Jane Fonda is doing, only she is one person and we're an organization of thirty people. We have six in the group, plus our staff, the guys who transport and run our light show, and by the time you add all the Groupies and girl friends and all, it takes a lotta money to move that much tonnage across the country. So we put all our money back into the group. If I go out and demonstrate with Abbie Hoffman or Jane Fonda, twenty-nine people sit around on their cans. So we stick together and promote peace through publicity, our interviews, and our music."

"Do you think rock will survive?" I asked.

"Well, the hardest thing about surviving is the outside influences, the dumb censorship from executives, and all the right-wing jerks who get uptight about nudity and dirty language and all that junk. The cops and even the record companies figure we take drugs and fornicate all the time, so they watch us pretty closely. RCA Victor has hassled us a lot. One time we got this idea for an album cover where everyone could draw something at the recording session and we'd put all the drawings together for the cover. Paul was eating a cupcake, so he took the holder and traced around it with a pencil, and RCA wouldn't let it go through because they said it looked like a woman's sex organs. Idiots! We're always going to the head of the RCA record division and saying, 'Show us proof that somebody is going to make trouble. Send us the letters and we'll answer them.' Adults all think it's a bunch of noise and the kids don't care anyway, so who do they think they're kidding? We had the four-letter word for defecation on *Eskimo Blue Day* and RCA had a fit. We left it in. Nobody ever complained, man. We're talking about leaving RCA to join up with Crosby, Stills and Nash and the Grateful Dead to form our own record company, the way the Beatles did when they left Capitol and formed Apple. The good thing about the Airplane, and the main reason we've outlasted most of the other rock groups, is that nobody plays God or tells anyone what to do. The boss is whoever has written the song we're doing that day. It's like a family, built on mutual trust."

Grace has had many offers to be a star at ten times the money she's making now. She's not interested. "I don't know one entertainer I would ever watch for more than two songs. That whole Judy Garland package is a bore. Even Streisand—one or two tunes and I say, 'Okay, I've heard *you*, baby!' Three hours of Sammy Davis, Jr. would be like *They Shoot Horses, Don't They?* So I wouldn't want to look at Grace Slick for three hours, either."

The only thing left dangling was the future. "You can last longer in rock than you can in something like opera because so few technical demands are made on your voice. Also, the fans don't judge you as harshly. If an opera singer hits the wrong half-note, she gets murdered. If they took out my vocal cords altogether, they'd probably say, 'Oh, wow, far out—she's singing through her ears now!' But I've had three operations on my vocal cords already. Janis Joplin had been yelling her head off for years, and she had no trouble. My vocal structure is weaker. I can't sing as long as I used to and my voice gives out fast. Five years ago, I could go over a song fifty times in a recording session. I can't do that anymore. I used to sound like Joan Baez, now I sound like Louis Armstrong. My voice gets lower all the time—it gets used, abused, knocked around. My days are limited. But if I blow it completely, I'll just do something else. Rock is not my life's work. I've been drawing lately and writing a lot, too. If I stop singing it won't mean a thing to me. I'll get into another scene."

Like what? "I'd really like to do a film. The Airplane was in a Godard movie, but I'd like to do a project of my own. I was sent a script for a movie called *Big Fauss and Little Halsey,* but it stank, so I said no. Now I learn Robert Redford and Michael J. Pollard are in it. Damn! I blew it. But I still don't want to do anything that means backing up. Mary looks at John, John kisses Mary—that's bull. Too many other things to say and do. That's why nobody slow dances or writes love songs anymore. People are getting killed, so who cares if John gets Mary in the end?"

I don't know who will get Grace Slick in the end, but as we rode an electric elevator-chair down a back staircase, it occurred to me he might have his hands full but he'll never be bored. "I'm crazy," she was saying at the door, "but I'm at peace with myself. The way we live in this crazy house, we're all nuts, man. But it's fun. We're too lazy to hassle anybody, even each other. That's why I don't shoot heroin. I'm too lazy to get into it. Like paying taxes. I just don't bother to keep recepits. I guess I'm also a bit old-fashioned. I still drink liquor, which is probably a throwback to the Establishment.

It's legal and easier to fool with than dope. Either way, I know where my head is. This is where I'm at."

There was a noise at the front door and two hippies came in looking like the gravediggers in *Hamlet*. The one with the red beard did all the talking. "Hey, Grace, we got a parade permit from the mayor's office to celebrate the Age of Aquarius. We got a ton of acid and we're gonna drop it on everybody in the street. We want you to be in the parade!"

She shot me a look: "Do you believe this, man?" Then she turned back to the hippies. "Far out, but we'll be on the road then. Try the Quicksilver Messenger Service or Pacific Gas and Electric."

Crestfallen, they shuffled past the broken toilet seat on the front porch and headed off down the street. They didn't want the Quicksilver Messenger Service or Pacific Gas and Electric. They wanted Grace Slick.

Frankly, I don't blame them. But give her time. If I know Grace, she can start her own parades.

*Study Guide*

1. Rex Reed is one of today's most successful interview writers. What characteristics exemplify his style?

2. How does Reed approach his subject? What attitude does he have toward Miss Slick? How is it revealed? What attitude does he want you to have toward her?

3. Superstars frequently reflect the attitudes and values of the culture that made them popular. What peculiarities of our era might account for the eminence of Miss Slick?

4. Read Warshow's "The Gangster as Tragic Hero" (selection 4) in this volume. Write a similar essay on the social significance of the rock singer in today's culture.

5. Many critics of rock feel that it encourages rebellion and antisocial behavior. Does such a causal relationship exist? You might consider whether or not the song "White Rabbit" (discussed in this interview) encourages the use of drugs. In an essay, analyze the lyrics of current popular songs. Do song writers attempt to shape cultural attitudes?

6. Gather recordings that exemplify the popular music of the 1940's, '50's and '60's. What do they tell us about the nature of our culture in each era? Combine these recordings on a tape which, through juxtaposition, comments on the values of each era and the changes that have taken place.

7. Create a collage that has the superstar as its theme. (You might make it in the shape of a phonograph record.) Try to show what characteristics of the '60's Grace Slick exemplifies.

8. Rewrite Reed's interview from the point of view of a moralistic individual; a cynical newspaper reporter; a writer for an underground newspaper. How might each reshape the facts contained in the article?

9. Select an interesting local figure or campus celebrity. Interview him. Then attempt to write an account of your interview in the style of Rex Reed.

# 19. The New Feminism

LUCY KOMISAR[1]

A dozen women are variously seated in straight-backed chairs, settled on a couch, or sprawled on the floor of a comfortable apartment on Manhattan's West Side. They range in age from twenty-five to thirty-five, and include a magazine researcher, a lawyer, a housewife, an architect, a teacher, a secretary, and a graduate student in sociology.

They are white, middle-class, attractive. All but one have college degrees; several are married; a few are active in social causes. At first, they are hesitant. They don't really know what to talk about, and so they begin with why they came.

"I wanted to explore my feelings as a woman and find out what others think about the things that bother me." Slowly, they open up, trust growing. "I always felt so negative about being a woman; now I'm beginning to feel good about it."

They become more personal and revealing. "My mother never asked me what I was going to be when I grew up." "I never used to like to talk to girls. I always thought women were inferior—I never *liked* women." "I've been a secretary for three years; after that, you

"The New Feminism," by Lucy Komisar, February 21, 1970 *Saturday Review*. Reprinted by permission of the author, copyright 1970 Saturday Review, Inc.

1 Lucy Komisar is a free-lance writer and a board member of the New York chapter of the National Organization for Women. Miss Komisar is currently writing a book on feminism.

begin to think that's all you're good for." "I felt so trapped when my baby was born. I wanted to leave my husband and the child."

Repeated a hundred times in as many different rooms, these are the voices of women's liberation, a movement that encompasses high school students and grandmothers, and that is destined to eclipse the black civil rights struggle in the force of its resentment and the consequence of its demands.

Some of us have become feminists out of anger and frustration over job discrimination. When we left college, male students got aptitude tests, we got typing tests. In spite of federal law, most women still are trapped in low-paying, dead-end jobs and commonly earn less than men for the same work—sometimes on the theory that we are only "helping out," though 42 per cent of us support ourselves or families.

Others have discovered that the humanistic precepts of the radical movement do not always apply to women. At a peace rally in Washington last year, feminists were hooted and jeered off the speakers' platform, and white women working in civil rights or anti-poverty programs are expected to defer to the black male ego. Many of us got out to salvage our own buffeted egos. However, most of the new feminists express only a general malaise they were never able to identify.

Nanette Rainone is twenty-seven, the wife of a newspaperman, the mother of a seven-month-old child, and a graduate of Queens College, where she studied English literature. She married while in graduate school, then quit before the year was out to become an office clerk at *Life* magazine. "I could have known the first day that I wasn't going to be promoted, but it took me eight months to find it out."

She spent the next five months idly at home, began doing volunteer public affairs interviews for WBAI radio, and now produces *Womankind,* a weekly program on the feminist movement.

"I always felt as though I was on a treadmill, an emotional treadmill. I thought it was neurotic, but it always focused on being a woman. Then I met another woman, who had two children. We talked about my pregnancy—my confusion about my pregnancy—and the problems she was having in caring for her children now that she was separated from her husband and wanted to work."

One evening Nanette Rainone's friend took her to a feminist meeting, and immediately she became part of the movement. "The child had been an escape. I was seeking a role I couldn't find on the outside," she says. "Then I became afraid my life would be over-whelmed, that I would never get out from under and do the things I had hoped to do.

"You struggle for several years after getting out of college. You know—what are you going to do with yourself? There's always the external discrimination, but somehow you feel you are talented and you should be able to project yourself. But you don't get a good job, you get a terrible job.

"I think I was typical of the average woman who is in the movement now, because the contradictions in the system existed in my life. My parents were interested in my education. I had more room to develop my potential than was required for the role I eventually was to assume.

"I don't put down the care of children. I just put down the fixated relationship that the mother has, the never-ending association, her urge that the child be something so that *she* can be something. People need objective projects. We all feel the need to actively partici-pate in society, in something outside ourselves where we can learn and develop.

"The closest I've been able to come to what's wrong is that men have a greater sense of self than women have. Marriage is an aspect of men's lives, whereas it is the very center of most women's lives, the whole of their lives. It seemed to me that women felt they couldn't exist except in the eyes of men—that if a man wasn't looking at them or attending to them, then they just weren't there."

If women need more evidence, history books stand ready to as-sure us that we have seldom existed except as shadows of men. We have rarely been leaders of nations or industry or the great contribu-tors to art and science, yet very few sociologists, political leaders, historians, and moral critics have ever stopped to ask why. Now, all around the country, women are meeting in apartments and conference rooms and coffee shops to search out the answers.

The sessions begin with accounts of personal problems and in-cidents. For years, we women have believed that our anger and frustration and unhappiness were "our problems." Suddenly, we dis-cover that we are telling *the same story!* Our complaints are not only common, they are practically universal.

It is an exhilarating experience. Women's doubts begin to dis-appear and are replaced by new strength and self-respect. We stop focusing on men, and begin to identify with other women and to analyze the roots of our oppression. The conclusions that are drawn challenge the legitimacy of the sex role system upon which our civilization is based.

At the center of the feminist critique is the recognition that women have been forced to accept an inferior role in society, and that we have come to believe in our own inferiority. Women are taught to be passive, dependent, submissive, not to pursue careers but to be taken care of and protected. Even those who seek outside work lack confidence and self-esteem. Most of us are forced into menial and unsatisfying jobs: More than three-quarters of us are clerks, sales personnel, or factory and service workers, and a fifth of the women with B.A. degrees are secretaries.

Self-hatred is endemic. Women—especially those who have "made it"—identify with men and mirror their contempt for women. The approval of women does not mean very much. We don't want to work for women or vote for them. We laugh, although with vague uneasiness, at jokes about women drivers, mothers-in-law, and dumb blondes.

We depend on our relationships with men for our very identities. Our husbands win us social status and determine how we will be regarded by the world. Failure for a woman is not being selected by a man.

We are trained in the interests of men to defer to them and serve them and entertain them. If we are educated and gracious, it is so we can please men and educate their children. That is the thread that runs through the life of the geisha, the party girl, the business executive's wife, and the First Lady of the United States.

Men define women, and until now most of us have accepted their definition without question. If we challenge men in the world outside the home, we are all too frequently derided as "aggressive" and "unfeminine"—by women as readily as by men.

A woman is expected to subordinate her job to the interests of her husband's work. She'll move to another city so he can take a promotion—but it rarely works the other way around. Men don't take women's work very seriously, and, as a result, neither do most women. We spend a lot of time worrying about men, while they devote most of theirs to worrying about their careers.

We are taught that getting and keeping a man is a woman's most important job; marriage, therefore, becomes our most important achievement. One suburban housewife says her father started giving her bridal pictures cut from newspapers when she was six. "He said that was what I would be when I grew up."

Most feminists do not object to marriage per se, but to the corollary that it is creative and fulfilling for an adult human being to spend her life doing housework, caring for children, and using her husband as a vicarious link to the outside world.

Most people would prefer just about any kind of work to that of a domestic servant; yet the mindless, endless, repetitious drudgery of housekeeping is the central occupation of more than fifty million women. People who would oppose institutions that portion out menial work on the basis of race see nothing wrong in a system that does the same thing on the basis of sex. (Should black and white roommates automatically assume the Negro best suited for housekeeping chores?) Even when they work at full-time jobs, wives must come home to "their" dusting and "their" laundry.

Some insist that housework is not much worse than the meaningless jobs most people have today, but there is a difference. Housewives are not paid for their work, and money is the mark of value in this society. It is also the key to independence and to the feeling of self-reliance that marks a free human being.

The justification for being a housewife is having children, and the justification for children is—well, a woman has a uterus, what else would it be for? Perhaps not all feminists agree that the uterus is a vestigial organ, but we are adamant and passionate in our denial of the old canard that biology is destiny.

Men have never been bound by their animal natures. They think and dream and create—and fly, clearly something nature had not intended, or it would have given men wings. However, we women are told that our chief function is to reproduce the species, prepare food, and sweep out the cave—er, house.

Psychologist Bruno Bettelheim states woman's functions succinctly: "We must start with the realization that, as much as women want to be good scientists or engineers, they want first and foremost to be womanly companions of men and to be mothers."

He gets no argument from Dr. Spock: "Biologically and temperamentally, I believe women were made to be concerned first and foremost with child care, husband care, and home care." Spock says some women have been "confused" by their education. (Freud was equally reactionary on the woman question, but he at least had the excuse of his Central European background.)

The species must reproduce, but this need not be the sole purpose of a woman's life. Men want children, too, yet no one expects them to choose between families and work. Children are in no way a substitute for personal development and creativity. If a talented man is forced into a senseless, menial job, it is deplored as a waste and a personal misfortune; yet, a woman's special skills, education, and interests are all too often deemed incidental and irrelevant, simply a focus for hobbies or volunteer work.

Women who say that raising a family is a fulfilling experience are rather like the peasant who never leaves his village. They have never had the opportunity to do anything else.

As a result, women are forced to live through their children and husbands, and they feel cheated and resentful when they realize that is not enough. When a woman says she gave her children everything, she is telling the truth—and that is the tragedy. Often when she reaches her late thirties, her children have grown up, gone to work or college, and left her in a bleak and premature old age. Middle-aged women who feel empty and useless are the mainstay of America's psychiatrists—who generally respond by telling them to "accept their role."

The freedom to choose whether or not to have children has always been illusory. A wife who is deliberately "barren"—a word that reinforces the worn-out metaphor of woman as Mother Earth— is considered neurotic or unnatural. Not only is motherhood not central to a woman's life, it may not be necessary or desirable. For the first time, some of us are admitting openly and without guilt that we do not want children. And the population crisis is making it even clearer that as a symbol for Americans motherhood ought to defer to apple pie.

The other half of the reproduction question is sex. The sexual revolution didn't liberate women at all; it only created a bear market for men. One of the most talked-about tracts in the movement is a pamphlet by Ann Koedt called "The Myth of the Vaginal Orgasm," which says most women don't have orgasms because most men won't accept the fact that the female orgasm is clitoral.

We are so used to putting men's needs first that we don't know how to ask for what *we* want, or else we share the common ignorance about our own physiology and think there is something wrong with us when we don't have orgasms "the right way." Freudian analysts contribute to the problem. The realization that past guilt and frustration have been unnecessary is not the least of the sentiments that draws women to women's liberation.

Feminists also protest the general male proclivity to regard us as decorative, amusing sex objects even in the world outside bed. We resent the sexual sell in advertising, the catcalls we get on the street, girlie magazines and pornography, bars that refuse to serve unescorted women on the assumption they are prostitutes, the not very subtle brainwashing by cosmetic companies, and the attitude of men who praise our knees in miniskirts, but refuse to act as if we had brains.

Even the supposedly humanistic worlds of rock music and radical politics are not very different. Young girls who join "the scene" or "the movement" are labeled "groupies" and are sexually exploited; the flashy pornosheets such as *Screw* and *Kiss* are published by the self-appointed advocates of the new "free," anti-Establishment lifestyle. *"Plus ça change. . . ."*

We are angry about the powers men wield over us. The physical power—women who study karate do so as a defense against muggers, not lovers. And the social power—we resent the fact that men take the initiative with women, that women cannot ask for dates but must sit home waiting for the phone to ring.

That social conditioning began in childhood when fathers went out to work and mothers stayed home images perpetuated in schoolbooks and games and on television. If we were bright students, we were told, "You're smart—for a girl," and then warned not to appear *too* smart in front of boys—"Or you won't have dates."

Those of us who persisted in reaching for a career were encouraged to be teachers or nurses so we would have "something to fall back on." My mother told me: "You're so bright, it's a pity you're not a boy. You could become president of a bank—or anything you wanted."

Ironically, and to our dismay, we discovered that playing the assigned role is precisely what elicits masculine contempt for our inferiority and narrow interests. *Tooth and Nail,* a newsletter published by women's liberation groups in the San Francisco area, acidly points out a few of the contradictions: "A smart woman never shows her brains; she allows the man to think himself clever. . . . Women's talk is all chatter; they don't understand things men are interested in."

Or: "Don't worry your pretty little head about such matters. . . . A woman's brain is between her legs. . . . Women like to be protected and treated like little girls. . . . Women can't make decisions."

The feminist answer is to throw out the whole simplistic division of human characteristics into masculine and feminine, and to insist that there are no real differences between men and women other than those enforced by culture.

Men say women are not inferior, we are just different; yet somehow they have appropriated most of the qualities that society admires and have left us with the same distinctive features that were attributed to black people before the civil rights revolution.

Men, for example, are said to be strong, assertive, courageous, logical, constructive, creative, and independent. Women are weak, passive, irrational, overemotional, empty-headed, and lacking in strong superegos. (Thank Freud for the last.) Both blacks and women are contented, have their place, and know how to use wiles —flattery, and wide-eyed, open-mouthed ignorance—to get around "the man." It is obviously natural that men should be dominant and women submissive. Shuffle, baby, shuffle.

Our "sexist" system has hurt men as well as women, forcing them into molds that deny the value of sensitivity, tenderness, and sentiment. Men who are not aggressive worry about their virility just as strong women are frightened by talk about their being castrating females. The elimination of rigid sex-role definitions would liberate everyone. And that is the goal of the women's liberation movement.

Women's liberation groups, which have sprung up everywhere across the country, are taking names like Radical Women or the Women's Liberation Front or the Feminists. Most start as groups of ten or twelve; many, when they get too large for discussion, split in a form of mitosis. Sometimes they are tied to central organizations set up for action, or they maintain communications with each other or cosponsor newsletters with similar groups in their area.

Some are concerned with efforts to abolish abortion laws, a few have set up cooperative day-care centers, others challenge the stereotypes of woman's image, and many are organized for "consciousness-raising"—a kind of group therapy or encounter session that starts with the premise that there is something wrong with the system, not the women in the group.

The amorphousness and lack of central communication in the movement make it virtually impossible to catalogue the established groups, let alone the new ones that regularly appear; many of the "leaders" who have been quoted in newspapers or interviewed on television have been anointed only by the press.

The one organization with a constitution, board members, and chapters (some thirty-five) throughout the country is the National

Organization for Women. Its founding in 1966 was precipitated by the ridicule that greeted the inclusion of sex in the prohibitions against job discrimination in the 1964 Civil Rights Act. (A staff member in the federal Equal Employment Opportunity Commission, which enforces the act, said it took pressure from NOW to get the EEOC to take that part of the law seriously.)

NOW members are not very different from women in other feminist groups, though they tend to include more professionals and older women. In general, they eschew "consciousness-raising" in favor of political action, and they are more likely to demonstrate for job equality and child-care centers than for the abolition of marriage or the traditional family unit.

NOW's president is Betty Friedan, who in 1963 published *The Feminine Mystique,* a challenge to the myth that a woman's place is either in a boudoir in a pink, frilly nightgown, on her hands and knees scrubbing the kitchen floor, or in a late model station wagon taking the kids to music lessons and Cub Scout meetings. (An article that previewed the theme of the book was turned down by every major women's magazine. "One was horrified and said I was obviously talking to and for a few neurotic women." When the book came out, two of these magazines published excerpts and several now have commissioned articles about the movement.)

Today, Betty Friedan says, the movement must gain political power by mobilizing the 51 per cent of the electorate who are women, as well as seeking elected offices for themselves. "We have to break down the actual barriers that prevent women from being full people in society, and not only end explicit discrimination but build new institutions. Most women will continue to bear children, and unless we create child-care centers on a mass basis, it's all talk."

Women are beginning to read a good deal about their own place in history, about the determined struggles of the suffragettes, the isolation of Virginia Woolf, and the heroism of Rosa Luxemburg. The Congress to Unite Women, which drew some 500 participants from cities in the Northeast, called for women's studies in high schools and colleges.

Present are all the accouterments of any social movement—feminist magazines such as *No More Fun and Games* in Boston, *Up from Under* in New York, and *Aphra,* a literary magazine published in Baltimore. (Anne Sexton wrote in the dedication, "As long as it can be said about a woman writer, 'She writes like a man' and that woman takes it as a compliment, we are in trouble.")

There are feminist theaters in at least New York and Boston, buttons that read "Uppity Women Unite," feminist poems and songs, a feminist symbol (the biological sign for woman with an equal sign in the center), and, to denounce specific advertisements, gum stickers that state, "This ad insults women."

With a rising feminist consciousness, everything takes on new significance—films, advertisements, offhand comments, little things that never seemed important before. A few women conclude that chivalry and flirting reduce women to mere sex objects for men. We stop feeling guilty about opening doors, and some of us experiment with paying our own way on dates.

Personal acts are matched by political ones. The National Organization for Women went to court to get a federal ruling barring segregated help-wanted ads in newspapers, and it regularly helps women file complaints before the EEOC and local human rights commissions.

A women's rights platform was adopted last year by the State Committee of the California Democratic Party, and the Women's Rights Committee of the New Democratic Coalition plans to make feminist demands an issue in New York politics. A women's caucus exists in the Democratic Policy Council, headed by Senator Fred Harris.

At Grinnell College in Iowa, students protested the appearance of a representative from *Playboy* magazine, and women from sixteen cities converged on Atlantic City to make it clear what they think of the Miss America Pageant. In New York, a group protested advertisements by toymakers that said "boys were born to build and learn" and "girls were born to be dancers."

Women's caucuses have been organized in the American Political Science, Psychological, and Sociological associations. At New York University, a group of law students won their fight to make women eligible for a series of coveted $10,000 scholarships.

Pro-abortion groups have organized around the country to repeal anti-abortion laws, challenge them in the courts, or openly defy them. In Bloomington, Indiana, New York City, and elsewhere, women's liberation groups have set up cooperative day-care centers, which are illegal under strict state rules that regulate child-care facilities.

Free child care is likely to become the most significant demand made by the movement, and one calculated to draw the support of millions of women who may not be interested in other feminist issues. About four million working mothers have children under six years of age, and only 2 per cent of these are in day-care centers.

Even Establishment institutions appear to reflect the new attitudes. Princeton, Williams, and Yale have begun to admit women students, though on an unequal quota basis—and not to the hallowed pine-paneled halls of their alumni clubhouses.

Nevertheless, most people have only a vague idea of the significance of the new movement. News commentators on year-end analysis shows ignored the question or sloughed it off uncomfortably. One said the whole idea frightened him.

Yet, the women's movement promises to affect radically the life of virtually everyone in America. Only a small part of the population suffers because it is black, and most people have little contact with minorities. Women are 51 per cent of the population, and chances are that every adult American either is one, is married to one, or has close social or business relations with many.

The feminist revolution will overturn the basic premises upon which these relations are built—stereotyped notions about the family and the roles of men and women, fallacies concerning masculinity and femininity, and the economic division of labor into paid work and homemaking.

If the 1960s belonged to the blacks, the next ten years are ours.

## Study Guide

1. How many varieties of discrimination against women does Miss Komisar discuss?

2. Select one area, such as discrimination against women in employment, and thoroughly investigate conditions in your own community. Write a research paper on the treatment of women in your area.

3. What are the chief means of perpetrating antifeminism? Who are the chief perpetrators?

4. Miss Komisar criticizes the dehumanization of women in advertising. Like many other women, she is offended by the reduction of the female to a sexual object. Gather a number of advertisements that depict women in this light. Then assemble them in a collage in which they are used to criticize themselves.

5. Create an imaginary dialogue between a fictitious women's liberationist and a Playmate of the month, in which the two discuss the role of women in society.

6. Write a defense of woman's traditional role in society.

# 20. *What It Means To Be a Homosexual*

MERLE MILLER[1]

Edward Morgan Forster was a very good writer and a very gutsy man. In the essay "What I Believe," he said: "I hate the idea of causes, and if I had to choose between betraying my country and betraying my friend, I hope I would have the guts to betray my country. Such a choice may scandalize the modern reader, and he may stretch out his patriotic hand to the telephone at once and ring up the police. It would not have shocked Dante, though. Dante places Brutus and Cassius in the lowest circle of Hell because they had chosen to betray their friend Julius Caesar rather than their country Rome."

It took courage to write those words, just as it does, at times, for anyone else to repeat them. In the early nineteen-fifties when I wanted to use them on the title page of a book on blacklisting in television that I wrote for the American Civil Liberties Union, officials of the A.C.L.U. advised against it. Why ask for more trouble, they said. Being against blacklisting was trouble enough. Those were timorous days. "What I Believe" was included in a book of essays used in secondary schools, but it disappeared from the book around 1954

[1] Merle Miller, the novelist, is also known for a book about his experiences as a TV scriptwriter, "Only You, Dick Daring!" Soon to be published are a novel called "What Happened" and the nonfictional "Marshalltown, Iowa."

and was replaced by something or other from the Reader's Digest. When I protested to the publisher, he said—it was a folk saying of the time—"You have to roll with the tide." The tide was McCarthyism, which had not then fully subsided—assuming it ever has or will. Forster was not a man who rolled with the tide. I met him twice, heard him lecture several times, was acquainted with several of his friends, and knew that he was homosexual, but I did not know that he had written a novel, "Maurice," dealing with homosexual characters, until it was announced last November. On top of the manuscript he wrote, "Publishable—but is it worth it?" The novel, completed in 1915, will, after 55 years and the death of Forster, at last be published.

Is it worth it? Even so outspoken a man as Forster had to ask himself that question. It is one thing to confess to political unorthodoxy but quite another to admit to sexual unorthodoxy. Still. Yet. A homosexual friend of mine has said, "Straights don't want to know for sure, and they can never forgive you for telling them. They prefer to think it doesn't exist, but if it does, at least keep quiet about it." And one Joseph Epstein said in Harper's only last September: ". . . however wide the public tolerance for it, it is no more acceptable privately than it ever was . . . private acceptance of homosexuality, in my experience, is not to be found, even among the most liberal-minded, sophisticated, and liberated people. . . . Nobody says, or at least I have never heard anyone say, 'Some of my best friends are homosexual.' People do say—I say—'fag' and 'queer' without hesitation—and these words, no matter who is uttering them, are put-down words, in intent every bit as vicious as 'kike' or 'nigger.' "

Is it true? Is that the way it is? Have my heterosexual friends, people I thought were my heterosexual friends, been going through an elaborate charade all these years? I would like to think they agree with George Weinberg, a therapist and author of a book on therapy called "The Action Approach," who says, "I would never consider a person healthy unless he had overcome his prejudice against homosexuality." But even Mr. Weinberg assumes that there is a prejudice, apparently built-in, a natural part of the human psyche. And so my heterosexual friends had it, maybe still have it? The late Otto Kahn, I think it was, said, "A kike is a Jewish gentleman who has just left the room." Is a fag a homosexual gentleman who has just stepped out? Me?

I can never be sure, of course, will never be sure, I know it shouldn't bother me. That's what everybody says, but it does bother me. It bothers me every time I enter a room in which there is anyone else. Friend or foe? Is there a difference?

When I was a child in Marshalltown, Iowa, I hated Christmas almost as much as I do now, but I loved Halloween. I never wanted to take off the mask; I wanted to wear it everywhere, night and day, always. And I suppose I still do. I have often used liquor, which is another kind of mask, and, more recently, pot.

Then, too, I suppose if my friends have been playing games with me, they might with justice say that I have been playing games with them. It took me almost 50 years to come out of the closet, to stop pretending to be something I was not, most of the time fooling nobody.

But I guess it is never easy to open the closet door. When she talked to the Daughters of Bilitis, a Lesbian organization, late last summer, Kate Millett, author of "Sexual Politics," said: "I'm very glad to be here. It's been kind of a long trip. . . . I've wanted to be here, I suppose, in a surreptitious way for a long time, and I was always too chicken. . . . Anyway, I'm out of the closet. Here I am."

Not surprisingly, Miss Millett is now being attacked more because of what she said to the Daughters of Bilitis than because of what she said in her book. James Owles, president of Gay Activists' Alliance, a militant, nonviolent organization concerned with civil rights for homosexuals, says: "We don't give a damn whether people like us or not. We want the rights we're entitled to."

I'm afraid I want both. I dislike being despised, unless I have done something despicable, realizing that the simple fact of being homosexual is all by itself despicable to many people, maybe, as Mr. Epstein says, to everybody who is straight. Assuming anybody is ever totally one thing sexually.

Mr. Epstein says, "When it comes to homosexuality, we know, or ought to know, that we know next to nothing"—and that seems to me to be true. Our ignorance of the subject is almost as great now as it was in 1915 when Forster wrote "Maurice," almost as great as it was in 1815 or, for that matter, 1715. Freud did not add much knowledge to the subject, nor have any of his disciples, none that I have read or listened to, none that I have consulted. I have spent several thousand dollars and several thousand hours with various practitioners, and while they have often been helpful in leading me to an understanding of how I got to be the way I am, none of them has ever had any feasible, to me feasible, suggestion as to how I could be any different.

And that includes the late Dr. Edmund Bergler, who claimed not only that he could "cure" me but get rid of my writer's block as well. He did neither. I am still homosexual, and I have a writer's block every morning when I sit down at the typewriter. And it's too late now to change my nature. At 50, give or take a year or so, I am afraid I will have to make do with me. Which is what my mother said in the beginning.

Nobody seems to know why homosexuality happens, how it happens, or even what it is that does happen. Assuming *it* happens in any one way. Or any thousand ways. We do not even know how prevalent it is. We were told in 1948 by Dr. Alfred C. Kinsey in "Sexual Behavior in the Human Male" that 37 per cent of all males have had or will have at least one homosexual experience between adolescence and old age. And last year a questionnaire answered by some 20,000 readers of Psychology Today brought the same response. Thirty-seven per cent of the males said that they had had one homosexual experience. (I will be speaking in what follows largely of male homosexuality, which has been my experience.)

Voltaire is said to have had one such experience, with an Englishman. When the Englishman suggested that they repeat it, Voltaire is alleged to have said, "If you try it once, you are a philosopher; if twice, you are a sodomite."

The National Institute of Mental Health says that between 3,000,000 and 4,000,000 Americans of both sexes are predominantly homosexual, while many others display what the institute delicately calls occasional homosexual tendencies.

But how do they know? Because the closets are far from emptied; there are more in hiding than out of hiding. That has been my experience anyway. And homosexuals come in all shapes and sizes, sometimes in places where you'd least expect to find them. If Jim Bouton is to be believed, in big league baseball and, if we are to go along with Dave Meggysey, in the National Football League. Nobody knows. The question as to who is and who isn't was not asked in the 1970 census.

A Harris survey indicates that 63 per cent of the American people feel that homosexuals are "harmful" to American society. One wonders, I wondered anyway, how those 37 per cent of the males with one admitted homosexual experience responded to the question. After how many such experiences does one get to be harmful? And harmful in what way? The inquisitive Mr. Harris appears not to have asked. Harmful. Feared. Hated. What do the hardhats find objectionable in the young? Their lack of patriotism and the fact that they are all faggots. Aren't they? We're in the midst of a "freaking fag revolution," said the prosecutor in the Chicago conspiracy trial. At least that seems to be the politically profitable thing to say in Chicago.

In the nineteen-fifties, McCarthy found that attacking homosexuals paid off almost as well as attacking the Communists, and he claimed they were often the same. Indeed, the District of Columbia police set up a special detail of the vice squad "to investigate links between homosexuality and Communism."

The American Civil Liberties Union recently has been commendably active in homosexual cases, but in the early fifties, when homosexuals and people accused of homosexuality were being fired from all kinds of Government posts, as they still are, the A.C.L.U. was notably silent. And the most silent of all was a closet queen who was a member of the board of directors, myself.

Epstein, a proclaimed liberal, said in Harper's: "If a close friend were to reveal himself to me as being a homosexual, I am very uncertain what my reaction would be—except to say that it would not be simple. . . . If I had the power to do so, I would wish homosexuality off the face of this earth."

I could not help wondering what Epstein, who is, I believe, a literary critic, would do about the person and the work of W. H. Auden, homosexual and generally considered to be the greatest living poet in English. "We must love one another or die." Except for homosexuals?

> Beleaguered by the same
> Negation and despair,
> Show an affirming flame.

The great fear is that a son will turn out to be homosexual. Nobody seems to worry about a Lesbian daughter; nobody talks about it anyway. But the former runs through every level of our culture. In the Arpège ad this Christmas: "Promises, husbands to wives, 'I promise to stop telling you that our youngest is developing effeminate tendencies.' "

And so on, and on. I should add that not all mothers are afraid that their sons will be homosexuals. Everywhere among us are those dominant ladies who welcome homosexuality in their sons. That way the mothers know they won't lose them to another woman.

And, of course, no television writer would feel safe without at least one fag joke per script. Carson, Cavett and Griffin all give their audiences the same knowing grin when *that* subject is mentioned, and audiences always laugh, though somewhat nervously.

Is homosexuality contagious? Once again, nobody seems to know for sure. The writer Richard Rhodes reports that those tireless and tedious investigators, Dr. William Masters and Mrs. Virginia Johnson of St. Louis, have got into the subject of homosexuality. And Masters *hinted* to Rhodes that his clinical work had shown that "homosexual seduction in adolescence is generally the predetermining factor in later homosexual choice."

One should not hold the indefatigable doctor to a "hint," but the Wolfenden Committee set up by the British Government in the fifties to study homosexuality and prostitution found the opposite:

"It is a view widely held, and one which found favor among our police and legal witnesses, that seduction in youth is the decisive factor in the production of homosexuality as a condition, and we are aware that this condition has done much to alarm parents and teachers. We have found no convincing evidence in support of this contention. Our medical witnesses unanimously held that seduction has little effect in inducing a settled pattern of homosexual behavior, and we have been given no grounds from other sources which contradict their judgment. Moreover, it has been suggested to us that the fact of being seduced often does less harm to the victim than the publicity which attends the criminal proceedings against the offender and the distress which undue alarm sometimes leads parents to show."

Martin Hoffman, a San Francisco psychiatrist who has written a book about male homosexuality called "The Gay World," said in a recent issue of Psychology Today: "Until we know about the mechanisms of sexual arousal in the central nervous system and how learning factors can set the triggering devices for those mechanisms, we cannot have a satisfactory theory of homosexual behavior. We must point out that heterosexual behavior is as much of a scientific puzzle as homosexual behavior. . . . We assume that heterosexual arousal is somehow natural and needs no explanation. I suggest that to call it natural is to evade the whole issue; it is as if we said it's natural for the sun to come up in the morning and left it at that. Is it possible that we know less about human sexuality than the medieval astrologers knew about the stars?"

I know this. Almost the first words I remember hearing, maybe the first words I choose to remember hearing, were my mother's, saying, "We ordered a little girl, and when you came along, we were somewhat disappointed." She always claimed that I came from Montgomery Ward, and when I would point out that there was no baby department in the Monkey Ward catalogue, she would say, "This was special."

I never knew what that meant, but I never asked. I knew enough. I knew that I was a disappointment. "But we love you just the same," my mother would say, "and we'll have to make do."

We had to make do with a great many things in those days. The Depression came early to our house, around 1927, when my father lost all his money in the Florida land boom, and once we got poor, we stayed poor. "You'll have the wing for supper, because this is a great big chicken and will last for days, and tomorrow you can take a whole leg to school in your little lunch pail and have it all to yourself." Day-old bread, hand-me-down clothes that had once belonged to more prosperous cousins, holes in the soles of my shoes—all of it. I was a combination of Oliver Twist and Little Nell.

They say that the Depression and the World War were the two central experiences of my generation, and that may be. I certainly had more than enough of both, but I was never really hungry for food. It was love I craved, approval, forgiveness for being what I could not help being. And I have spent a good part of my life looking for those things, always, as a few psychologists have pointed out, in the places I was least likely to find them.

My baby blankets were all pink, purchased before the disaster, my birth. The lace on my baby dress was pink; my bonnet was fringed with pink, and little old ladies were forever peering into the baby buggy and crib, saying, "What an adorable little girl." They kept on saying that until I got my first butch haircut, at 4, just before I started kindergarten. Until then I had long, straight hair, mousebrown, lusterless, and long hair was just as unpopular in Marshalltown then as it is now.

Not until college did I read that Oscar Wilde's mother started him down the garden path by letting his hair grow and dressing him as a little girl. As Oscar said, "Children begin by loving their parents; as they grow older they judge them; sometimes they forgive them."

I was 4 years old when I started school. My mother had told them I was 5; I was somewhat precocious, and she may just have wanted to get me out of the house. But butch haircut or not, some boys in the third grade took one look at me and said, "Hey, look at the sissy," and they started laughing. It seems to me now that I heard that word at least once five days a week for the next 13 years, until I skipped town and went to the university. Sissy and all the other words—pansy, fairy, nance, fruit, fruitcake, and less printable epithets. I did not encounter the word faggot until I got to Manhattan. I'll tell you this, though. It's not true, that saying about sticks and stones; it's words that break your bones.

I admit I must have been a splendid target, undersized always, the girlish voice, the steel-rimmed glasses, always bent, no doubt limp of wrist, and I habitually carried a music roll. I studied both piano and violin all through school, and that all by itself was enough to condemn one to permanent *sissydom.*

When I was doing a television documentary of Harry Truman's life, he said at one point: "I was never what you'd call popular when I went to school. The popular boys were the athletes with their big, tight fists, and I was never like that. . . . I always had a music roll and wore thick glasses; I was wall-eyed, you know. . . . I stopped playing the piano when I was 14 years old. Where I come from, playing the piano wasn't considered the proper thing for a boy to do."

I said, "Mr. President, did they ever call you 'four-eyes' when you were a little boy?"

"Oh, yes," he said, " 'four-eyes,' 'sissy,' and a lot of other things. When that happens, what you have to do is, you have to work harder than they do and be smarter, and if you are, things usually turn out all right in the end."

As a child I wanted to be the girl my mother had had in mind —or else the All-American boy everybody else so admired. Since sex changes were unheard of in those days, I clearly couldn't be a girl; so I tried the other. I ate carloads of Wheaties, hoping I'd turn into another Jack Armstrong, but I still could neither throw nor catch a baseball. I couldn't even see the thing; I'd worn glasses as thick as plate-glass windows since I was 3. ("You inherited your father's eyes, among other weaknesses.") I sold enough Liberty magazines to buy all the body-building equipment Charles Atlas had to offer, but it did no good. I remained an 89-pound weakling year after year after year. And when the voices of all the other boys in my class had changed into a very low baritone, I was still an uncertain soprano, and remained that until I got to the University of Iowa in Iowa City and, among other disguises, lowered my voice at least two octaves so that I could get a job as a radio announcer on the university station.

I also became city editor of The Daily Iowan and modeled myself after a character out of "The Front Page," wearing a hat indoors and out, talking out of the corner of my mouth, never without a cigarette, being folksy with the local cops, whom I detested, one and all. I chased girls, never with much enthusiasm I'm afraid, and denounced queers with some regularity in the column I wrote for the Iowan. What a fink I was—anything to avoid being called a sissy again.

I was afraid I would never get into the Army, but after the psychiatrist tapped me on the knee with a little hammer and asked how I felt about girls, before I really had a chance to answer, he said, "Next," and I was being sworn in. For the next four years as an editor of Yank, first in the Pacific and then in Europe, I continued to use my deepest city editor's-radio announcer's voice, ordered reporters and photographers around and kept my evenings to myself, especially in Paris.

After the war, I became as much a part of the Establishment as I had ever been, including servitude as an editor of Time. I remember in particular a long discussion about whether to use the picture of a British composer on the cover because a researcher had discovered that he was. . . . I am sure if there was a vote, I voted against using the picture.

A little later, after finishing my first successful novel, "That Winter," which became a best seller, I decided there was no reason at all why I couldn't be just as straight as the next man. I might not be able to play baseball, but I could get married.

Petr Ilich Tchaikovsky had the same idea. Maybe marriage would cure him of what he called "The." But, afterwards, in a letter to his friend Nadejda von Meck, he wrote, ". . . I saw right away that I could never love my wife and that the *habit* on which I had counted would never come. I fell into despair and longed for death. . . . My mind began to go. . . ."

Petr Ilich's marriage lasted only two weeks. My own lasted longer and was not quite so searing an experience, but it could not have succeeded.

Lucy Komisar says in Washington Monthly that this country is obsessed by what she calls "violence and the masculine mystique," which is certainly true enough. "The enemies of national 'virility' are called 'effete,' a word that means 'sterile, spent, worn-out,' and conjures up the picture of an effeminate pantywaist." Also true, but Americans are certainly not the first people to get uptight about "virility."

Philip of Macedon was forever fussing at Olympias because he claimed she was making their son Alexander effeminate. And, to be sure, Alexander turned out to be at least bisexual, maybe totally homosexual. How else could one explain his grief at the death of his lover, Hephaestion? According to Plutarch, "Alexander was so beyond all reason transported that, to express his sorrow, he immediately ordered the manes and tails of all his horses and mules cut, and threw down the battlements of the neighboring cities. The poor physician he crucified, and forbade playing on the flute or any other musical instrument in the camp a great while. . ."

Gore Vidal has been quoted as saying: "The Italians are sexual opportunists. Anything that feels goods, they're for it." Which may be true, but I cannot imagine an Italian father who would not be devastated if he found that his son was homosexual. Or, for that matter, a father in any country in Western society. In England, where the Sexual Offenses Act has been on the law books since 1967, 10 years after the recommendations of the Wolfenden Committee, Anthony Gray, director of an organization that helps sexual minorities, says that even today ". . . the briefest experience is enough to convince one that discrimination against known homosexuals is still the rule rather than the exception." Gray notes that homosexuals still cannot belong to the Civil Service and are still likely to lose their jobs if "found out."

Most members of the Gay Liberation Front appear to believe that Marxism is the answer, which is odd because in Communist China homosexuals are put in prisons for brainwashing that are called "hospitals for ideological reform." Chairman Mao has said: "Our object in exposing errors and criticizing shortcomings is like that of a doctor in curing a disease." In Cuba homosexuals have been placed in concentration camps.

Still, as Huey P. Newton, Supreme Commander of the Black Panther Party, has said, there is no reason to think a homosexual cannot be a revolutionary. Late last summer, shortly after the New York chapter of the Gay Liberation Front gave a $500.00 donation to the Panthers, Newton in a rambling, rather tortured statement said: "What made them homosexual? Some people say that it's the decadence of capitalism. I don't know whether this is the case; I rather doubt it. . . . But there's nothing to say that a homosexual cannot also be a revolutionary. . . . Quite the contrary, maybe a homosexual could be the most revolutionary."

On the other hand, Eldridge Cleaver in "Soul on Ice" gives what I am sure is a more prevalent view among the Panthers: "Homosexuality is a sickness, just as are baby-rape or wanting to become head of General Motors."

Of course, the Soviet Union claims not to have any homosexuals. I cannot comment on the validity of that claim never having been there, but I do know that when one of the Russian ballet companies is in town, you can hear a great many Russian accents on West 42d Street and at various gay bars.

Growing up in Marshalltown, I was allowed to take out as many books as I wanted from the local library and I always wanted as many as I could carry, 8 or 10 at a time. I read about sensitive boys, odd boys, boys who were lonely and misunderstood, boys who really didn't care all that much for baseball, boys who were teased by their classmates, books about all of these, but for years nobody in any of the books I read was ever tortured by the strange fantasies that tore at me every time, for instance, my mother insisted I go to the "Y" to learn how to swim. They swam nude at the Y, and I never went. Lead me not into temptation. In gym—it was required in high school—I always tried to get in and out of the locker room before anybody else arrived.

And in none of the books I read did anybody feel a compulsion, and compulsion it surely was, to spend so many hours, almost as many as I spent at the library, in or near the Minneapolis & St. Louis railroad station where odd, frightening things were written on the walls of the men's room. And where in those days, there were always boys in their teens and early 20's who were on their way to and from somewhere in freight cars. Boys who were hungry and jobless and who for a very small amount of money, and sometimes none at all, were available for sex; almost always they were. They needed the money, and they needed someone to recognize them, to actually see them.

That was the way it happened the first time. The boy was from Chicago, and his name was Carl. He was 17, and I was 12 and the aggressor. I remember every detail of it; I suppose one always does. Carl hadn't eaten, said he hadn't eaten for two days. His father was a plumber, unemployed, and his mother was, he said rather vaguely, "away, hopefully forever." I remember once I said, "But why don't you go home anyway?" And he said, "Where would that be?"

Years later a boy I met on West 42d Street said it best, about the boys in my childhood and the boys on all the streets of all the cities where they wait. He was the next-to-youngest child in a very poor family of nine, and once he ran away from home for two days and two nights, and when he got back, nobody knew that he had been gone. Then, at 19, he discovered The Street, and he said, "All of a sudden here were all these men, and they were looking at me."

The boys who stopped by at the M. and St. L. in Marshalltown all had stories, and they were all anxious to tell them. They were all lonely and afraid. None of them ever made fun of me. I was never beaten up. They recognized, I guess, that we were fellow aliens with no place to register.

Like my three friends in town. They were aliens, too: Sam, whose father ran a grocery store my mother wouldn't patronize. ("Always buy American, Merle, and don't you forget it. We don't know *where* the Jews send the money you spend in one of their stores.") A girl in a wheel chair, a polio victim; we talked through every recess in school. And there was the woman with a clubfoot who sold tickets at the Casino, a movie house, and let me in for free—tickets couldn't have been a dime then, but they were—until I was 16, and, as I say, skipped town.

The black boy and the black girl in my high school class never spoke to me, and I never spoke to them. That was the way it was. It never occurred to me that that was not necessarily the way it was meant to be.

There were often black boys on the freight trains, and we talked and had sex. Their stories were always sadder than anybody else's. I never had any hangups about the color of somebody's skin. If you were an outcast, that was good enough for me. I once belonged to 22 organizations devoted to improving the lot of the world's outcasts. The only group of outcasts I never spoke up for publicly, never donated money to or signed an ad or petition for were the homosexuals. I always used my radio announcer's voice when I said "No."

I was 14 when I happened on a book called "Winesburg, Ohio." I don't know how. Maybe it was recommended by the librarian, a kind and knowing woman with the happy name of Alice Story. Anyway, there at last, in a story called "Hands," were the words I had been looking for. I was not the only sissy in the world: "Adolf Myers was meant to be a teacher . . . In their feeling for the boys under their charge such men are not unlike the finer sort of women in their love of men."

Sherwood Anderson's story ended unhappily. Of course. How else could it end? "And then the tragedy. A half-witted boy of the school becomes enamored of the young master. In his bed at night he imagined unthinkable things and in the morning went forth to tell his dreams as facts. Strange, hideous accusations fell from his loose-hung lips. Through the Pennsylvania town went a shiver. Hidden, shadowy doubts that had been in men's minds concerning Adolf Myers were galvanized into beliefs."

I must have read "Hands" more than any story before or since. I can still quote it from beginning to end. "They had intended to hang the schoolmaster, but something in his figure, so small, white, and pitiful, touched their hearts and they let him escape."

Naturally. If you were *that way*, what else could you expect? Either they ran you out of town or you left before they got around to it. I decided on the latter. I once wrote that I started packing to leave Marshalltown when I was 2 years old, which is a slight exaggeration.

"As he ran into the darkness, they repented of their weakness and ran after him, swearing and throwing sticks and great balls of soft mud at the figure that screamed and ran faster into the darkness."

"Winesburg" was published in 1919, and one of the terrifying things is that the people in any town in the United States, quite likely any city, too, would react very much the same way today, wouldn't they?

Look what happened only 15 years ago, in 1955, in Boise, Idaho, when a "homosexual underworld" was uncovered. The "upright" citizens panicked, and some people left town, some were run out of town, and others were sentenced to long prison terms.

In a perceptive and thorough account of what happened, "The Boys of Boise," John Gerassi reports that a lawyer told him that during the height of the hysteria the old American custom of a night on the town with the boys disappeared entirely: "You never saw so many men going out to the bars at night with their wives and girl friends . . . we used to have poker games once a week. Well, for a few weeks we canceled them. Then one of the guys got an idea:

'We'll invite a girl to play with us. You know, it's not very pleasant to play poker with women, not when you're in a serious game. But that's what we had to do.' "

I have been back to Marshalltown only briefly in all the years since my escape, but a few years ago, I did return to a reunion of my high school class. I made the principal speech at the banquet, and at the end there was enough applause to satisfy my ego temporarily, and various of my classmates, all of whom looked depressingly middle-aged, said various pleasant things, after which there was a dance.

I have written about that before, but what I have not written about, since I was still not ready to come out of the closet, is that a little while after the dance began, a man whose face had been only vaguely familiar and whose name I would not have remembered if he had not earlier reminded me came up, an idiot grin on his face, his wrists limp, his voice falsetto, and said, "How about letting me have this dance, sweetie?" He said it loud enough for all to hear.

I said, "I'm terribly sorry, but my dance card is all filled up." By no means the wittiest of remarks, but under the circumstances it was the best I could manage.

Later, several people apologized for what he had said, but I wondered (who would not?) how many of them had been tempted to say the same thing. Or would say something of the kind after I had gone. Fag, faggot, sissy, queer. A fag is a homosexual gentleman who has just left the room.

And the man who said it was a successful newspaper executive in Colorado, in his mid-40's, a father of five, I was told, a grandfather. After all those years, 27 of them, was he still . . . what? Threatened by me? Offended? Unsettled? Challenged? No children or grandchildren around to be perverted. Was his own sexual identity so shaky that . . . ? A closet queen at heart? No, that's too easy. And it's too easy to say that he's the one who needs treatment, not me. George Weinberg says, "The 'homosexual problem,' as I have described it here, is the problem of condemning *variety* in human existence. If one cannot enjoy the fact of this variety, at the very least one must learn to become indifferent to it, since obviously it is here to stay."

The fear of it simply will not go away, though. A man who was once a friend, maybe my best friend, the survivor of five marriages, the father of nine, not too long ago told me that his eldest son was coming to my house on Saturday: "Now please try not to make a pass at him."

He laughed. I guess he meant it as a joke; I didn't ask.

And a man I've known, been acquainted with, let's say, for 25 years, called from the city on a Friday afternoon before getting on the train to come up to my place for the weekend. He said, "I've always leveled with you, Merle, and I'm going to now. I've changed my mind about bringing—[his 16-year-old son]. I'm sure you understand."

I said that, no, I didn't understand. Perhaps he could explain it to me.

He said, "—is only an impressionable kid, and while I've known you and know you wouldn't, but suppose you had some friends in, and. . . . ?"

I suggested that he not come for the weekend. I have never molested a child my whole life through, never seduced anybody, assuming that word has meaning, and, so far as I know, neither have any of my homosexual friends. Certainly not in my living room or bedroom. Moreover, I have known quite a few homosexuals, and I have listened to a great many accounts of how they got that way or think they got that way. I have never heard anybody say that he (or she) got to be homosexual because of seduction.

But then maybe it is contagious, floating in the air around me, like a virus. Homosexuals themselves often seem to think so. How else can you explain the self-pitying "The Boys in the Band"?

Martin Hoffman, the San Francisco therapist I mentioned earlier, says: "Self-condemnation pervades the homosexual world and, in concert with the psychodynamic and biological factors that lead toward promiscuity, makes stable relationships a terrific problem. In spite of the fact that so many homosexuals are lonely and alone, they can't seem to find someone with whom to share even part of their lives. This dilemma is the core problem of the gay world and stems in large measure from the adverse self-definitions that society imprints on the homosexual mind. Until we can change these ancient attitudes, many men—including some of our own brothers, sons, friends, colleagues and children yet unborn—will live out their lives in the quiet desperation of the sad gay world."

Perhaps. None of my homosexual friends are any too happy, but then very few of my heterosexual friends—supposed friends, I should say—are exactly joyous, either. And as for the promiscuity and short-term relationships, neither of those has been quite true in my case, and only recently I attended an anniversary party of two homosexuals who had been toegther for 25 years, reasonably constant, reasonably happy. They still hold hands, though not in public, and they are kind to each other, which is rare enough anywhere these days.

Late in October members of the Gay Activists' Alliance staged an all-day sit-in at Harper's to protest the Epstein article surely the first time in the 120-year history of the magazine that that has happened. And as Peter Fisher, a student at Columbia who helped organize the sit-in, kept saying, "What you don't understand is that there's been a revolution."

I'm not sure it's a full-scale revolution yet, but there's been a revolt, and for thousands of young homosexuals, and some not so young, the quiet desperation that Hoffman talks about is all over. They are neither quiet nor desperate.

The whole thing began with an event that has been compared to the Boston Tea Party or the firing on Fort Sumter: the Stonewall Rebellion. On June 28, 1969, the police started to raid a gay bar in the West Village, the Stonewall Inn. The police are forever raiding gay bars, especially around election time, when they also move in on West 42d Street. And in the past, what you did was, you took the cops' abuse, and sometimes you went off with only a few familiar epithets or a hit on the head. And sometimes you were taken to the station on one charge or another and, usually, released the next morning.

But that is not what happened on June 28, 1969. A friend of mine who was there said, "It was fantastic. The crowd was a fairly typical weekend crowd, your usual queens and kids from the sticks, and the people that are always around the bars, mostly young. But this time instead of submitting to the cops' abuse, the sissies fought back. They started pulling up parking meters and throwing rocks and coins at the cops, and the cops had to take refuge in the bar and call for reinforcements. . . . It was beautiful."

That was the beginning, and on the anniversary last summer between 5,000 and 15,000 gay people of both sexes marched up Sixth Avenue from Sheridan Square to the Sheep Meadow in Central Park for a "gay-in." Other, smaller parades took place in Chicago and Los Angeles, and all three cities survived the sight and sound of men with their arms around men and women kissing women, chanting, "Shout it loud, gay is proud," "3-5-7-9, Lesbians are mighty fine," carrying signs that said, "We Are the People Our Parents Warned Us Against," singing "We Shall Overcome."

And something else perhaps even more important happened last

June. When Arthur J. Goldberg paid what was to have been a routine campaign visit to the intersection of 85th and Broadway, more than three dozen members of the G.A.A. were waiting for him. They shook his hand and asked if he was in favor of fair employment for homosexuals and of repeal of the state laws against sodomy. Goldberg's answer to each question was, "I think there are more important things to think about."

But before the election Goldberg had issued a public statement answering yes to both questions, promising as well to work against police harassment of homosexuals. Richard Ottinger and Charles Goodell also issued statements supporting constitutional rights for homosexuals. Of course, Rockefeller and Buckley, the winners, remained silent on those issues, but Bella Abzug, one of the earliest supporters of G.A.A., won, and so did people like Antonio Olivieri, the first Democrat elected in the 66th Assembly District in 55 years. Olivieri took an ad in a G.A.A. benefit program that served to thank the organization for its support.

Marty Robinson, an extremely vocal young man, a carpenter by profession, who was then in charge of political affairs for G.A.A., said that "this election serves notice on every politician in the state and nation that homosexuals are not going to hide any more. We're becoming militant, and we won't be harassed or degraded any more."

John Francis Hunter, one of the alliance's founders, said: "G.A.A. is a political organization. Everything is done with an eye toward political effect. . . . G.A.A. adopted this policy because all oppression of homosexuals can only be ended by means of a powerful political bloc."

For an organization only a little more than a year old and with only 180 paid-up members, G.A.A. has certainly made itself heard. And that, according to Arthur Evans, another fiery member, is just the beginning. He said: "At the end of June we had a statement that gay is good. We had a joyous celebration, as is right. But today we know not only that gay is good, gay is angry. We are telling all the politicians and elected officials of New York State that they are going to become responsible to the people. We will make them responsible to us, or we will stop the conduct of the business of government." Well.

Small wonder that the Mattachine Society, which for 20 years has been trying to educate straight people to accept homosexuals, is now dismissed by some members of G.A.A. and the Gay Liberation Front as "the N.A.A.C.P. of our movement."

Laws discriminating against homosexuals will almost surely be changed. If not this year, in 1972; if not in 1972, in 1976; if not in 1976 . . .

Private acceptance of homosexuals and homosexuality will take somewhat longer. Most of the psychiatric establishment will continue to insist that homosexuality is a disease, and homosexuals, unlike the blacks, will not benefit from any guilt feelings on the part of liberals. So far as I can make out, there simply aren't any such feelings. On the contrary, most people of every political persuasion seem to be too uncertain of their own sexual identification to be anything but defensive. Fearful. And maybe it is contagious. Prove it isn't.

I have never infected anybody, and it's too late for the head people to do anything about me now. Gay is good. Gay is proud. Well, yes, I suppose. If I had been given a choice (but who is?), I would prefer to have been straight. But then would I rather not have been me? Oh, I think not, not this morning anyway. It is a very clear day in late December, and the sun is shining on the pine trees outside my studio. The air is extraordinarily clear, and the sky is the color it gets only at this time of year, dark, almost navy blue. On such a day I would not choose to be anyone else or any place else.

## Study Guide

1.   Why does Miller begin his essay with the quotation from E. M. Forster? How does the quotation qualify your response to the remainder of the essay?

2.   To what extent does the experience of the homosexual in America parallel that of members of racial or ethnic minorities? How is it different?

3.   What attitude does the author have toward his own homosexuality? What attitude does he want the reader to have toward him?

4.   To what extent does Miller succeed in undercutting the traditional prejudices against sexual deviation? Why does he succeed or fail?

5.   Does our society's treatment of homosexuals parallel its treatment of women?

6.   Miller concludes his essay with the statement: "If I had been given a choice (but who is?) I would prefer to have been straight." How does this admission affect your response to his essay?

7.   Investigate the local and state laws that attempt to regulate sexual conduct in your community. Are such laws just or do they infringe upon private morality? Present your conclusions in a documented essay.

8.   Do you feel that laws that discriminate against homosexuals are comparable to those laws that might discriminate against blacks or women or some other minority group in our society? Present your opinion in the form of a letter to the editor of your local newspaper.

9.   Homosexuals are frequently stereotyped by our society. Describe that stereotype in a brief paragraph. Then try to determine whether or not Merle Miller succeeds in convincing you that the stereotype is inaccurate. Present your opinion in a brief essay.

# 21. The Feast

DANIEL WRIGHT

## Author's Note

The Feast, *it must be mentioned, was written with a particular
performance situation in mind—a situation in which this play
was to be one of several short plays produced before an audience.
In this sense it is a self-conscious play; it seems to comment upon
the nature of drama. It seems to make fun not only of its own
inherent pretense as a play but of the pretense of the other plays
produced along with it. As the play begins, it literally tears
down the flats and machinery of the play which preceded it.
As for itself, it is apologetic. The character Blue Jeans, who
introduces it and is, in a sense, the major-domo of the play, is
not a self-assured actor—he is not an actor at all, but a bashful,
stumbling underling of the theater. Timidly he wishes to communicate a special emotion he feels and a special vision he sees.
Consistently, his two characters are insignificant like himself.*
 *The play is the lunch hour of two construction workers.
The Old Man has led a life which we may guess has been unsuccessful in a material sense—in old age he is still a manual
laborer. The Young Man can see perhaps little more than such a*

*menial life ahead of him. Both characters possess a measure of pride, and they are both great pretenders because of this pride, though in different ways. The Young Man disclaims any part of the world he is in; his pseudo–anger comes from this disclaimer. The Old Man, on the other hand, has learned to glorify his life out of insignificance, through his imagination, and so to reconcile himself with his life.*

*The major technique of the play, seemingly to create itself out of nothing, acts as a metaphor of the Old Man's imaginative process. The Old Man becomes a teacher and the Young Man, in spite of himself, a willing student of this art of imaginative reconciliation. Blue Jeans sympathizes with his characters and helps them with their illusions. The lunch hour becomes a feast indeed. Yet, the play leaves with a trembling, perhaps tragic, realization: surely there is strength in the Old Man to accept the joy of the Feast as untarnished by the fact that it springs only from desire and illusion.*

## CHARACTERS

BLUE JEANS
OLD MAN
ANGRY YOUNG MAN
ELF WITH CHAMPAGNE (*Blue Jeans disguised*)
DROWSY CELLIST (*likewise*)

*The curtains open . . . and . . . it must be some kind of mistake. The stage crew is still putting up sets. But no one seems to be much bothered by the fact. It might be a nice touch, though, to have a director, troubled species, to look up and notice. He might shout some muffled expletive off stage about who was the fool who opened the curtains etc., when they weren't ready. But in any case, the stage work-lights remain on, the stage work continues, somebody's complaining about a costume that doesn't fit, and damnitall if the curtains don't stay open. Now some character in blue jeans and spotted shirt comes out along the front of the stage. He is carrying an easel over his shoulder, a large piece of cardboard in his hand, and a pot of paint. For the sake of somebody's reputation, he might smile an apology to the audience. At any rate, when he gets to the opposite end of the stage, he sets up his easel, places the cardboard upon it facing the audience, and paints—rather scrawls, "THE FEAST." He puts his pot of paint aside and sits down on the stage next to his easel. He looks out at the audience and, twirling his glasses in his hand, begins:*

BLUE JEANS.    Well, now . . . no one said it was going to be an extraordinary sort of play . . . I mean, as a matter of fact, it's quite an ordinary sort of . . . Believe me, it doesn't deserve much of . . . You know, come to think of it, it's such an ordinary . . . I mean, I, for one, wouldn't feel so bad about dispensing with . . . uh . . . that is, I don't want to bother them for the sake of the feast. After all, you start stomping around on the grounds of every whim and . . . well, people get mad. So, we'll just let them go on working . . . go on, go right on and . . . then we can maybe sneak in this bit . . . (*He saunters back among the stagemen and, in a pantomime, wangles two tin buckets, which he brings forward, arranging them about five feet apart.*) . . . I've got friends . . . or, sometimes I seem to . . . CHARLIE (*Calls over audience.*) hey . . . HEY CHARLIE . . . (*A spot comes on, and* BLUE JEANS *waves it over to where he is standing between the buckets. The stage work-lights remain on.* B.J. *places a can on top of one of the buckets.*) I've got characters too, or sometimes I seem . . . they are supposed to arrive . . . (*Factory whistle.* BLUE JEANS *holds up his hand to the audience, nods his head.*) . . . a whistle, if you hadn't guessed, and it signals the start of this play. It makes a suitable sound to start a play? . . . right? It blows, and people change . . . you know, it toots, and people are possessed by it. It beckons in the harbor, and people look up expectant. Maybe it calls from the factory stacks . . . feet move, sometimes a smile . . . and you know it's our own creation, but we pray in our exertion to . . . A CHERUB OUT THERE perhaps. He looks down and chuckles at our business, but the takes up his horn and sounds pause, "take pause" . . . (*The whistle blows again.* B.J. *is about ready to climb down in the orchestra—but one final word.*) . . . and so on, so forth. (*He makes himself comfortable in the first row.* OLD MAN *is heard humming outside.*)
OLD MAN (*enters through the audience down the center aisle. He is*

*wearing spotted, baggy work pants supported from the shoulders of a red plaid wool shirt by suspenders. He is characterized by an ambling, joyful gait, and when he speaks, it is with the friendly, booming quality of a man who has found a sense of self-assurance and contentment. Go ahead and ham him up . . . no danger. You might as well. He walks all the way down the center aisle, swinging a lunch pail at his side, singing. He sings to the tune of "Freight train, freight train . . .").*   Lunch hour, lunch hour, goin' so faaaast . . . Lunch hour, lunch hour, goin' so faaast . . . Dum de dum, de dum de donn . . . so they won't know where I've gone . . . *(Climbs stage, eventually sees the tin can on the one bucket.)* . . . AH HA! Miserable tin can of a man that I am . . . counting the minutes till your lunch hour comes . . . *(Kicks the can off the bucket.)* TAKE THAT! . . . (OLD MAN *gazes after the can and chuckles contentedly.*)

*(Several of the stage crew members are still working on the sets, but they are making less noise now. One of the crew calls "Lights!" off stage, and the stage work-lights go off. The red and white border lights remain on, along with the spot centered on the* OLD MAN *and on the two buckets . . .* OLD MAN *puts his lunch pail in front of him, and as he opens it,* ANGRY YOUNG MAN *enters from the side. He is wearing old pants and a denim jacket—on his head a battered tweed golf cap. He sits down on the second bucket and . . . facing the audience like the* OLD MAN, *explores the contents of his paper bag. During the conversation that follows,* OLD MAN *eats his lunch out of his lunch pail,* YOUNG MAN, *out of his paper sack.* OLD MAN *chews his lunch in delight.* YOUNG MAN *rips at his lunch in anger. They are about finished with lunch by the time the "feast" begins.* YOUNG MAN *is characterized by brooding, suspicious expressions of a rebelliousness which, I guess, he considers attractive. Certainly he holds no distinct notions of revolt, because you see, indications are that* YOUNG MAN *isn't all that bright. But anyway,* OLD MAN *hums;* YOUNG MAN *broods, and neither seems conscious of the other until* OLD MAN *glances over at* YOUNG MAN *and says offhandedly:*)

Ah, you are here too . . . So you have come to join in the Great, Green Lunch Hour—that moment of rapture and dizzy joy, that . . . uh, moment of freedom! and . . . *(No response from* ANGRY YOUNG MAN.) . . . so you have come too?

YOUNG MAN (*glances around, realizes that* OLD MAN *has spoken to him*). Yeah, sure, I mean, what do you mean? . . . of course I am here . . . I mean I DON'T EVEN KNOW YOU, OLD MAN!

OLD MAN. As you wish . . . was just trying to make conversation.

YOUNG MAN. Humph. (*Lights begin to fade.*)

OLD MAN. There's this little game, see, that I know . . . makes new acquaintances come much easier . . .

YOUNG MAN. Humph. (*Spot remains on.*)

OLD MAN. It starts out, you see, by me asking a question . . . I ask you, "What did you have for breakfast this morning, stranger?"

YOUNG MAN. Yeah?

OLD MAN. Well, what did you have for breakfast this morning, stranger?

YOUNG MAN (*suspiciously*). Well, let me see now . . . I had a big bowl of Sugar Crisp—yes, and a cup of coffee from the machine.

OLD MAN. Now I tell you what I had for breakfast. I had this magnificent combination of Wheat Chex . . . I really like Wheat Chex . . . and orange juice, sausage, eggs—poached with pepper—and toast with plenty of kumquat jam . . .

YOUNG MAN. Look here, what kind of a game is this?

OLD MAN. Why . . . it's called the comparative breakfasts game.

YOUNG MAN (*throwing his hat to the floor*). LOOK HERE, OLD MAN . . . WHAT DIFFERENCE DOES IT MAKE WHAT I HAD FOR BREAKFAST ANYWAY . . . I mean, A MAN'S BREAKFAST IS HIS OWN BUSINESS . . . (Y.M. *sputters, dusts off his hat and goes back to his lunch bag.*)

OLD MAN. Exactly . . . you see, disclosing one's breakfast, a very intimate matter indeed, presumes acquaintance and avoids all sorts of embarrassment. Now if I were to tell you what I'm having for lunch . . . for instance, I say, "Well, lemme see, I've got a boiled egg and a thermos of vegetable beef soup and . . . a salomy 'n' lettuce on rye . . . (*Gleefully exhibits the contents of his lunch pail.*)

YOUNG MAN. LOOK HERE . . . I don't happen to be interested in your breakfast, or your lunch, or even your fridgin' dinner, for that matter . . .

(*Long pause.*)

OLD MAN. It's such a pleasant day out. I just thought maybe . . .

YOUNG MAN. Hey, Dad . . . So happens I think it's a lousy rotten day, and so happens I don't like eating lunch out here in this lousy, rotten storage lot . . . out of a lousy, rotten paper bag. So happens it's a grubby, lousy city in a grubby, rotten world filled up with a lotta grubby, lousy, rotten people . . . try that out for size on the old wazoo.

(OLD MAN *takes a crunchy bite from an apple.*)

OLD MAN. Why, I'd say you are bitter . . . you are bitter, aren't you?

YOUNG MAN. Yeah . . . I am . . . I'm real bitter (*Throws hat on floor again.*) WHAT'YA MEAN BITTER, ANYWAY? . . . WHAT KIND OF QUESTION'S *THAT?* AND WHAT IF I AM . . . (*Turns his back on* O.M., *who shrugs his shoulder. They go back to their lunch.*)

OLD MAN. Well . . . I was just interested, you know . . . I mean bitter people don't usually . . . don't come here, that is . . .

YOUNG MAN (*challenged*). What do you mean?

OLD MAN. But . . . come to the feast, of course.

YOUNG MAN. The WHAT?

OLD MAN. . . . the feast . . .

YOUNG MAN. Oh, "the feast" . . . look, if that's some underhanded way of telling me you don't like my company, it don't wash, see Dad . . . I've got as much right to this crummy can as the next Joe . . . and so maybe you don't like me, well that's just tough potatoes.

OLD MAN. Oh, you can do what you like . . . the feast is quite open, you know . . . I don't mean to say you weren't invited, in fact this very moment I ask you to be my special guest.

YOUNG MAN. Guest?

OLD MAN. Yes, at the feast.

YOUNG MAN. Yeah, sure, what feast?

OLD MAN. Right now . . . here.

YOUNG MAN. What the fat kind of a feast you expect to have out in this crummy lot . . . I know about feasts, you think I'm dumb or something? . . . You think I'm dumb? My old lady used to tell me about feasts. She used to work at the Regis, and she used to bring junk back to the place and tell me about all the food and the people getting potted and dancing and smoking big cigars.

OLD MAN. Well, you see, this feast is a little different. I mean, your mother . . .

YOUNG MAN. You can leave her out of this. What gives you the right to sit there and . . .

OLD MAN. Really, I'm sure your mother is a very fine woman. I just want to explain . . .

YOUNG MAN. Well, for your information, so happens the old lady can take it in the ear for all I'm concerned.

(*Long pause.*)

OLD MAN. Let me explain about the feast.

YOUNG MAN. OK, OK, I'm willing to go along with a gag . . . the feast . . . shoot.

OLD MAN. Well take, for example, that little fellow over there on the corner playing the flute.

YOUNG MAN. Where . . . you mean that corner?

OLD MAN. Yes, over there . . . the little fellow with the flute.

YOUNG MAN. Oh, yeah. You mean the traffic cop—sure, I see the traffic cop.

OLD MAN. NO! NO! Not the traffic cop . . . "traffic cop" . . . the little fellow on the corner with a red bandana on his head playing the *flute!*

YOUNG MAN. The newsboy . . . maybe?

OLD MAN. NO! Not the newsboy . . . you mean to say you don't see a little man wearing a green coat and a red bandana, dancing around the bus stop sign, playing a flute? (*He makes a motion as if playing a flute.*)

YOUNG MAN. LOOK! I don't see any little guy in a green coat and a red bandana dancing around any bus stop sign, playing any fridgin' flute on THAT CORNER!

OLD MAN. Well, I suppose that's understandable.

YOUNG MAN. OK. What's the catch?

OLD MAN. My fine young man, any fool, if he uses his eyes, can plainly see that there is no little man with a flute and a bandana . . . quite obviously, he is not there.

YOUNG MAN (*pause, nods his head, barely restraining his impulse to throw his hat on the floor*). Yes, I . . . I see . . . yes, that . . . come to think of it . . . that's surely the reason why I couldn't see the guy with the flute.

OLD MAN. Now, the feast is about the same as the little man with the flute, you know.

YOUNG MAN. Yeah, I get it, you mean I'm not going to be able to see the feast either . . . well, you didn't have to tell me that!

OLD MAN. NO, NO . . . not in the least . . . you see the feast is like the little man because it is not . . . for the most part, essentially and in *factum* . . . there.

YOUNG MAN. Yeah, sure . . . but, uh . . . how we going to have the feast if it is not there? . . . or here?

OLD MAN. Ah . . . no more time to explain . . . the feast is about to begin. But there's one small matter to settle first.

YOUNG MAN. And what's that?

OLD MAN. Why, the sort of feast that you prefer, of course.

YOUNG MAN. Now, don't tell me we have a choice even . . . of feasts, that is.

OLD MAN. Absolutely! You have the broadest choice of all the choices, so you just say which it is that you prefer, and we will see what we can do.

YOUNG MAN. Yes, well . . . I'm not exactly up on this feast jazz. What sort of choices do I have?

OLD MAN. GREAT SCOTT! Let's see . . . you have wedding feasts, birthday feasts, feasts for coronation celebrations, vengeance feasts, mercy feasts and . . . funeral feasts, war feasts, peace feasts . . . whether you win or lose, you always have a feast . . . and you have feasts for kings, feasts for thieves, demagogues, churchmen, salesmen, boatmen, law men, small men . . . let's see, there are New Year feasts, Easter feasts, Christmas, Halloween, Arbor Day, Ground Hog's Day . . .

YOUNG MAN. Yes, but there's really no fridgin' reason to have a feast, come right down to it.

OLD MAN. I was hoping you'd say that, because you see, that's the best sort of feast to have.

YOUNG MAN. Sure . . . what's that?

OLD MAN. Why, the feast for no fridgin' . . . er, Phrygian reason, as you put it.

YOUNG MAN. Yeah, sure . . . that's bound to be the best . . . uh, feast.

OLD MAN. Certainly the best . . . no red tape of emotion to tangle up the revelry, no sticky cause, you see . . . no cloud of duty hanging overhead . . . yes, the feast for feast's sake is, without a doubt, the best.

YOUNG MAN. Anything you say, Dad . . . it's your show, but seriously, how're you going to have any kind of a feast when all you've got left is half a salomy 'n' lettuce, and me . . . (*Holding up his sandwich fragment.*) . . .

OLD MAN. Come, lad . . . the feast is not essentially a matter for eating. Food is but a key to the door where most any key will fit, you see . . . It is that moment when the appetite is satisfied, when hunger is bubbled away (*Slaps his stomach.*), and the door opens on the magical landscape of the FEAST! (OLD MAN *strikes a dramatic pose and slowly lifts his hands to the ceiling.* YOUNG MAN *sits awed at the* OLD MAN'S *invocation. The spotlight is by now the only light on the stage.*) OH, BACCHUS! SPIRIT OF MIRTH! SPIRIT OF SONG! LOOK DOWN WITH FAVOR UPON US . . . SMILE THE SMILE OF MERRIMENT, for why have we come but for the sake of merriment? Do we come to honor the living or the dead? Do we come to goad ourselves to victory or to cheer the victory already won? NO! Do we come in the guise of charity and pity? Or do we come in the guise of business and serious matters? NO! NONE OF THESE! WE HAVE COME TO THIS GRAND FEAST FOR NO FRIDGING . . . er, PHRYGIAN REASON AT ALL! . . . so to speak—but for the sake of merriment. Let us, oh Bacchus, celebrate this moment!

YOUNG MAN (*whispering to* OLD MAN). Hey, cut it out! You want somebody to see us and think we're nuts? You want to be shipped off to the booby hatch or something?

OLD MAN. . . . I look upon the vaulted hall, the ranks of bountiful tables smiling in their candlelight. I see kindred faces, expectant faces . . . How best to celebrate this occasion which is, of course, no occasion, we ask. I present to you our special guest (OLD MAN *waves an arm in* YOUNG MAN'S *direction.* YOUNG MAN *shrinks back.*) Here is a mind of vigor and youth. He represents a promise for our age . . .

YOUNG MAN (*whispering*). *Look here, Old Man,* I don't know what you're up to, but I sure as fat don't like it. I didn't ask to get into this. I . . . I was sucked into this flaming feast, you know damn well I was . . . come on now.

OLD MAN. Ladies and gentlemen, I present to you a young man with depth of spirit, breadth of heart, and fullness of imagination . . .

YOUNG MAN (*still whispering*). This is no fair, you tricked me . . . you trapped me . . . you . . . (*Shouts in* OLD MAN'S *ear.*) . . . FRUITCAKE! (OLD MAN *not fazed.* YOUNG MAN *hastily stoops to pick up his bag and lunch papers, puts on his cap in preparation for flight.*)

OLD MAN. . . . in short, I present to you the Angry Young Man. (OLD MAN *catches* YOUNG MAN *by the sleeve and leads him into the spotlight.*)

YOUNG MAN. Look here, this gag of yours has gone far enough . . .

go right ahead and spout off if you want, just leave me out of it . . . uh, just feast it by yourself, why don't you?

OLD MAN (*whispering*).   Don't spoil it all . . . this is part of the bit. There always has to be some sort of a keynote speech at every feast.

YOUNG MAN.   But really, Dad. This is ridiculous . . . I mean, really.

OLD MAN.   I don't know what you're so worried about. All you have to do is to say a few words to them . . .

YOUNG MAN.   To WHO?

OLD MAN.   To them . . . (*Indicates the audience.*) It's just part of the bit, you know.

YOUNG MAN.   OK, OK. Nobody's going to say I'm not a good sport, a good Joe, an all right guy . . . just so long as you agree that if someone happens to come by, it's all a joke, see . . . Let's make this short . . . what am I supposed to say?

OLD MAN.   Well, let me see . . . you ought to say something about the reason for the feast which, of course, will be a hard part . . . you just say what you like. Yes, and add something about how distinguished the audience is . . . appeal to the emotions, their pity, amuse them, flatter them, agree with them . . .

YOUNG MAN.   OK, anything you say. Remember, I'm just going along with the gag. (*Takes off his hat and faces the audience with an embarrassed smile, then turns towards the* OLD MAN *again.*) Aw, come on. This is crazy.

OLD MAN (*whispering*).   Go on, go on . . .

YOUNG MAN (*turns to the audience, smiling again*).   Ladies and gentlemen . . . I'm not much on speeches really . . . (*Turns.*) How's that?

OLD MAN.   Fine, fine. Their sympathy is already with you.

YOUNG MAN (*facing the audience again*).   . . . and believe me, it's like a great honor to be here at this moment before you. Now let me tell you about a funny thing that happened to me during my lunch hour. I was sitting there, see, and this old geezer invites me to this feast, just for a gag (*Glances at* OLD MAN.) and so . . . uh, here I am. And the introduction that the Old Man gave me was way out . . . I mean it was too much. But, consider the reason why we are all here . . . What is the reason we're all here, after all? . . . Damned if I know. Man, the whole thing is really . . . uh, crazy. (*Glances at* OLD MAN.) Well, there doesn't seem to be any reason for being here—how about all the reasons for not being here? Just put that in your pipe and smoke it. Just think of all the things you might be doing instead of wasting your time at this, uh . . . feast. You could be putting the garbage out. You could be running over rabbits in your car (*Whispers "Pity" to* OLD MAN, *who nods his head in approval.*) . . . you could be shoplifting in a super-market or thinking up nasty comments to make to your mother-in-law. Just THINK of all the temptations you might be yielding to if you weren't wasting your time here, feasting it up . . . It's great to have you here and . . . So go right ahead and feast it up because it's great to be here (*Glances at* OLD MAN *for approval.*) and besides that, you are all really great people, and I really agree with you about everything . . . thank you. (*Turns to* OLD MAN.) How was that?

OLD MAN.  That was great, just great . . . but wait, you may be called on to make a few toasts.

YOUNG MAN (*brow-beaten and confused*).  Just give the word, Dad . . . I can't make any more a fool of myself. (*He sits down, shaking his head.*)

OLD MAN.  We thank the Angry Young Man for his remarks, always apt, well-chosen, short, and to the point. But the time for invocation has passed; the moment of preparation is accomplished . . . Therefore, GIVE US WINE! Let us lift up our glasses and so lift up our hearts. (OLD MAN *looks down at the front row seat where* BLUE JEANS *is sitting.*) PSSSSST! That's your cue . . . the wine . . . (BLUE JEANS *gets up from his seat, goes back up the ladder, and is to be seen at one end of the stage, putting on a short green coat and wrapping a red bandana around his head, both of which were handed out to him from the wings.*)

YOUNG MAN.  Wine?

OLD MAN.  Of course. How can you drink a toast without wine?

YOUNG MAN.  Yeah, sure. This I gotta see. (*Follows* BLUE JEANS *off stage in amazement.*)

OLD MAN.  . . . Bring flushes to our cheeks and so flush the general spirit with unemcumbered mirth. (*A cart is pushed out onto the stage, and* BLUE JEANS *trundles it out towards the spotlight. The cart holds a bucket of ice with a bottle of champagne and several glasses.*) Sniff gently the wine's bouquet and rejoice in its sweet vapor. Smile, laugh . . . feel warmth. (ELF *with champagne, i.e.,* BLUE JEANS, *rolls the cart into the spotlight.* YOUNG MAN *stares* at him wide-eyed. BLUE JEANS *answers the stare with an embarrassed shrug.* B.J. *pours out two glasses and hands one to* OLD MAN, *one to* YOUNG MAN.) I PROPOSE A TOAST . . . (*Lifts up his glass*) . . . TO THE FEAST . . . THE FEAST FOR NO FRIDGIN' . . . PHRYGIAN REASON, so the expression goes. (*Drinks, motioning to* YOUNG MAN *to do the same.*)

YOUNG MAN (*after lowering his glass*). This is ridiculous . . .

OLD MAN. TO THE RIDICULOUS, THEN! (*They drink.*)

YOUNG MAN. This is UNREAL!

OLD MAN. TO THE UNREAL, IF YOU LIKE! (*They drink again.*)

YOUNG MAN. But I mean . . . really . . .

OLD MAN. DRINK! (*Drinks again. As* BLUE JEANS *refills the glasses,* OLD MAN *whispers to* YOUNG MAN.) Now it's your turn to make the toast . . . (YOUNG MAN *hesitates.*) Go on, go on.

YOUNG MAN. Well, OK . . . I propose a toast to, uh . . .

OLD MAN. WHY NOT?!

YOUNG MAN (*slumping down on the bucket*). This is too much . . . (BLUE JEANS *has been sneaking a few drinks himself.*)

OLD MAN. All right, all right. So much for the toasts. (*Smacks his lips.*) Let's on to the reading of the ode.

YOUNG MAN. Yeah, sure, "The Ode"!

OLD MAN. Any kind of feast that's worth its salt has a reading of a commemorative ode . . . (*Takes a piece of paper from his shirt pocket and unfolds it.*) . . . You don't want to read the ode, do you? Some people say the special guest should always read the ode.

YOUNG MAN. Oh, no . . . uh, you just go right ahead, and I'll just sort of sit here and listen.

OLD MAN. As you prefer. (*During this time,* BLUE JEANS *has taken off his green coat and bandana, handing them off stage. He runs to the other side of the stage and slips into a tails coat and buttons on a white tie. He carries a cello and a small stool out to the edge of the spotlight, sits down and prepares to play. He yawns and stretches, waiting for* OLD MAN *to begin the reading of the ode.*) I present to you the ODE, forever commemorating this feast . . . our feast without reason or occasion.

(OLD MAN *motions for the* CELLIST *to begin his background music, waits a moment, then sighing, begins. As the ode progresses,* CELLIST *falls almost asleep, bowing of cello is spasmodic, but recorded music plays on.*)

Oh Bacchus, look this way!
See the anger mapping lines upon our brow, trace the print of trouble's foot around our eyes—
Dismal creatures we must seem, cowering behind the day's affairs,
Grasping tight to tin toy soldiers of our objective lives, staring, as imagination dies;
See our mental siege and send down laughing legions to set us free.

Thus did we call out to Bacchus, and he raised a drunken eyebrow to our plea.
He sent to us, not legions, but a Cherub from his troop,
One small, fat, sodden Cherub (*Looks at* BLUE JEANS.) from his troop.

Oh Cherub, harken to our woe!
Listen, minor spirit of the feast, fledgling sent by Bacchus giving answer to our plea,
Thou, who now would far rather be thronged among thy master's ranks,
Voicing his choral praise, or tipping the Olympian cup upon your lip to drain his liquid revelry,
*Listen to our labor's chant, and grant, at least, a momentary feast!*
Thus, did we call out to the Cherub Bacchus sent, still pouting from his journey,
He blinked his eyes, and then his pudgy mouth gaped open in a yawn,
But he gave us music, and he gave us wine before our time was up.

(*Factory whistle blows. All characters look up. The lights begin to fade on again.* BLUE JEANS *takes his cello and stool off stage, along with his costume. He comes back out and grabs the glasses away from* YOUNG MAN, *who resists, and from* OLD MAN, *who is resigned.* BLUE JEANS *trundles the champagne cart off stage. The lights come up quickly now. The stage work-lights are flipped on. The stage crew members begin to return to their task of putting up sets.*)

YOUNG MAN (*looking around him, bewildered*). The wine . . . the guy with the . . . uh, violin? Where have they gone? The feast . . . what happened?

OLD MAN. Time was up, that's all.

YOUNG MAN. What do you mean, the time was up . . . I mean they were all here . . . and your ode? Where's your ode?

OLD MAN (*checking through his pockets*). I guess I lost it . . . (*He had set it down on the cart.*) . . . anyway, you heard the whistle, didn't you . . . back to work, you know. (*Cheerful.*)

YOUNG MAN. I guess so . . . (OLD MAN *climbs down the ladder after gathering up his things.* YOUNG MAN *puts his lunch papers in the paper bag and crumples it up. He gazes up the aisle as* OLD MAN *leaves.*)

OLD MAN (*turns somewhere up the aisle*). So long, Young Man . . .

YOUNG MAN. So long, Old Man . . . (*Turns and walks slowly off stage pondering something. As he goes,* BLUE JEANS *bustles out from the wings, gathers up his easel and cardboard and ladder. In his rush he bumps into* YOUNG MAN, *says, "Excuse me . . .".* YOUNG MAN *barely notices.*)

(BLUE JEANS *bustles off the other side of the stage; someone among the stage crew looks up, and noticing that some damn fool has opened the curtain when they weren't ready, shouts some expletive off stage.*)

(*The curtains close hurriedly.*)

## Study Guide

1.  The author tells us that *The Feast* is a self-conscious play that comments on the nature of the theater and makes fun of its pretenses. Explain and illustrate the meaning of these assertions.

2.  In his first speech, the old man describes his lunch hour as his moment of freedom. From what is he freed? How does he achieve freedom?

3.  At the old man's insistence, the two characters engage in the comparative breakfast game. What does this concentration on the trivial tell us? How do we respond to the excitement the old man finds in the game and in the contents of his lunch?

4.  How do you account for the young man's reaction to the old, and the manner in which it changes during the play?

5.  What reasons might the old man have for celebrating the feast?

6.  Why does the young man let himself be drawn into the fantasy? Consider his speech to the audience.

7.  The young man has been a reluctant, even hostile participant in the feast. How do you account for his sorrow at its conclusion? How do you account for the old man's cheerful return to work?

8.  Are the characters in the play contending with any of the problems that Fromm discussed?

9.  Can you find parallels between what happens in the play and what happens to you when you attend a film or a theatrical presentation?

10. In this play, the old man engages the young man in an elaborate game, forcing him into a fantasy world. In what situations do we play games to escape from reality?

11. Select some game that you or someone you know may play and construct a play around it.

# "Whose Country Is America"

# 22. Whose Country is America

ERIC HOFFER

## The Young and the Middle-Aged

The conspicuous role played by the young in our society at present has prompted a widely held assumption that the young constitute a higher percentage of the population than they did in the past. Actually, in this country, the percentage of the under-25 age group has remained fairly constant through several decades—it hovers around 47 per cent. The high-school and college age group—14 to 24—has remained close to 15 per cent. The nation as a whole has not been getting younger. The median age of all Americans in 1910 was 24. Today it is 27, and it is likely to go up since the birth rate right now is very low.

The conspicuousness of the young is due to their greater visibility and audibility. They have become more flamboyant, more demanding, more violent, more knowledgeable and more experienced. The general impression is that nowadays the young act like the spoiled children of the rich. We are discovering that there is such a thing as an "ordeal of affluence," that diffused affluence subjects the social

Adapted from Chapters 5 and 6 of *First Things, Last Things,* by Eric Hoffer. (Originally appeared in *The New York Times Magazine,* Nov. 1970 under the title "Whose Country is America"). Copyright © 1970 by Eric Hoffer. Reprinted by permission of Harper & Row, Publishers, Inc.

order to greater strain and threatens social stability more than does diffused poverty. Order and discipline have up to now been attributes generated in the battle against want. Society itself originated in the vital need for a joint effort to wrest a livelihood from grudging nature. Not only our material but our moral and spiritual values are predicated on the immemorial curse: "In the sweat of thy face shalt thou eat bread." Thus diffused affluence unavoidably creates a climate of disintegrating values with its fallout of anarchy.

In the past, breakdowns of value affected mainly the older segment of the population. This was true of the breakdown of the Graeco-Roman civilization, of the crisis that gave birth to the Reformation, and of the periods of social disintegration that preceded the French, the Russian and the Nazi revolutions. That our present crisis particularly affects the young is due partly to the fact that widespread affluence is robbing a modern society of whatever it has left of puberty rites to routinize the attainment of manhood. Never before has the passage from boyhood to manhood been so difficult and explosive. Both the children of the well-to-do and of families on welfare are prevented from having a share in the world's work and of proving their manhood by doing a man's work and getting a man's pay. Crime in the streets and insolence on the campus are sick forms of adolescent self-assertion. The young account for an ever-increasing percentage of crimes against persons and property. The peak years for crimes of violence are 18 to 20, followed by the 21 to 24 age group.

Even under ideal conditions the integration of the young into the adult world is beset with strains and difficulties. We feel ill at ease when we have to adjust ourselves to fit in. The impulse is to change the world to fit us rather than the other way around. Only where there are, as in primitive societies, long established rites of passage, or where the opportunities for individual self-assertion are fabulous, does growing up proceed without excessive growing pains.

Can a modern affluent society institute some form of puberty rites to ease the passage from boyhood to manhood? It is of interest in this connection that among the Bantu tribes in South Africa work is replacing the ritual related to puberty. It used to be that a young man had to kill a lion or an enemy to prove his manhood. Today many young natives do not feel they have become full-fledged adults until they have put in a stint in the mines. Could not a ritual of work be introduced in this country? Every boy and girl on reaching 17, or on graduating from high school, would be given an opportunity to spend two years earning a living at good pay. There is an enormous backlog of work to be done both inside and outside the cities. Federal, state and city governments, and also business and labor would pool their resources to supply the necessary jobs and training.

The routinization of the passage from boyhood to manhood would contribute to the solution of many of our pressing problems. I cannot think of any other undertaking that would dovetail so many of our present difficulties into opportunities for growth.

Though the percentage of the young, as pointed out, has remained constant through several decades, there has been a spectacular increase in the percentage of adolescents. At present, adolescence comprises a wider age range than it did in the past. Affluence is keeping persons in their late 20's in a state of delayed manhood, while television has lowered the threshold of adolescence. Nowadays, 10-year-olds have the style of life and the bearing of adolescents. Even children under 10 have an astounding familiarity with the intricacies and the mechanics of the adult world. By the time a child enters kindergarten, he has spent more hours learning about his world from television than the hours he will spend later in classrooms earning a college degree. It is a paradox that at a time when youths rioting in Chicago are called "mere kids," there are actually few genuine kids any more.

The contemporary blurring of childhood is not unprecedented. During the Middle Ages, children were viewed and treated as miniature adults. Nothing in medieval dress distinguished the child from the adult. The moment children could walk and talk they entered the adult world, and took part in the world's work. In subsequent centuries, the concept of childhood became more clearly defined. Yet even as late as 1835 schoolbooks in this country made no concession to childhood in vocabulary or sophistication. Child labor, so widely practiced in the first half of the 19th century, and which we find abhorrent, was not totally anomalous in a society that did not have a vivid view of childhood as a sheltered, privileged age.

To counteract an old man's tendency to snort at the self-important young, I keep reminding myself that until the middle of the 19th century the young acted effectively as members of political parties, creators of business enterprises, advocates of new philosophical doctrines and leaders of armies. Most of the wars that figure in our history books were fought by teen-agers. There were 14-year-old lieutenants in Louis XIV's armies. In one of his armies the oldest soldier was under 18. The middle-aged came to the fore with the Industrial Revolution. The experience and capital necessary to make an industrialist required a long apprenticeship. One might say that from the middle of the 19th to the middle of the 20th century the world was run by and for the middle-aged. The post-industrial age seems to be groping its way back to an immemorial situation interrupted by the Industrial Revolution.

. . .

The middle-aged came to the fore with the Industrial Revolution. Another way of putting it is that the middle-aged came into their own with the full entrance of the middle class onto the stage of history. The present discomfiture of the middle-aged is a symptom of a downturn in the fortunes of the middle class.

Adolescence as a clearly marked phase in the life of the individual, and the practice of keeping physically mature males in a state of delayed manhood are middle-class phenomena. The young of the working class and of the aristocracy come early in touch with the realities of life, and are not kept waiting in the wings. In neither the working class nor the aristocracy does age have the vital meaning it has in the middle class.

Industrialization was the creation of the middle class. It is questionable whether the spectacular "mastery of things," the taming of nature on a global scale, could have been achieved by other human types. No other ruling class succeeded so well in energizing the masses, and infusing them with an automatic readiness to work. Aristocrats and intellectuals know how to generate in a population a readiness to fight and die, but they cannot induce an uncoerced, wholehearted participation of the masses in the world's work.

Indeed, it is doubtful whether a nonmiddle-class society can be modern. Domination by aristocrats, intellectuals, workers or soldiers results in a return to the past—to feudalism, the Middle Ages, or even the ancient river-valley civilizations. It is not as yet certain whether it is possible to have a free-wheeling science, literature and art, or even a genuine machine age, without a middle class.

Yet, despite its unprecedented achievements, the middle class is just now on the defensive, unsure of its footing. With the consummation of the Industrial Revolution and the approach of affluence the middle class seems to have nowhere to go. It no longer feels itself in possession of the true and only view possible for sensible people. One begins to wonder whether the unglamorous, hard-working middle class, so essential to the process of production in a climate of scarcity, is becoming anachronistic in an age of plenty where distribution is the chief problem. Middle-class society is being strained to the breaking point not, as Marx predicted, by ever-increasing misery but by ever-increasing affluence. The coming of affluence has found the middle class unequipped and unprepared for a return to Eden.

Early in the 19th century, Saint-Simon characterized the coming of the industrial age as the passage "from the management of men to the administration of things." He did not foresee that once the industrial revolution had run its course there would have to come a reversion from the administration of things to the management of men. Up to quite recently, the middle class did not have to bother overmuch with the management of men since scarcity (unfulfilled needs), the factory, long working hours, etc. tamed and disciplined people automatically. Now, with affluence and leisure, people are no longer kept in line by circumstances. Discipline has to be implanted and order enforced from without. It is at this point that "men of words" and charismatic leaders—people who deal with magic—come into their own. The middle class, lacking magic, is bungling the job.

Thus, as the postindustrial age unfolds, we begin to suspect that what is waiting for us around the corner is not a novel future but an immemorial past. It begins to look as if the fabulous century of the middle class and the middle-aged has been a detour, a wild loop that turns upon itself, and ends where it began. We are returning to the rutted highway of history, which we left 100 years ago in a mad rush to tame a savage continent and turn it into a cornucopia of plenty. We see all around us the lineaments of a preindustrial pattern emerging in the postindustrial age. We are rejoining the ancient caravan, a caravan dominated by the myths and magic of élites, and powered by the young.

In this country, the coming of the postindustrial age may mean the loss of all that made America new—the only new thing in the world. America will no longer be the common man's continent. The common people of Europe eloped with history to America and have lived in common-law marriage with it, unhallowed by the incantations of "men of words." But the élites are finally catching up with us. We can hear the swish of leather as saddles are heaved on our backs. The intellectuals and the young, booted and spurred, feel themselves born to ride us.

The phenomenal increase of the student population is shaping the attitudes and aspirations of the young. There are now more students in America than farmers. For the first time in America, there is a chance that alienated intellectuals, who see our way of life as an instrument of debasement and dehumanization, might shape a new generation in their own image. The young's sympathy for the Negro and the poor goes hand in hand with an élitist conceit that pits them against the egalitarian masses. They will fight for the Negro and the poor, but they have no use for common folk who work and moonlight to take care of their own. They see a free-wheeling democracy as a society stupefied by "the narcotic of mass culture." They reserve their wrath for the institutions in which common people are most represented: unions, Congress, the police and the Army. Professor Edgar Z. Friedenberg thinks that "élitism is the great and distinctive contribution students are making to American society." Democracy is for the dropouts; for the élite, an aristocratic brotherhood.

Yet one cannot help but wonder how inevitable is the future that seemingly is waiting for us around the corner. Might not the common people, so cowed and silent at this moment, eventually kick up their heels, and trample would-be élitists in the dirt? There is no earthly reason why the common people who for more than a century have been doing things here that in other countries are reserved for élites, should not be capable of overcoming the present crisis.

## Whose Country?

Nowhere at present is there such a measureless loathing of educated people for their country as in America. An excellent historian thinks Americans are "the most frightening people in the world," and our foremost philologist sees America as "the most aggressive power in the world, the greatest threat to peace and to international cooperation." Others call America a "pig heaven," "a monster with 200 million heads," "a cancer on the body of mankind."

Novelists, playwrights, poets, essayists and philosophers depict America as the land of the dead—a country where sensitive souls are starved and flayed, where nothing nourishes and everything hurts. Nowhere, they say, is there such a boring monotony: monotony of talk, monotony of ideas, monotony of aim, monotony of outlook on the world. One American writer says: "America is no place for an artist. A corn-fed hog enjoys a better life than a creative artist." One she-intellectual maintains that "the quality of American life is an insult to the possibilities of human growth."

It is hard to believe that this savage revulsion derives from specific experiences with persons and places. What is there in America that prevents an educated person from shaping his life, from making the most of his inborn endowments? With all its faults and blemishes, this country gives a man elbowroom to do what is nearest to his heart. It is incredible how easy it is here to cut oneself off from vulgarity, conformity, speciousness, and other corrupting influences and infections. For those who want to be left alone to realize their capacities and talents, this is an ideal country.

The trouble is, of course, that the alienated intellectual does not want to be left alone. He wants to be listened to and be taken seriously. He wants to influence affairs, have a hand in making history, and feel important. He is free to speak and write as he pleases, and can probably make himself heard and read more easily than one who would defend America. But he can neither sway elections nor shape policy. Even when his excellence as a writer, artist, scholar, scientist or educator is generally recognized and rewarded he does not feel himself part of the power structure. In no other country has there been so little liaison between men of words and the men of action who exercise power. The body of intellectuals in America has never been integrated with or congenial to the politicians and businessmen who make things happen. Indeed, the uniqueness of modern America derives in no small part from the fact that America has kept intellectuals away from power and paid little attention to their political views.

The nineteen-sixties have made it patent that much of the intellectual's dissent is fueled by a hunger for power. The appearance of potent allies—militant blacks and students—has emboldened the intellectual to come out into the open. He still feels homeless in America, but the spectacle of proud authority, in cities and on campuses, always surrendering before threats of violence, is to him a clear indication that middle-class society is about to fall apart, and he is all set to pick up the pieces.

There is no doubt that in our permissive society the intellectual has far more liberty than he can use; and the more his liberty and the less his capacity to make use of it, the louder his clamor for power—power to deprive other people of liberty.

• • •

The intellectual's allergy to America shows itself with particular clarity in what has happened to many foreign intellectuals who found asylum here during the Hitler decade. It is legitimate to assume that they had no anti-American preconceptions when they arrived. They were, on the contrary, predisposed to see what was best in their host country. Though no one has recorded what Herbert Marcuse said when he landed in New York in 1934, it is safe to assume that he did not see Americans as one-dimensional men, and did not equate our tolerance with oppression, our freedom with slavery, and our good nature with simple-mindedness.

We have a record of what some other foreign intellectuals said when they arrived in the nineteen-thirties. It is worth quoting in full the words of Olga Schnitzler, the widow of Arthur Schnitzler: "So much is here to learn and to see. Everyone has been given an opportunity. Everyone who has not been completely worn out experiences here a kind of rebirth. Everyone feels what a grandiose, complex and broad-minded country America is, how well and free one can live among these people without perfidy and malice. Yes, we have lost a homeland, but we have found a world."

Once they had settled down and found their place, many of these intellectuals began to feel constrained and stifled by the forwardness and the mores of the plebeian masses. They missed the aristocratic climate of the Old World. Inevitably, too, they became disdainful of our lowbrow, practical intelligence. They began to doubt whether Americans had the high-caliber intelligence to solve the problems of a complex, difficult age. Hardly one of them bethought himself that in Europe, when intellectuals of their kind had a hand in shaping and managing affairs, things had not gone too well. There was something that prevented them from sensing the unprecedented nature of the American experiment; that the rejected of Europe have come here together, tamed a savage continent in an incredibly short time and, unguided by intellectuals, fashioned the finest society on a large scale the world has so far seen.

Scratch an intellectual and you find a would-be aristocrat who loathes the sight, the sound and the smell of common folk. Professor Marcuse has lived among us for more than 30 years and now, in old age, his disenchantment with this country is spilling over into book after book. He is offended by the intrusion of the vulgar, by the failure of egalitarian America to keep common people in their place. He is frightened by "the degree to which the population is allowed to break the peace where there is still peace and silence, to be ugly and uglify things, to ooze familiarity and to offend against good form." The vulgar invade "the small reserved sphere of existence" and compel exquisite Marcusian souls to partake of their sounds, sights and smells.

To a shabby would-be aristocrat like Professor Marcuse there is something fundamentally wrong with a society in which the master and the worker, the typist and the boss's daughter do not live totally disparate lives. Everything good in America seems to him a sham and a fraud.

. . .

An interesting peculiarity of present-day dissenting intellectuals is their lack of animus toward the rich. They are against the Government, the Congress, the Army and the police, and against corporations and unions, but hardly anything is being said or written against "the money changers in the temple," "the economic royalists," "the malefactors of great wealth" and "the maniacs wild for gold" who were the butt of vituperation in the past. Indeed, there is nowadays a certain rapport between the rich and the would-be revolutionaries. The outlandish role the rich are playing in the affluent society is one of the surprises of our time. Though the logic of it seems now fairly evident, I doubt whether anyone had foreseen that affluence would radicalize the upper rich and the lowest poor and nudge them toward an alliance against those in the middle. Whatever we have of revolution just now is financed largely by the rich.

In order to feel rich, you have to have poor people around you. In an affluent society, riches lose their uniqueness—people no longer find fulfillment in being rich. And when the rich cannot feel rich they begin to have misgivings about success—not enough to give up the fruits of success, but enough to feel guilty, and emote soulfully about the grievances of the disadvantaged, and the sins of the status quo. It seems that every time a millionaire opens his mouth nowadays he confesses the sins of our society in public.

Now, it so happens that the rich do indeed have a lot to feel guilty about. They live in exclusive neighborhoods, send their children to private schools, and use every loophole to avoid paying taxes. But what they confess in public are not their private sins, but the sins of society, the sins of the rest of us, and it is our breasts they are beating into a pulp. They feel guilty and ashamed, they say, because the mass of people, who do most of the work and pay much of the taxes, are against integrated schools and housing, and do not tax themselves to the utmost to fight the evils that beset our cities. We are discovering that in an affluent society the rich have a monopoly of righteousness.

Moreover, the radicalized rich have radical children. There is no generation gap here. The most violent cliques of the New Left are made up of the children of the rich. The Weathermen, to whom workingmen are "honky bastards," have not a member with a workingman's background. The behavior of the extremist young makes sense when seen as the behavior of spoiled brats used to instant fulfillment who expect the solutions to life's problems to be there on demand. And just as in former days aristocratic sprigs horsewhipped peasants, so at present the children of the rich are riding roughshod over community sensibilities. The rich parents applaud and subsidize their revolutionary children, and probably brag about them at dinner parties.

As I said, the alienated rich are one of the surprises of our time. It is not surprising to be told that America is a country where intellectuals are least at home. But it is startling to realize that the rich are not, and probably never have been, wholly at ease in this country. The fact that it is easy to get rich in America has not made it a rich man's country. The rich have always had it better elsewhere—better service, more deference, and more leisure and fun. In America, the rich have not known how to savor their riches, and many of them have not known how to behave and have come to a bad end.

There is a story about a British intellectual who traveled through this country toward the end of the last century. He was appalled by the monotony and unimaginativeness of the names of the towns he saw through the train window: Thomasville, Richardsville, Harrysville, Marysville and so on. He had not an inkling of the import of what he was seeing: namely, that for the first time in history common people—any Tom, Dick and Harry—could build a town and name it after his own or his wife's name. At one station, an old Irishwoman got on the train and sat next to him. When she heard his muttering and hissing she said: "This is a blessed country, sir. I think God made it for the poor." Crèvecœur, in the 18th century, saw America as an asylum where "the poor of Europe have by some means met together." The poor everywhere have looked on America as their El Dorado. They voted for it with their legs by coming over in their millions.

Yet during the nineteen-sixties, poverty became one of the chief problems that plague this country: one of several nagging problems—

like race relations, violence, drugs, inflation—which defy solution. From being a land of opportunity for the poor, America has become a dead-end street for some 15 million unemployables—80 per cent of them white, and most of them trapped in the cores of big cities. Money, better housing, and special schooling have little effect. Our society is showing itself unduly awkward in the attempt to turn the chronically poor into productive, useful citizens. Whereas, in the not too distant past, it was axiomatic that society lived at the expense of the poor, the present-day poor, like the Roman proletariat, live at the expense of society.

We have been transferred by affluence to a psychological age. Impersonal factors, including money, no longer play a decisive role in human affairs. It seems that, by mastering things, we have drained things of their potency to shape men's lives. It is remarkable that common people are aware of this fact. They know that at present money cannot cure crime, poverty, etc., whereas the social doctors go on prescribing an injection of so many billions for every social ailment.

In the earliest cities, suburbs made their appearance as a refuge for dropouts who could not make the grade in the city. When eventually the cities decayed, the suburbs continued as the earliest villages. In our cities, the process has been reversed. The dropouts are stagnating in the cores of the cities, while people who are ideally suited for city life seek refuge in the suburbs. The indications are that we shall not have viable cities until we lure the chronically poor out of the cities and induce the exiled urbanites to return.

The diffusion of affluence has accelerated the absorption of the majority of workingmen into the middle class. The unemployable poor, left behind, feel isolated and exposed, and it is becoming evident that a middle-class society, which hugs the conviction that everyone can take care of himself, is singularly inept in helping those who cannot help themselves. If the rich cannot feel rich in an affluent society, the poor have never felt poorer.

* * *

Whose country, then, is America? It is the country of the common—the common men and women, a good 70 per cent of the population—who do most of the work, pay much of the taxes, crave neither power nor importance, and want to be left alone to live pleasurable humdrum lives. "The founders of the United States," said Lord Charnwood, "did deliberately aspire to found a commonwealth in which common men and women should count for more than elsewhere."

Again and again, you come up against the mystery of what happens to common folk when they land on our shores. It is like a homecoming. They find here their natural habitat, their ideal milieu that brings their energies and capacities into full play.

Tasks that in other countries are reserved for a select minority, for a specially trained élite, are in this country performed by every Tom, Dick and Harry. Not only did common Americans build and name towns, but they also founded states, propagated new faiths, commanded armies, wrote books, and ran for the highest office. It is this that has made America unprecedentedly new.

It tickled me no end that the astronauts who landed on the moon were not élite-conscious intellectuals but lowbrow ordinary Americans. It has been the genius of common Americans to achieve the momentous in an unmomentous matter-of-fact way. If space exploration remains in their keeping, they will soon make of it an everyday routine accessible to all.

The intellectuals call this giving access to the vulgar—vulgarization. The intellectuals' inclination is to complicate things, to make them so abstruse and difficult that they are accessible only to the initiated few. Where the intellectuals are in power, prosaic tasks become Promethean undertakings. I have yet to meet an intellectual who truly believes that common people can govern themselves and run things without outstanding leaders. In the longshoremen's union the intellectuals have a nervous breakdown anytime a common, barely literate longshoreman runs for office and gets elected.

To me it seems axiomatic that the common people everywhere are our natural allies, and that our chief contribution to the advancement of mankind should be the energizing and activation of common folk. We must learn how to impart to common people everywhere the technological, political and social skills that would enable them to dispense with the tutorship of the upper classes and the intellectuals. We must deflate the pretensions of self-appointed élites. These élites will hate us no matter what we do, and it is legitimate for us to help dump them into the dustbin of history.

Our foreign aid to backward countries in Asia, Africa and Latin America should be tailored to the needs of common people rather than of the élites. The élites hanker for the trappings of the 20th century. They want steel mills, airlines, skyscrapers, etc. Let them get these trappings from élitist Russia. Our gift to the people in backward countries should be the capacity for self-help. We must show them how to get bread, human dignity and strength by their own efforts. We must know how to stiffen their backbone so that they will insist on getting their full share of the good life and not allow themselves to be sacrificed to the Moloch of a mythical future.

There is an America hidden in the soil of every country and in the soul of every people. It is our task to help common people everywhere discover their America at home.

## Study Guide

1. Hoffer relates the problems of youth in America to what he describes as the ordeal of affluence. What is the nature of this ordeal? Is this concept related to the ideas of MacLeish and Fromm?

2. Hoffer thinks adolescence now extends from the preteen years into the late 20's. What evidence can you find in our society that supports this view?

3. The author suggests that the middle classes played a significant role in the industrial age. Explain this role. What change does Hoffer see forthcoming in the American class structure? What effect does he think this change will have on America?

4. What does Hoffer feel is the present attitude of the young toward the common man?

5. How does Hoffer explain the alliance that links the rich and intellectual elements in our society with the revolutionaries in our culture?

6. Why does Hoffer refute those individuals who deride America?

7. Why does Hoffer distrust the elitist movement in our culture?

8. What goals does Hoffer attribute to the elite? To the common man?

9. Is Hoffer's faith in the common man justified?

10. Hoffer suggests that our society lacks a significant initiation ritual. Do you think this statement is true?

11. Various young writers or writers representing our youth culture are included in this book. Are their ideals and ideas indicative of adolescent attitudes?

12. In your opinion, what might Hoffer's attitude be toward any one of the specific minority groups represented in this book?

13. For what audience did Hoffer write? How does this influence his style?

14. Assume the persona of a Chicano laborer, a Negro militant, or a student activist. Then write an essay in which you refute Hoffer's criticisms.

15. Hoffer places great faith in the common man. In your opinion,

who is the common man? Describe him in an essay. You might consider how his goals differ from yours or how they are similar.

16.  Hoffer suggests that "Every boy and girl on reaching 17, or on graduating from high school, [should] be given an opportunity to spend two years earning a living at good pay." He suggests that they might be employed by the government to solve problems in both urban and rural areas. Such a plan would provide a significant initiation ritual for the young and also provide our country with the means of accomplishing much necessary work. In an essay, debate the merits of Hoffer's proposal.

17.  In an essay, attempt to determine whether the rebellion of the young, as it is described by Hoffer, can be related to the weaknesses in our society that were described by Fromm and MacLeish. To what extent does the rebellion of the young reflect or result from their depersonalization?